S0-BBE-911

"Love Of Shopping" Is Not A Gene

dedicated to the memory of Charles Darwin

a true scientist

who documented his theory with verifiable facts

Anne Innis Dagg

"Love Of Shopping" Is Not A Gene

Problems With Darwinian Psychology

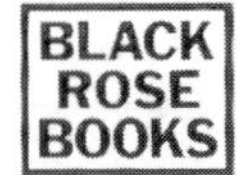

Montréal/New York/London

Black Rose Books No. HH330

National Library of Canada Cataloguing in Publication Data

Dagg, Anne Innis, 1933-

"Love of shopping" is not a gene : problems with Darwinian psychology / Anne Innis Dagg

Includes bibliographical references and index.

Hardcover ISBN: 1-55164-257-3 (bound) Paperback ISBN: 1-55164-256-5 (pbk.)

1. Evolutionary psychology. 2. Human behavior. 3. Animal behavior. I. Title.

BF698.95.D33 ~~2004~~ 2005 155.7 C2004-905037-0

Every effort has been made to secure permission for materials reproduced herein.

Cover design: Associés libres

BLACK ROSE BOOKS

C.P. 1258	2250 Military Road	99 Wallis Road
Succ. Place du Parc	Tonawanda, NY	London, E9 5LN
Montréal, H2X 4A7	14150	England
Canada	USA	UK

To order books:

In Canada: (phone) 1-800-565-9523 (fax) 1-800-221-9985
email: utpbooks@utpress.utoronto.ca

In United States: (phone) 1-800-283-3572 (fax) 1-651-917-6406

In the UK & Europe: (phone) London 44 (0)20 8986-4854 (fax) 44 (0)20 8533-5821
email: order@centralbooks.com

Our Web Site address: http://www.web.net/blackrosebooks

A publication of the Institute of Policy Alternatives of Montréal (IPAM)

Printed in Canada

The Canada Council for the Arts | Le Conseil des Arts du Canada

Contents

Acknowledgements

I am grateful to all those people who provided or helped provide specific information for this book, or who read and suggested improvements for parts of the text. They include Thomas Abler, Marc Bekoff, Fred Bodsworth, Alan Cairns, Wendy Campbell, Roland Chrisjohn, Phyllis Dolhinow, Brian Ferguson, Gary Griffin, Matthew Griffin, Frédéric Loyer, Peter Klopfer, Martin McGreal, Jessica Menéndez, Bev Sawyer, Victoria Serda, Elaine Sim, Robert Sussman and Paul Vasey. Many thanks also to the many friendly librarians who made my work easier, to Dimitri Roussopoulos, the publisher, and to Linda Barton, my editor.

Introduction

Shopping: "It must be in our genes as former hunters and gatherers," a journalist writes cheerfully in her regular column (Gagnon, 2001). "There is no qualitative difference between gathering fruits and shopping for food, clothes, houseware or knickknacks. As for men, they like to shop for big ticket items such as cars and computers: the modern version of big game."

Although few people have studied genetics, our culture is full of casual references to genes; in my files I can read not only about the "shopping gene" (early women's ability to locate food plants is correlated with an aptitude enabling them to "spot and remember which object might eventually go on sale"), but also about the "reading gene," the "humility gene," the "coaching gene," the "selfless gene" (as in women), the "God gene" (for religious belief), a "non-visiting gene" (in people who won't visit hospitalized friends) and a gene for "meditative sky-watching." This is pop science, fostered by Darwinian psychology, run amok. What are we to make of it?

This book is a critique of Darwinian psychology, alias evolutionary psychology, alias sociobiology—the study of social behavior of animals and people based on evolution. Darwinian psychology rests on the premise that the current social behavior of human beings largely evolved genetically during the six million years since our ape-like ancestors split into two lineages, one leading to ourselves and the other to chimpanzees and bonobos. An alternate possibility, and the one to which I subscribe, is that as our ancestors developed large brains they became increasingly able to react in appropriate ways to their environment with reason rather than instinct. As hominid groups spread into different regions around the world, their intellectual ability resulted in the development of many diverse behaviors and cultures.

Genes vs Culture. There is no certain proof, one way or the other, that we act largely according to our culture and our individual personalities (which do have a genetic component) rather than to our general genetic inheritance, but there are four major reasons that suggest we do: a) the myriad of errors present in data claiming to support Darwinian psychology which this book will detail, b) the difficulty of even defining a social behavior in order to search for genes that might cause it, c) the dearth of possible genes for social behavior from extensive examination of the human genome, and d) the profound distance mentally between non-human and human animals. (For simplicity, the former group in this book will be referred to simply as animals and the latter as human beings.)

a) Charles Darwin would have been aghast at the often shoddy data used to support Darwinian psychology; he was much too good a scientist to tolerate inaccurate information. He worked meticulously, gathering relevant facts and checking them out, one at a time, thousands each year, to build his theory of evolution. He spent *eight years* studying barnacles through a microscope so that he would understand exactly how evolution worked in this one complex order. One highlight was the discovery of a male sixteen-hundredths of an inch living in the valve of a female—her "little husband" (Desmond and Moore, 1991, 355). His research was so central to his family's life that his son out visiting once asked another child, "Where does your father do his barnacles?" (Browne, 1995, 473). Darwin would have shuddered at a "science" such as Darwinian psychology in which an academic could grab an idea out of thin air and then marshall only data which supported it, not negated it, to declare the hypothesis likely valid.

b) Although it is easy to talk casually about genes for such things as infanticide, war, rape and criminality, as some Darwinian psychologists do, how are these characteristics defined? If there is a gene(s) for infanticide, as Larry Milner (2000) claims in his book *Hardness of Heart, Hardness of Life*, how would we be able to track it down when few people actually kill children? If a teenage father shakes his baby to death because it cries too much, would we assume that he possesses the infanticide gene(s)? Would a mother suffering from postpartum depression who smothers her newborn also have the gene(s)? What if a bachelor possesses the gene(s) but has no children to kill? How would we know to include him in the small population whose DNA could be studied?

c) The past few decades have been flooded with the importance of genetics to human beings, fostered in large part by hype from the multi-billion dollar Human Genome Project. Yet after decades of work, thousands of highly paid researchers have failed to locate significant social behavioral attributes in our genetic inheritance. Briefly and to much fanfare scientists initially claimed to have discovered genes governing characteristics such as aggression, criminality and homosexuality, but with further research these claims have not been substantiated.

d) Darwinian psychology focuses on the inheritance of human social behavior from our primate ancestors. The common ancestors of chimpanzees, bonobos and human beings lived about six million years ago at which time the future ape group and the future hominid group (which would evolve into human beings) split apart. The former evolved into chimpanzees and bonobos who continue to live in the forests of central Africa; the latter initially migrated from forests to African savannahs in small nomadic bands. Because the members of this lineage were now adapting to an entirely new environment and in the process developing an enlarged brain and greater intellectual powers, the hominid individuals developed different behaviors than those of their ape-like "cousins."

Because social behavior is genetically based in most animals even if not in human beings, proponents of Darwinian psychology often use results from animal behavioral research to bolster hypotheses about human behavior. This is especially true for chimpanzees, but also for many other species so that the activities of a few random species including fish or insects (for example in rape studies) are used to shed light on human behavior, which is too much of a stretch to make sense. A discussion of animal behavior *is* included in this book when it highlights topics that involve a wide spectrum of species such as infanticide (to show that its rationale for animals and human beings is entirely different) and homosexual behavior (to prove that it is so widespread that to call it "unnatural" in people is not logical).

Another dilemma clouding the discipline of Darwinian psychology is that its proponents and opponents tend to come from either end of the political spectrum (Segerstråle, 2000). The view that human social behaviors are correlated with our human genes is largely held by people who are right wing politically. Opponents of Darwinian psychology, by contrast, tend to be liberals and democratic socialists who believe that the enlarged human brain enabled individuals and cultures to adopt these same behaviors not through genetic inheritance, but because they were best suited to their lives. While these opponents feel that Darwinian psychologists are politically motivated, the latter feel the same about their critics (Gander, 2003, 238). The left-wingers would like to see the world change for the betterment of all, an aspiration more feasible if human behavior is not biologically determined but plastic enough to adapt to new conditions as they arise. For individuals whose lives are in disarray, blame can then tend to rest with conditions and cultures that caused this dysfunction. Can a discipline be truly scientific if it so readily reflects political rather than academic precepts?

Related to this political bias is a sexual/poverty/homosexual bias which pervades Darwinian psychology. Research on animals is usually concerned with how natural selection works for a species in respect to living a healthy life, choosing a mate, producing young and caring for these offspring to ensure they will function well as adults. By contrast, of the scores of topics that Darwinian psychologists could study in human beings, they tend to research those which have social repercussions. These include domination, aggression and competition which often have a positive appeal for men; aggression, rape, infanticide and sperm competition within their wombs which have a negative connotation for women; crime and IQ studies which can be made to reflect badly on blacks and the poor; and homosexuality which is given a negative spin against gay men and lesbians.

Another dilemma for Darwinian psychology is that research findings are virtually impossible to test; human behavior is infinitely complex and it is unethical to carry out intrusive research on people. One can theorize, but can seldom carry out realistic experiments to prove that a particular behavior is either genetically or culturally based.

Opponents of Darwinian psychology claim that its practitioners tend to rationalize what they already wish for and/or believe. Their catholic approval of evolutionary possibilities means that virtually any theory can be (and often is) postulated and presented with little or no proof. Sometimes two views that are 180 degrees at variance are both accepted. For example, Darwinian psychology has long held the belief that female birds and mammals are coy and choosy about whom they mate with; because they have relatively few offspring in their lifetime on which they expend much care, they want them sired by a superior father. However, recent evidence showing that many females cheat on their mate is also accepted by Darwinian psychologists for several possible reasons: to ensure pregnancy in case the first male is infertile, to foster sperm competition, and to increase genetic diversity and kinship relationships on behalf of their offspring (Tang-Martinez, 2000, 268). Proponents of Darwinian psychology seem happy to agree that white is white and that black is white too, as long as it makes, in theory, evolutionary sense.

To illustrate the unnerving flexibility of Darwinian psychology, Professor Steve Jones plays a parlor game with his university classes, asking them first to list human phenomena beginning with the letters A to Z, then to attribute an evolutionary reason for each (Levin, 2001). So A is for Acne, which may prevent young people from having sex until they are old enough to care for possible children responsibly, while Z is for Zoophilia, a sexual attraction for animals. An elaboration of this game is given in Appendix A.

Most of the chapters of this book highlight problems that undermine the credibility of Darwinian psychology. These include supporting a hypothesis by collecting only research data that back it, not refute it (Chapter 1 on lion infanticide); using largely anecdotes to "prove" a hypothesis (Chapter 3 on aggression); equating animal with human behavior (Chapter 5 discussing chimpanzees and war); championing a hypothesis by citing references inaccurately (Chapter 9 on rape); titillating the reader with soft porn (Chapter 11 on sperm competition); adopting a moral bias (Chapters 12 and 13 on homosexuality); bypassing accepted academic standards (Philippe Rushton's work on race in Chapter 14); adopting a political bias (Chapter 15 on race and IQ); and hijacking a valid theory (fluctuating asymmetry in Chapter 16).

Darwinian psychology considers itself a science, so why do its proponents countenance such biases and errors? In some cases researchers are so busy collecting data supporting their hypothesis that they do not step back to consider alternate explanations for animal behavior (for example, infanticide in lions). In others, proponents seem to have a political agenda which seeks to "prove" that blacks and the poor have an inheritance that tends toward violence and stupidity (Chapters 8 on crime and 15 on IQ) and that women are by their inheritance subordinate to men both as individuals (Chapter 7 on dominance) and as baby producers (Chapter 11 on sperm competition).

If there is so much wrong with Darwinian psychology, why does it even exist? Why does anyone pay any attention to it? Science is supposed to be self-correcting, with each new published hypothesis being studied, weighed in the balance by other scientists, discarded if it is wrong, and accepted and refined if it is right. Researchers involved with sociobiology and Darwinian psychology originally had difficulty publishing their articles because editors of mainstream journals refused to accept them, finding them scientifically inadequate (Rose and Rose, 2001, 2). Darwinian psychologists have apparently banded together to found their own journals in which to publish their articles and those of their students and other adherents. The journals include *Ethology and Sociobiology* (changing its name more recently to *Evolution and Human Behavior*) founded in 1979 and *Human Nature* founded in 1990.

As well as publishing their "scientific" papers, proponents of Darwinian psychology give public lectures and interviews. They publish books, anthologies and popular commentaries which sell well because their message is music to the ears of the many millions of nonscientific readers delighted to have their (often invalid) stereotypes confirmed—that men are by nature aggressive and dominant to women, that it is in men's nature to rape, that stepfathers are all too likely to abuse and kill their stepchildren, that blacks are dumber and more criminal than whites. Darwinian psychologists are perplexed by gay men and lesbians because they are unable to determine how the existence of homosexuals who do not have children can be explained by evolution, as we shall see in Chapter 13.

Because of widespread media exposure, people begin to believe what Darwinian psychologists say, even when it has been shown to be incorrect. And what they say can have a drastic effect on society. For example, when researchers in 1980 declared that girls were less inherently able to do math than boys, a fact later shown to be incorrect, there was a decline in the number of female college students expressing interest in technical courses (Allen, 1997, 520). As another example, male proponents of Darwinian psychology who devalue women, and especially feminists, in their pronouncements, help impede women's equality in Western society as Susan Faludi describes in her 550-page book *Backlash: The Undeclared War Against American Women* (1991). ("Why do so many men seem to begrudge [women's independence], resent it, fear it, fight it with an unholy passion?" Faludi [1999, 40] asks?) Women working full-time still earn on average only seventy-two cents for every dollar men earn (U.S. government statistics, 2000).

This book will, I hope, make readers ponder the many anomalies at the heart of the Darwinian psychological debate.

- Why is it that when chimpanzee males are known to be somewhat violent and the females highly promiscuous, human beings are said to emulate them in male violence but not in female randiness? Might it be that men are happy to envision themselves as aggressive, but don't fancy women acting out a promiscuous evolutionary trait? In his paper describing how female chimpanzees cuckold their home-group males, Richard Wrangham (1997, 774) concludes "Chimpanzee and human social systems differ importantly in the characteristics of the female relationships, so there are certainly no direct analogies for human sociobiology."
- Why is it that Darwinian psychologists claim that human beings behave very like chimpanzees in aggression, although these two species do not even belong to the same mammalian family, but don't expect gregarious lions to act like unsociable tigers when both are members of the same genus and sometimes interbreed in zoos?
- Why is it that if Darwinian psychologists really think women are subservient to men, they have to expend so much effort combatting feminism to "prove" this? Would it not be obvious?

I shall show in this book that although Darwinian psychology for animals has been a fruitful topic for biology, Darwinian psychology for human beings has not; it is faulty because it is largely based not on facts, but on fallacies. If we hope to succeed in addressing social issues in the future, we must deal with scientific data, not flawed misconceptions.

Chapter 1

A Strange Tale Of Non-Darwinian Lions

Scientists are supposedly a rational lot, seeking truth wherever they find it. Right? Well, perhaps not when their subject matter is too dear to their heart, almost a religion. Not necessarily when they are proponents of Darwinian Psychology, the "science" whose creed is that evolution (Darwin) is responsible not only for our anatomy and physiology passed along to us from our ape-like ancestors, but for human behavior (psychology) as well. Why do I think this? Here is my strange story.

No matter how I tried, I couldn't believe male lions were as malevolent as they were made out to be. Biologists Craig Packer and Anne Pusey were publishing scientific papers from Africa blaming male lions for killing thousands of lion cubs, each to further his own evolutionary destiny. Packer (1994, 75) would later state that "Every lion in the world has a father who is a murderer."[1] Not that the lion could help himself. He had genes, a genetic inheritance, that made him kill every cub he came across not sired by him or his pride mates.

This behavior was thought to be an excellent (if gory) example of Darwinian psychology whereby one's behavior is inherited from one's ancestors. If a chance genetic mutation caused a male to kill other males' offspring, if the male with this mutation then fathered more young than his peers, if these cubs were raised to maturity, then eventually his progeny (who also carried the gene(s) for infanticide) would swamp those of other males. When this happened, all males would indeed practise infanticide. This is what Packer and Pusey believed had happened.

At the time in 1982, as a biologist in feminist mode, I was researching the subject of sexism in the reports of scientists studying the behavior of animals in the wild. Each day I would troop with my daughter to the University of Queensland library in Brisbane, Australia, where I was then staying, to read in articles, monographs and books, descriptions of the activities of as many different species of animals as possible. The most eye-opening work was that of Walter Bagehot who wrote in the 1800s that throughout the animal kingdom the sexes differed in boldness, pugnacity, adventurousness, restlessness, mildness, gentleness and inoffensiveness—the former characteristics belonging to males and the latter to females (in Sayers, 1980, 40). I knew that female lions would never go for this. Bagehot noted that these characteristics fitted males and females for the different tasks assigned them by nature, and that "the attempt to alter the present relations of the sexes is not a rebellion against some arbitrary law instituted by a despot or a majority—not an attempt to break the yoke of a mere convention; it is a struggle against Nature." Yeah, right.

What about lions? I knew of the hypothesis that male lions were supposed to kill cubs other than those of their own pride, and looked forward to reading about this for the book and article I was writing on sexual bias to see if the authors gave this material a sexist spin (Dagg 1983, 1984a). Aside from the scientific papers being produced by Packer and Pusey, the two primary sources of information on lion behavior were the books *The Serengeti Lion* (1972a) by George Schaller and *Pride of Lions* (1978) and scientific papers by Brian Bertram.

Schaller had been the first to study lion behavior in depth, living on the Serengeti Plains of Tanzania from 1966 to 1969 during which time he put ear tags on 156 individuals so that he could always recognize them. He spent most of his time observing the activities of the lions belonging to two prides, the Seronera and the Masai. Brian Bertram continued this research for the next five years; his observations on individual lions were "less intensive, visits to the prides' areas being made once or twice a week" (Bertram, 1975, 465).

Bertram was much less likely than Schaller to refer to individual lions in his book, so I read Schaller's book first. He reported that at least half of all lion cubs died before they reached adulthood. Most of the causes of death were unknown, but some cubs had been killed by lions. I hunted through the text to discover that four had been killed by males passing through the area, one by a male rolling accidentally on a pride cub, and five by females (Dagg, 1998). This last fact startled me. If one discounted the accident, then more cubs had been killed by females than males. Yet the hypothesis of infanticide by male lions touted by Packer and Pusey made no mention that females were involved in infanticide.

The hypothesis of infanticide by male lions is tied in with the way in which lion society works. Each pride is composed of related females—daughters, mothers, grandmothers, sisters, aunts, nieces—and one or a few males unrelated to the females. The females reproduce and look after the cubs while the males' job is to protect the pride from other males who might harm the cubs or the females. The pride males' status is so coveted that every few years new males try and often succeed in replacing them as pride males. During the turmoil of new males fighting to take over the pride, many cubs die. It is these cubs who are assumed to have been killed by the new males so that the females would come into estrus and mate with the new males to produce their cubs. However, the cubs could equally well have died because of starvation, because their mothers' milk dried up from stress, because of maternal neglect or because they were killed by females. No one knows.

The hypothesis of infanticide by male lions indicates that the cubs are killed by males newly joining a pride, but there is little evidence for this. Only about a dozen cubs of the many thousands born during twenty-five years of field study have actually been seen killed by males (Packer 1994). Packer and Pusey do not mention any cubs being killed by females which would not fit into the hypothesis, although there is no doubt that many such deaths must have occurred, given Schaller's observations.

Far from believing that many or most cubs were killed by male lions (and he had no reason to suspect this because the theory of infanticide by males had not yet been formulated), Schaller (1972a) reported that many other causes of death were common. He found lionesses to be not only murderers, but often bad mothers. Many cubs died of starvation not because the mothers themselves were starving (p. 190), but because they would not share food with their young. Schaller wrote (1972b 86): "It was depressing to see a starving cub totter to its mother, each rib sharply outlined beneath its unkempt hide, and receive a vicious cuff instead of a bite to eat." At a time when their cubs were starving, the females did not hunt more to provide food for them as long as they had enough meat for themselves (p. 100).

Schaller concluded that many cubs died not because males killed them, but because of maternal neglect. He noted (1972b, 84) that "Many cubs simply disappeared, often whole litters of vigorous youngsters, and I think that in some instances they were simply abandoned. Perhaps leaving them to die in the obscurity of a thicket, their mothers returned to the pride's conviviality." He wrote (1972a:190) "Probably more cubs died as a result of having been abandoned by their mothers than through any other cause, but I have no data to support this assumption." However he did document examples of certain and probable abandonment by lion mothers (pp. 190-191). How ironic that we speak allegorically of the fierce lioness protecting her cubs!

When I finished reading *The Serengeti Lion* I realized that there was no sexist problem with the text itself (although I was unsettled by the female lions' questionable maternal behavior), but that there was a huge problem with the hypothesis of infanticide by male lions. There were no data in Schaller's book to support this hypothesis, yet much information describing the large number of cub deaths caused by other factors, especially maternal neglect.

Schaller's lion research in Tanzania was continued by Brian Bertram from late 1969. Bertram gives few data on how individual cubs died, but ponders if his research can support the infanticide hypothesis first formulated by Sarah Hrdy for monkeys (as we shall see shortly) in 1974, the year Bertram wrapped up his research. He concluded that if males had indeed killed all the cubs in a pride they were newly joining, they might have an evolutionary advantage. However, he was doubtful about males killing cubs as an evolutionary strategy. He writes (1978:99):

> Certainly the new males do not indulge in wholesale slaughter of cubs, but on the other hand the takeover of a pride does result in an increase in the mortality of cubs of any age in that pride. Some of these deaths may be only indirectly due to the new males. Possibly, for example, their presence causes stress for the lionesses who therefore hunt less efficiently, or produce less milk, or waste time and effort trying in vain to guard their cubs...

If we consider the logistics of the infanticide hypothesis, it is clear that males must do more than merely kill a cub. To be an evolutionary strategy, the males must then mate with the cub's mother and stay with the pride until his young are born and grow old enough (at least two years) to look after themselves; if the males do not do this, some other male or males will "take over" the pride and in turn kill their cubs to start a new cycle of death and life.

If the propensity of males to kill cubs is inherited, then it must be correlated with some gene or genes. How would this work? The infanticide gene(s), let's call it/them INF, would presumably be on one of the sex chromosomes, either X or Y, because the hypothesis is that males but not females have it/them.

> If the INF gene(s) were on the Y chromosome, males would have it/them but this does not fit with Schaller's observations that as many or more females as males killed cubs.
>
> If INF were on the X chromosome, it would occur in males (who do not have a second X chromosome to mask its effects), but when two X chromosomes with INF genes were present in females, these females would presumably, like males, be driven also to kill alien cubs. Because Packer (1994, 75) writes that every male is a murderer who kills cubs, all X chromosomes in the population must have the INF genes and all females

would therefore also have INF genes and would be murderers too, which does not fit with the hypothesis. Why would males but not females need INF gene(s) to kill alien cubs?

Killing is a way of life for all predators. It is difficult or impossible to believe that male lions would have special genes connected to the killing of cubs as opposed to genes connected to the killing of adult lions, antelope or buffalo.

Packer and Pusey (1984) describe the seven known cases of infanticide by males from the first seventeen years of lion research (strangely ignoring the five cases of infanticide by females noted by Schaller in the first four years). In NO instance is there evidence that the males who killed the cubs then mated with their mothers and remained with the mothers' pride for two years to protect their new cubs until they were more or less independent.

I was so intrigued by what I had discovered about lions and what seemed to be a misrepresentation of their lives, that I decided to take time away from my research into sexism to write a paper on infanticide in lions which I titled, rather aggressively perhaps, "Lying about Lions." I now felt sure that this was not an evolutionary strategy, with all males having genes that made them kill certain cubs, but a result of stress and turmoil in prides whenever new males were trying to oust the pride males by force.

I sent my paper to several biological journals but none was interested in publishing an article that took issue with the, by then, widely accepted Darwinian hypothesis of infanticide by males. Soon I received a letter from Craig Packer, the lion researcher himself. He told me simply that the thesis of my paper was wrong. At that point he might have realized that there was a problem with his collection of data—that females killed cubs too and that it made no sense for a hypothesis to focus on one group of killers (male) and ignore another (female). He chose instead to disregard my work. Packer continues to reject the fact that female lions kill the young of other lions although he must know, at the very least because of Schaller's work, that this is so (Dunham, 2001).

Because Packer at the time was fortunate enough to be actually in Africa watching the lions rather than just reading about them in the library, I decided he must have collected information not yet published that supported his hypothesis. With a sigh, I put my article away in a desk drawer and began to look forward with interest to what Packer's next articles would say that vindicated his stand. No such articles appeared that persuaded me I was wrong.

Unbeknownst to me, a professor thousands of miles away at the University of Colorado in Boulder, Marc Bekoff, *did* accept the thesis and logic of my paper. He, too, filed it away in a desk drawer where it stayed for the next fifteen years.

At this pause in my story, we should consider the history of the hypothesis of infanticide by male adults. It was formulated first by Sarah Hrdy (1974), a colleague of E.O. Wilson while he was in the process of writing his book *Sociobiology* which launched the modern discipline which would become Darwinian psychology. At her research site of Abu in Rajasthan, India, where she was studying the behavior of langur monkeys, some local people while she was away saw four unidentified adult males kill langur infants. An earlier scientist had also seen males killing infants. There was no evidence that the males were necessarily killing the young of other males or mating soon after with the infants' mothers. However, because these theoretical activities would fit into a hypothesis of infanticide as an evolutionary strategy, Hrdy assumed in her report that they were in fact being carried out.

There was some negative feedback to Hrdy's langur data. Several experts believe that localized infanticide in some langur populations such as those of Abu is caused not by Darwinian forces within the males, but by the great stress of increasing human pressure on langur habitat (Curtin and Dolhinow, 1978; Dolhinow, 1999); langurs are now forced to live very different lives than they did a million to a few thousand years ago during the course of their evolution. Langurs living at more normal, uncrowded sites such as at Orcha and Junbesi in India have not had their societies devastated by males killing infants. However, such negative critiques of the infanticide hypothesis were largely ignored.

In general, Hrdy's paper caused a firestorm of excitement in the world of animal behavior. It was horrendous that adults would kill infants of their own species, but if this was a Darwinian strategy then the behavior made sense. Soon biologists from around the world were reporting that "their" species *also* practised infanticide for the cause of evolution, even if the only evidence was that a male killed an infant. However, as we have seen, this is insufficient testimony to constitute a Darwinian strategy for the higher social mammals. Females also killed infants, but this roused little interest because it did not fit into such a seductive hypothesis.

Some of the examples of infanticide occurred among animals that the researcher did not recognize individually. In normal small mammal populations in the field, it is impossible to know if the male who kills a newborn is the same one who later mates with the female, if indeed the female is actually the mother whose young was killed. Indeed it is virtually impossible to observe any of these activities which take place among vegetation or in underground burrows.

Other examples came from research laboratories: A small mammal in a cage gives birth to a litter of young. A male allowed access to the female kills the young.

Later the two copulate to produce more young. Darwinian psychologists may see this as a clear-cut example of an evolutionary strategy at work; skeptics see animals in the abnormal condition of captivity behaving abnormally.

The most credible data for infanticide come from relatively large social species that have been thoroughly studied by researchers who can recognize each individual in a population and so know what he or she is up to. The most obvious possibilities are monkeys, apes and lions.

Researchers first addressed the question of infanticide in primates; the behaviors of scores of species have been investigated in the field for many years by biologists, psychologists and anthropologists because of interest in the activities of our closest relatives. Many anthropologists were concerned that the infanticide hypothesis was widely promulgated and accepted when in fact there were few data to back it up. To look into the matter further, Thad Bartlett, Robert Sussman and James Cheverud (1993) carried out an extensive analysis of all the records of infanticide that had been published for species of monkeys and apes. They found that infanticide was *not* a widespread Darwinian strategy for males, but that instances of infanticide in primates "come from a very small number of species, and a careful examination of the specific context of each of these episodes [of male killing] fails to support the interpretation of infanticide as a primate wide adaptive complex." Of the forty-eight descriptions of primate infanticide in the literature, only six provide evidence consistent with the sexual-selection hypothesis (p. 976). Hrdy, however, refused to accept their data although she could not deny it. In her book *Mother Nature* (1999) she expounds throughout on infanticide by male langurs as an evolutionary strategy but does not cite the study of Sussman and his colleagues which found the behavior to be insignificant in this species.

Several years later one of these authors, Robert Sussman of Washington University in St Louis, decided that lion society, too, should be investigated to see if it also debunked the infanticide hypothesis. While chatting with his colleague at another university, Marc Bekoff, he heard of my paper on lions that Bekoff had filed away. Maybe the author would be willing to rewrite the paper in the light of research that had taken place since 1983? Sussman phoned me at my university to propose such a possibility which I immediately accepted. I had been following further research on lions from Africa but as far as I could see, none of it had given definitive support to the hypothesis of infanticide by male lions.

By that time, the lion researchers had organized a camera crew to follow for six weeks two lionesses with young cubs, day after day and into the night, to capture footage of cubs being killed by males (Packer 1994, 73). Eventually a male did kill a cub which the camera recorded. This scene of the killing was played and replayed on television leaving no doubt in viewers' minds that males did indeed kill cubs. However, to be an evolutionary strategy as we have seen, the male lion must then mate with the female to produce cubs and stay with her pride for several years while these cubs grow old enough to become independent. Anyway, being stalked by a camera crew for weeks at a time probably stressed the males, females and cubs so much that infant slaughter was inevitable. (Human behavior is known to negatively affect the behavior of animals observed. For example, in the northern elephant seal, females respond to the approach of human observers by threatening and biting both their own and other seal pups [Klopfer and Gilbert, 1966]. It was only when researchers decided to stand far back from the seals and observe them with binoculars that their normal unaggressive behavior resumed.)

For my new lion project I collected all the scientific information that had been published about lions and again analyzed the results to see if I agreed with the infanticide hypothesis. I did not. After completing my scientific article entitled "Infanticide by Male Lions Hypothesis: A Fallacy Influencing Research into Human Behavior" I sent it to the prestigious academic journal *American Anthropologist*. Because of its contentious nature, the journal editor had the article read and approved by five reviewers and a number of other readers to make sure it was completely accurate. It was finally published in the December 1998 issue of that journal.

Because my paper criticized a Darwinian psychological hypothesis, and a popular one at that (Packer's work on infanticide in lions has been cited hundreds of times by other scientists), proponents of this hypothesis immediately jumped into action. Two anthropologists, Joan Silk (Chair of the Department of Anthropology at the University of California, Los Angeles) and Craig Stanford (Associate Professor in the Department of Anthropology at the University of Southern California, Los Angeles), neither of whom were biologists or had ever studied lions in the field, wrote a critique of my paper and circulated it along with a petition to over ninety scholars asking if they wanted to add their names to those who objected to its content, although only a few were biologists or had ever studied lions or read the literature on lion behavior.[2]

Silk and Stanford then published an edited version of this critique in *Anthropology News* (1999), a weighty newsletter that goes out each month to the large membership of the American Anthropological Association. This version was accompanied by the approving signatures of seventeen academics, virtually all non-biologists, from

Scotland, England, Canada and the United States. My response justifying my article was published in the December 1999 issue of this newsletter. Before this issue came out, the controversy had received so much publicity that it was written up in another scholarly journal called *Lingua Franca* (Shea 1999), which specializes in providing information on academic controversies. Eventually lion researcher Packer himself wrote a critique of my original article which was published in the December 2000 issue of *American Anthropologist*, along with my response to this response.

Craig Packer has refused to countenance the fact that infanticide is not an innate behavior of male lions. When I sent him comments recently about an article he had published in *Nature* which continued to state that it was (Whitman et al., 2004), he replied to me angrily that if my remarks were ever published he would "be very harsh in dismissing you as a fringe scientist with some sort of bizarre obsession with a subject you seem to know nothing about." So much for rational scientific discourse.

What can one make of this flurry of activity? An important inference is that the facts of any debate are not necessarily important. I had supplied data backed up completely with references in my 1998 article, but scholars unconnected with biology and with lion research were willing to sign a statement saying that I was wrong. How did they know? Had they themselves read the fifty-two scientific books and articles that I cited as well as many articles beyond these? There would not have been time for them to do so. These scholars were some of the many consulted by Silk and Stanford who were known to be sympathetic to the tenets of Darwinian psychology. It is disturbing that adherence to a biological hypothesis takes precedence over the facts of a particular case. My hypothesis right or wrong? Can this be a proper way to conduct scientific debate?

Notes

1. We'll assume here that the lions' victims include not zebras and antelope but only other lions, just as human beings don't count as murder victims the individuals of other species that they kill—the cows they eat or the deer they shoot.
2. What is it about anthropologists? This activity recalls the denouncement of Derek Freeman's well-documented book *Margaret Mead and Samoa: The Making and Unmaking of an Anthropological Myth* (1983) at a special session of the American Anthropological Association to which he was not invited. Because Margaret Mead is an icon to most anthropologists and therefore not to be maligned no matter what the evidence against her, the book was pronounced in his absence to be "poorly written, unscientific, irresponsible and misleading." He responded that "to seek to dispose of a major scientific issue by a show of hands is a striking demonstration of the way in which belief can come to dominate the thinking of scholars" (Shaw, 2001).

Chapter 2

Theory Driving The Data—Infanticide

> A young divorced mother of two young lads has the chance to hook up with an attractive wealthy man. The only impediment is her sons; her new heart throb doesn't like children. One night she loads her sons into her car, straps them into their car seats, drives to a lake and, after climbing out of the vehicle and slamming the door, watches as it slowly slides into the water, drowning the terrified youngsters.

It is odd that although proponents of Darwinian psychology write a great deal about infanticide, the killing of dependent young by adults of the same species, and describe it as a clever evolutionary strategy of hundreds of species, the cases of infanticide we read about every few weeks in the newspaper are of parents killing their *own* children, a completely anti-evolutionary activity. A teenager shakes his baby—it wouldn't stop crying!—so hard that its brain stops functioning. A woman, overwhelmed by the responsibilities of parenthood, grabs her children one by one and drowns them in the bathtub. A husband, enraged at his wife's plan to leave him for another man, shoots her and their two children before turning the gun on himself.

Darwinian psychologists are great on extrapolating the behavior of human beings from that of other species, so let's consider the difference between infanticide in animals where adults kill the young of other adults (behavior that can confer an evolutionary benefit to the killer), and infanticide in modern human beings where parents usually murder their own children (which is obviously counterproductive from a hereditary point of view).

The concept of infanticide in animals as a Darwinian strategy, as we have seen for monkeys, apes and lions, is a fairly new hypothesis first postulated in 1974. However, in the short time it has been around it has become immensely popular. Immediately all sorts of researchers began reporting that "their" species, too, practised infanticide—what a great way to add another publication to one's credit with little effort! Many of these species really did seem to do so for evolutionary reasons, but many did not; in any case the desire to leap onto the Darwinian infanticide bandwagon was so great that one article on wild gibbons has "infanticide" in the title even though this behavior is unknown in this species. This lengthy paper proves that gibbons are not monogamous as has long been believed; rather, females mate with neighbors as well as with their partners which enables them "to confuse paternity and *forestall* infanticide" (Reichard and Sommer, 1997).

We know relatively little about infanticide in the wild for most species because it is almost impossible to observe—newly-born animals are small, so it doesn't take much time or effort to kill them. This is true even for lions, as we have seen. Since 1966 when successive biologists began to research the behavior of prides of lions on the open savannahs of Tanzania, tens of thousands of cubs have been born and have died, but fewer than two dozen have been seen or known (because of tell-tale tracks) to be killed by adult male and female lions (Dagg, 1998). In secretive or small mammals and birds, infanticide may be present but never even suspected by human observers. (Of course biological researchers themselves may cause stress and possibly infanticide in a population of animals they are studying, as we have noted for elephant seals.)

Nor is infanticide easy to understand in captivity although it is more readily observed. Newborn pups of small mammals in cages can be joined under scientific conditions by their mothers, their fathers or unrelated adults, but whether or not the young will be killed depends on such things as their age, the number of young, how much all the animals were handled before and during an experiment, the paternal interest of the male and the amount of stress experienced by the adults (Elwood, 1991). Because conditions in captivity are artificial, there is no way to determine if such infanticide would occur in the wild and if it did, whether it would represent a Darwinian strategy rather than a random act of aggression.

Infanticide as a Darwinian strategy has not been shown to occur in thoroughly-researched species of monkeys, apes and lions as we have seen, presumably because these are relatively large mammals whose young take two years or more to raise to independence. By contrast, animals in which infanticide *does* seem to be an evolutionary strategy raise their young to independence in a year or less; their tactic involves only a quick killing, not a long-term commitment of several years during which time many events can derail a male's agenda.

The reason for infanticide as a Darwinian strategy is resource competition. Depending on the species, young are killed for four main reasons: primarily as a response to food shortage as we shall see in the examples below, but also because of high population density, a shortage of nesting sites or the need for a partner.

Many infants die for lack of food, a basic requirement of life, such as lion cubs which starve for want of meat. In the far north, the arctic fox produces a litter of up to fourteen kits a year; if it is a year of plenty with abundant populations of lemmings and arctic hares, most of these kits will grow to be adults, but if populations of these prey species have crashed, then few of the young foxes will survive the famine.

Rather than some or most young dying slowly because of too little food, one solution is to kill individuals who are going to die anyway so that one or a few lucky siblings can prosper. This is the Darwinian solution that has evolved in many raptors. The "Cain Syndrome," the killing of one newly-hatched young by its older sibling, is named after Cain in the Bible who killed his brother Abel because of petty jealousy (Mock, 1984). The first egg of an eagle pair begins to develop as soon as it is laid, which means the nestling of a second egg is smaller than its sibling born several days earlier. The first nestling typically attacks the second, injuring or killing it and often pushing it out of the nest. This is an evolutionary adaptation because if it were not genetically beneficial in the long run, the offspring would not hatch at different times. Presumably the likelihood of the eagle parents finding enough food to produce two strong young is problematic, so by having one young kill the other all the food supplied by the parents is consumed by this one offspring. If the first egg does not hatch for some reason, the second acts as insurance so that the parents still have an eaglet to raise.

Nor is the Cain Syndrome restricted to birds. It also occurs in spotted hyenas who routinely produce twins in a litter. In one study, a twin was killed by its sibling born only an hour or so earlier in about one-quarter of litters (Frank, 1994); this siblicide was most common when both twins were females (the more aggressive and dominant sex in this species) and least common when both were males. Newborn hyenas were so vicious that they even tried to demolish a rolled towel of about their own size with their sharp teeth, or a brother or sister still encased in its amniotic sac. However, when there are lots of prey species available, siblicide may be unknown (Wachter et al., 2002). Again it is assumed that, when food is limited, sibling deaths are a product of evolution.

Sometimes food shortage will trigger family infanticide not by siblings, but by parents. In Heermann's gull which breeds in Mexico, the smaller last egg (second or third) that a female lays may hatch a chick that is killed by its parents if there is little available food (Urrutia and Drummond, 1990). From a distance observers saw parents pecking these smaller chicks on the head if they were begging, or all over the body if they were lying down. When the nestlings were dead, their bodies were pushed or tossed away from the family nest.

Concern about food also triggers an alpha female wolf to kill not any of her own cubs, but young born to subordinate females in her pack (McLeod, 1989). As there is only so much meat to go around, she wants to ensure that her cubs benefit from whatever is available. Instead of raising their own offspring each year, subordinate adults are reduced to helping the alpha pair raise theirs.

Sometimes infanticide seems to be a reaction not to limited food, but to too dense a population, as occurred in the urban populations of langurs in India mentioned earlier. Similarly (although here the rural and urban characteristics are reverse), in agricultural areas of France where there are dense populations of farm cats, transient males sometimes kill the young of resident females, something that they don't do in urban areas where there are fewer cats (Pontier and Natoli, 1999).

In ground-nesting skimmers and terns in Texas and Ontario crowded together in colonial sites, chicks who wander away from their home broods are sometimes killed by neighbors, although they are occasionally adopted instead (Quinn et al., 1994). This raises an evolutionary conundrum. Why would both types of behavior have evolved in these birds, one of which (adoption) is genetically non-productive? A Darwinian hypothesis is that young birds have inherited the tendency to leave their nest site and approach neighbor pairs if they are not being well cared for by their biological parents (Pierotti, 1991). To counteract this conduct, adult pairs have inherited the tendency to kill unrelated young, although sometimes this instinct doesn't kick in and they adopt and feed them instead. (Of course, this scenario may have no evolutionary aspect at all. Perhaps it is only by chance that a chick wanders away from "home" and is greeted by neighbors who, depending of their mood, either feed it or kill it.)

Less commonly, infanticide is an evolutionary response to a tight market for nesting sites. An example occurred in little swifts nesting in a colony on the ceiling of a passageway in Shimizu City, Japan, where each nest took several months to construct (Hotta, 1994). On a number of occasions, new swift arrivals killed the nestlings of resident pairs after one member of each pair had disappeared and probably died. Most of these new males or females then replaced the missing bird, mating with the remaining resident to produce new young. Nests were at a premium, so infanticide was a way to obtain one along with a new partner.

Finally, individuals in some species crave a mate although not necessarily a nest. One such species is the wattled jacana, a tropical shorebird in whom the sex roles are reversed with a polyandrous (a female mating with several males) mating system whereby males rather than females care for the eggs and the young (Emlen et al., 1989). When researchers removed a resident female, a replacement female soon killed the absent female's young and solicited mating with several males before laying eggs to be raised by one of the males.

The hypothesis of infanticide as an evolutionary strategy originally blamed males for killings as in the lion—it was assumed that the males would then mate with the mothers to produce their own progeny—but as some of the above examples show, females may be equally deadly. In the Columbian ground squirrel males were initially blamed in a field study as the perpetrators of infanticide before careful observation indicated rather that it was females who were killing young (Hare, 1991). Similarly, in a seven-year field study of black-tailed prairie dogs in South Dakota, fifty-one percent of all the litters born were wiped out partly or entirely, with most of the killers being lactating females presumably anxious to reduce competition for food for their own progeny (Hoogland, 1985).

As we have seen for lions and primates, infanticide need have no evolutionary purpose at all. In lions it happens when prides are in a state of chaos caused by a change in pride males. In species of bears, infanticide exists not because of societal chaos, but because hungry males who happen across cubs undefended by their mothers kill them for food (as Derocher and Wiig, 1999). In Jane Goodall's chimpanzees at Gombe two of the females, mother Passion and her daughter Pom, killed and ate up to nine infants belonging to other members of their troop (Goodall, 1986), even though the troop did not lack food. Random infanticide also occurs in fish and other "lower" forms where many young are produced but not guarded by their parents. These are all situational killings. If individuals did inherit behavior which made them routinely seek out and kill conspecific young, whole populations could be wiped out.

Among animals, we have seen that infanticide may be random and without scientific reason, but it also may be a strategy by which males and females improve their chances of having young who will carry on their genetic inheritance to the next generation. Does this apply also to human beings?

Long ago nomadic societies from which modern people evolved practised infanticide not because men and women had a genetic imperative to do so, but in order for the group to survive. Nomads move constantly from one food source to another—to feed on a kill too large to move easily, to hunt out edible tubers and roots, to visit fruiting trees. The males must have their arms free to scavenge or hunt or fight against predators the group chances upon, so the females must carry their children. It was impossible for a woman to carry two children at once for a long distance or usually to provide enough milk for both, so if a second child was born too close in age to another, it was routinely killed (Graber et al., 2000, 172). Or if twins were born, at least one would die (Milner, 2000, 160). Such infanticide also helped ensure that a group remained small enough to feed itself. If abnormal children were born, they too would be killed which removed a possible genetic disorder from the group (Milner, 2000, 161).

Societies changed for most people after horticulture and agriculture were invented by our human ancestors beginning about 10,000 years ago. Infanticide was no longer essential; there was usually food enough for everyone and children were valuable for manual labor on farms. As human populations increased and diversified during the past few thousands years, however, infanticide often reappeared, now for cultural rather than essential or evolutionary reasons (Harris and Ross, 1987).

Infanticide became an all too common feature of preindustrial societies of Europe and Asia where a mother or biological parents did not have the resources to raise their child. In Europe, infanticide was carried out in a number of ways (Harris and Ross, 1987, 90ff). Often a mother who could not look after all her children smothered a newborn by lying on it in the family bed. This was called "overlaying." In medieval Europe laws were passed to try to prevent mothers and babies from sleeping in the same bed, but such laws could not be enforced and no one could prove that the mother intended to harm her child.

Large numbers of infants were simply abandoned because their mothers were unable to care for them. Some of these were rescued and placed in a foundling hospital, the first established in 787 in Milan. However, children in these institutions also died at a high rate because they received poor care. As late as the eighteenth century, of 15,000 abandoned infants admitted to London's first foundling hospital, only 4,400 survived to adulthood.

Other unwanted infants were killed in other ways—given lethal drugs, buried alive or not fed. The English Parliament in 1624 passed a law "to prevent the murdering of bastard children," but this was ineffectual. Unmarried women tried to hide the fact that they were pregnant; if their condition was discovered but no baby was subsequently registered, juries proved sympathetic to the women, accepting almost any excuse for the babies' deaths.

Thousands of babies from families that could afford to do so farmed them out to wet nurses to suckle. Preferably these were women who had lost their own infants at birth so that all their milk would go to the new charge; however, country women were sometimes so poor that they killed their own infants so they could earn as much money as possible as wet nurses. Some of these women felt little obligation to the babies they were nursing; they could earn more money with a rapid turn-over of their charges, so the rate of infanticide for them was also high (Harris and Ross, 1987, 91).

Cases of modern infanticide in which a mother or father causes the death of their progeny go against Darwinian psychology in that the parents' genotypes are extinguished along with the child. In theory, parents should produce as many children as they can raise in order for their genetic inheritance to be passed on to the next generation, yet in his book *Hardness of Heart/Hardness of Life*, Larry Milner (2000, 549) argues that human infanticide, which was not uncommon in the past, still reflects a carrying out of a Darwinian psychological agenda: modern parents kill their children because they, like the rest of us, have a genetic code for infanticide that evolved in our nomadic ancestors. He writes (p. 548) that "Without excusing the commission of infanticide, we have to realize that there is a natural tendency for parents to kill their newborn child." By contrast, I believe infanticide was and is a function of culture or environment, triggered because of the harsh conditions in which a child was born or because of incredible stress which drove parents to such drastic behavior.

In nomadic days an infant was killed so that a group could thrive, but more recently regional infanticide has been practised to carry out a cultural agenda which often focuses on the baby's sex. In the cases noted above, whether a newborn was a male or a female usually did not matter; an infant of either sex was killed because its parents lacked the resources to raise it. More recently, especially in rural areas, either boys or usually girls were killed preferentially; in demographic charts this latter possibility is known as EFM, for "excess female mortality." It is impossible to tabulate the killing of infants when it occurs, but a biased ratio of boys to girls in a population gives a handy measure of which sex has been unwanted and which valued. In populations not subject to infanticide, a normal birth rate is about 106 boys born for every 100 girls. When the ratio of boys to girls increases, then female infanticide has occurred or else girls at an older age have died because of such things as receiving little food, little care, much work and/or too little dowry. Among some castes of Gujarat in India in the past, the male/female ratio was as great as 400:100, while other castes refused to raise any girls at all—a total anti-evolutionary practice (Harris and Ross, 1987, 97).

The direct and varying role of culture related to infanticide is well illustrated by data from Japan and from India. In Japan infanticide was widespread because there was no physical room or resources in this small nation for large families (p. 98). Young couples were especially likely to destroy firstborn sons because they needed daughters to help raise later sons. Older couples, by contrast, were more likely to kill daughters to make sure the family remained small.

More recently in areas of south and east India where rice paddies predominate, infanticide of females was reduced because women were important in weeding, harvesting, threshing and processing rice. By contrast, female infanticide was significantly greater in areas further north where wheat and other dry-land crops were grown. Here muscle power was important which increased male survival. Girls do less heavy agricultural work and when they marry, they move away from home and are of little further use to their birth family.

According to Darwinian psychological theory, parents should not kill their own progeny although to a small extent some do, as we have seen. Perhaps it could be shown that adoptive parents kill even more of their children than biological parents because they have no genetic connection with them? This would help to some extent to bolster the hypothesis. Psychologists Martin Daly and Margo Wilson decided to carry out research on this question which they describe at length in their book *The Truth About Cinderella*: *A Darwinian View of Parental Love* (1998) and their many articles on the subject. At first, their discoveries were exciting. The statistical data from Canada, the United States and Britain did show that stepparents (usually fathers because mothers are more likely to stay with their biological children) have a much higher rate of infanticide than biological parents.

However, more recent research invalidates their results. Three researchers from Sweden have discovered that in their country stepparents are not any more malevolent than biological parents (Temrin et al., 2000). By analyzing the data of all child homicide victims in Sweden during a twenty-year period, they found *no* increased murder rate of children who lived with a stepparent rather than with biological parents. This makes sense from another evolutionary perspective: a woman is unlikely to want to stay and have more offspring with a man who has murdered one of her children.

What could cause this difference between countries? In Sweden, the frequency of unwanted births is low because of the country's long history of widely-accepted legal abortions. By contrast, in Canada (and presumably in the United States and Britain), the frequency of unwanted births was about twice as high and especially common among young mothers who often lived in unstable social situations involving stepfathers. Hans Temrin and his colleagues (2000) found that children were killed for a variety of reasons—revenge against the other parent, jealousy, a lost court case, drug abuse, psychiatric problems. Because parents kill their children for personal or cultural reasons, infanticide in human families cannot be said to be an evolutionary phenomenon.

Proponents of Darwinian psychology are eager to study any human behavior that seems to fit into evolutionary theory, but they usually ignore data that do not do so. Infanticide by stepparents has been the focus of many research articles, but the proponents are largely silent on why almost eight times as many children are killed by biological parents (Jason et al., 1983). (Although Daly and Wilson found that the *rate* of killing was greater for stepparents, relatively few children live with stepparents). In Canada, parents killed 860 children under the age of twelve between 1974 and 2000 (Fedorowycz, 2002):

Biological fathers killed 410
Biological mothers killed 395
Biological parents killed 94 percent

Stepfathers killed 50
Stepmothers killed 5
Stepparents killed 6 percent

In Germany, the number of baby killings reached such a peak recently that thirty "baby boxes" have been established in urban areas (Buck, 2002). One is located in the bushy area around a side entrance of a large Berlin hospital where a mother can leave her newborn to be adopted with no questions asked.

Other related problems that go against Darwinian psychological theory have also been little studied including slave owners who, after raping African women slaves, were usually brutally indifferent to the fate of their genetic offspring (Rose, 2001, 123) and women world-wide who each year seek abortions by the millions.

In nomadic societies infanticide made sense, but today it does not. One could argue that biological parents might feel unready to raise their infant, or the mother might be depressed, or the infant might have a disability. However, there are thousands of childless couples desperate to adopt a child and if the Darwinian imperative to pass one's genetic inheritance were strong, one would imagine that parents who didn't want their child would find some way to give it up for adoption or state care (as in a baby box) rather than murder it.

Although human and non-human animals are similar in that both have individuals who practise infanticide, in animal species adults usually kill young that are not their own which often makes evolutionary sense. In human beings adults are likely to kill their own children, which does not. Human behavior in modern society confounds Darwinian psychology.

Chapter 3

Stereotypes—Aggression

> A young female baboon sits on Monkey Hill at the London Zoo in early January of 1927 beside her much larger mate, looking nervously about (Zuckerman, 1932, 224). She is becoming the object of attention of a second male who suddenly attacks her partner. Several other males join in the battle, biting each other and her, all screaming in excitement. When her mate is too injured to carry on the combat she is grabbed by another male while the biting and brawling swirls on. This male too is soon fatally injured. A third male clutches her victoriously and drags her to the pool of water where he is attacked by the remaining male. When the battle dies down, three males are dead. Even the remaining male isn't successful in his quest for a female because she dies the next day from her injuries. Is this scene of mayhem relevant to human aggression, here defined for simplicity as a wilful act or acts of violence directed toward members of the same species with intent to harm? Is violence an innate characteristic of humans beings?

In 1925 officials at the London Zoo "liberated" 100 hamadryas baboons (*Papio hamadryas*) into a rocky enclosure 100 feet long and sixty wide called Monkey Hill, where visitors and later researcher Solly Zuckerman could watch their behavior (Zuckerman, 1932, 218ff). Only six of the baboons were females. Unhappily, over the next years during which thirty more females and a few males were added to the crowded group, the males battled over the females so single-mindedly that thirty of the females died from injuries inflicted by them. Some had legs, ribs and even skulls fractured, along with bites and gashes on their bodies. Of the fifteen young known to be born only one survived, the others being strangled during attacks, crushed or bitten to death. In addition, sixty-two males were killed. Over two-thirds of the population was annihilated, much to the consternation of the keepers and the public. Little was known at the time about how apes and monkeys behaved in the wild, so people who heard about the baboon chaos from the media or from Zuckerman's book *The Social Life of Monkeys and Apes* (1932) began to think of large primates as natural killers.

This book had another effect, too. When Zuckerman described the various baboons in his book he used words such as "overlord," "bigamous family party," "harem," "an adult male with his family," "bachelor" (meaning celibate male) and "prostitution," indicating that baboons were almost human. Readers must have asked themselves why would he use such words if the baboons weren't very like people? Of course he enraged feminists because all of these words were used stereotypically (as well as incorrectly) (Dagg, 1983).

Zuckerman has a lot to answer for, although he didn't know that. With his book he encouraged a male obsession with aggression and violence which continues to this day, to the detriment of society, women and children. It is not only that males act out more aggressively than females and therefore are especially interested in the topic. It is that by worshipping aggression as we have done for several generations, females are subtly devalued at the same time. They may not feel the physical effects of male violence, but they must live in a society that often countenances values of "might is right."

In hindsight we know that the all-encompassing title of Zuckerman's book *The Social Life of Monkeys and Apes* indicates that he had no idea how unrepresentative his observations were of the actual behavior of the 200 or so different species of primates, research on which has kept thousands of scientists engrossed and financed for the past fifty years.

Nor did Zuckerman realize that a species' behavior in captivity and in the wild was not the same (p. 216). A comparison of the activities of wild and of caged baboons of another species (*Papio cynocephalus*) shows that they are quite different, with social interactions among captive animals far more common and the captive baboons more stressed because of their unnatural surroundings and their inability to escape from the group (Rowell, 1967). Zuckerman's study was of baboons crowded far too closely together, and with an unnatural sex ratio, who reacted to each other in highly abnormal ways. His conclusion that baboons were natural killers was unfounded, yet it influenced many people's perceptions of our early ancestors and of human nature. (Maybe men in positions of power wanted to be so influenced? Later on in his career Zuckerman was awarded a knighthood.) If men were aggressive because of their genetic inheritance, there was no point trying to eradicate this trait; women would have to realize they would always be at risk from men in general and must seek to find a husband to protect them.

Zuckerman remained intransigent to the end. As a patriarch at a 1962 conference on primates in London, he listened to Jane Goodall's first report on wild chimpanzee behavior with disdain. He insisted that all his own earlier observations had been confirmed, which was completely untrue, and that "...a few presumed facts which I have heard today have indeed been little better than anecdote picked up second hand" (Haraway, 1989, 268-9).

During the 1930s and 1940s, perhaps people were too focused on the Great Depression and on the second World War to worry philosophically about whether aggression was an innate part of human nature, although Hitler was a prime example of how violent and evil a man could be. Nor was there much focus on aggression in the 1950s; service people returning from war and immigrants moving to a new continent were happy to settle down and begin raising the baby boomer generation. Women accepted their limited place in society—as wives and mothers, lovers and caregivers. It was in the 1960s, spurred in part by the civil rights movements for blacks, that women began to revolt and also demand identities of their own.

It was also in the 1960s that journalists and scientists began to publish popular books about aggression, their theme often interlaced with the allegedly vicious behavior of our relative the baboon. Popularizing authors using a Darwinian perspective began to explain human behavior by likening it most often to that of the "killer" baboon. In his book *African Genesis: A Personal Investigation into the Animal Origins and Nature of Man* (1961), journalist Robert Ardrey could have compared human behavior with that of our closest relatives the apes, but he chose instead to highlight the presumably ferocious baboon. (He mentions baboons on four times as many pages as he does chimpanzees with whom we share much more DNA.) Like early human ancestors, baboons live in large savannah areas of Africa in social groups of fifty to sixty, eat mostly vegetable matter and scavenge meat when possible (Washburn and DeVore, 1961). However, in other ways the two groups were very different. Our early ancestors shared food, bonded more in couples, nursed the sick, used tools, cared for young for many years and related to each other in an egalitarian manner.

In his next book, *The Territorial Imperative: A Personal Inquiry into the Animal Origins of Property and Nations* (1966), Ardrey extended the theme of the "universality of innate aggressive behavior in the animal world" including human beings (p. 300). In support of this thesis he discusses baboons on twice as many pages as chimpanzees. Although both these primates are primarily vegetarians, he stresses the presumed importance of hunting to our ancestors. He noted that our male forebears actively enjoyed the chase and the kill, that they shared the meat of the animals they killed which encouraged bonding, and that hunting obliged males to cover much more territory than they would otherwise, given the mobile and erratic nature of their prey (Washburn and Avis, 1958).

Ardrey was a journalist, so his books were taken less seriously than that of zoologist Konrad Lorenz, *On Aggression*, published earlier in German and translated in 1966 into English. It was a smash hit, reprinted many times with multiple copies bought for university, school and public libraries and still used as a class text at the University of Toronto. Everyone had a soft spot in their heart for Lorenz, whose Nazi activities during the second World War were at that time little known. They'd seen pictures of him, bearded and loveable, trudging in rubber boots across his Austrian farmyard followed by a mesmerized gaggle of greylag geese who believe they were human, too, and that Lorenz was their beloved leader.

In *On Aggression* Lorenz (1967, 45) describes individual acts of aggression in the unlikely person of his old-fashioned aunt, who used to hire a maid but would never keep her for as long as a year. At first the aunt would be delighted with the new servant, but then she would find more fault with her month by month until finally she discovered a climactic hateful quality that sparked a violent quarrel, after which the bemused maid was fired without a reference. The story of Lorenz's aunt who could not keep a maid is a touching one, but not necessarily an example of inbred aggression building up to periodic explosions. What seems more likely is that she was a spoiled tyrant who insisted on always having her own way which was difficult for a maid or anyone else to cope with.

Lorenz also includes in his book examples of aggression in human groups such as the Ute Indians of the American West who had a "wild life consisting almost entirely of war and raids" which continued for several centuries (p. 210). He states that they could only have developed their "extreme aggressiveness" by "extreme selection pressure" over several centuries. This means that he thought the men had genes for violence which would have enhanced their reproductive success. It also implies inbreeding—that Utes had children with their own women rather than with foreign women they had captured.

Lorenz's information about the Ute Indians makes exciting reading but is incorrect. Omer Stewart (1968) who studied this tribe for thirty-five years claims that Lorenz's picture of them is "completely false," while John Beatty (1968) takes issue with Lorenz's opinion that aggression among them is genetically controlled. He points out that far from mating only among themselves, the Ute Indians stole women from other tribes to become their wives. Moreover government documents show that murder by Utes was rare; most homicides were of Utes by white men and by other tribes.

Lorenz used the anecdotes about his aunt and the Ute Indians to explain his theory of aggression based largely on observations of fighting in birds and cichlid fish. He believed that animals, including human beings such as his aunt and the Ute Indians, had inherited an instinct for aggression independent of experience (Berkowitz, 1990, 25). He thought that violence was triggered not necessarily by an external stimulus (such as drinking too much alcohol or being taunted or hit), but by excitations generated spontaneously in the nervous system. Therefore human aggression was an inbred part of human nature that made individuals erupt periodically to release their internal tension. His aunt could only put up with each maid for eight or nine months before she could no longer tolerate her and "blew," like a pressure cooker. He felt that Ute males in more recent civilized times had become neurotic because they could not discharge the aggression building up within them by injuring or killing members of other tribes (but not of their own). He did not wonder if any neurotic behavior might more likely have come from ostracism, extreme poverty and alcoholism fostered by their colonial status.

Fig 3.1 Konrad Lorenz's Psychohydraulic Model Applied to Aggression

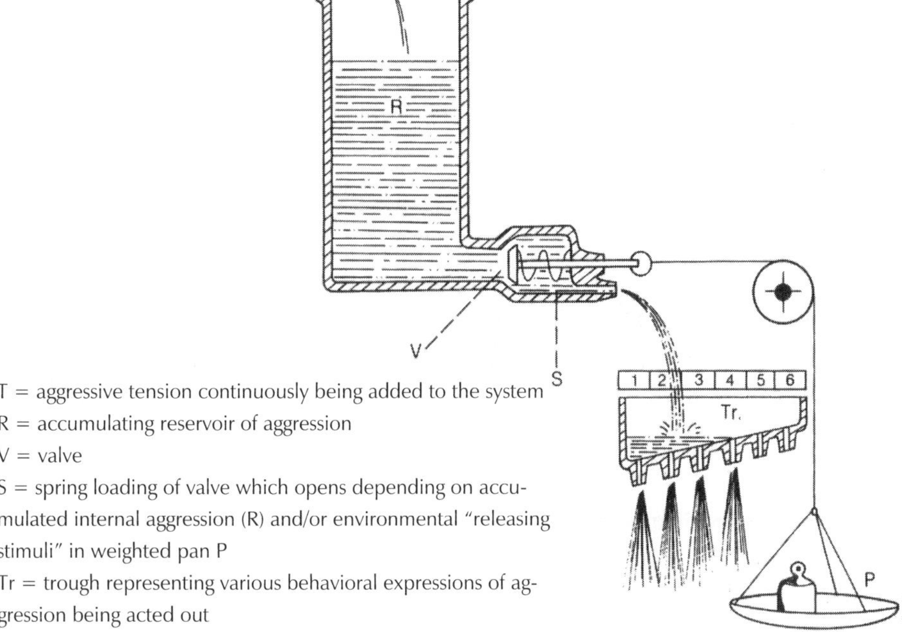

T
R
V
S
1 2 3 4 5 6
Tr.
P
T = aggressive tension continuously being added to the system
R = accumulating reservoir of aggression
V = valve
S = spring loading of valve which opens depending on accumulated internal aggression (R) and/or environmental "releasing stimuli" in weighted pan P
Tr = trough representing various behavioral expressions of aggression being acted out

Source: The Society of Experimental Biology, by permission.

Lorenz's description of the behavior is called a psychohydraulic model because the more aggressive tension (water) that accumulates, the more pressure is exerted and the more likely the person is to erupt in anger (Klama, 1987, 106). Lorenz felt that a civilized society should provide ways in which the invariable build-up of aggressive energy could be discharged—perhaps for a surgeon operating with a knife, or an academic "struggling" with a research problem, or for athletes games of sport (although these solutions would probably not have suited his aunt or the Utes).

The idea of sport dispersing aggression is doubtful, though. Sport is, itself, becoming increasingly violent with arenas and fields often filled with animosity. Instead of athletes getting rid of their aggression during competition, in some it fosters violence. One study carried out at ten American universities found that although only 3.3 percent of male undergraduates were athletes, they accounted for nineteen percent of sexual assaults on campus (Charbonneau, 2001).

Lorenz's psychohydraulic model works for some types of human behavior—it is valid for hunger and thirst because people become more insistent for food and water the longer they go without it—but not for aggression (Klama, 1987, 107ff). Men who do fight don't have to wait for their internal aggression level to build up, nor does a desire to fight necessarily build up over time, nor do they fight without any reason at all except that their aggression level has reached a climax.

With *On Aggression* so popular, there was obviously a huge market for books featuring aggression in human beings and other primates. In their book about human nature, *The Imperial Animal* (1971), two other scientists with the delightfully zoological names Lionel Tiger and Robin Fox paid even more attention than did Ardrey's books to "our cousin" the baboon. They discuss baboons on six times as many pages as chimpanzees, arguing that if baboons had weapons such as hand grenades (which the authors are sure baboons could quickly learn how to use), they would surely kill each other just as men do (p. 210). They admit that since baboons don't have weapons, they tend to flee if attacked.[1]

If one wants to trace human aggression from a Darwinian psychological perspective, then the best way to do so is to consider not the behavior of baboons and other monkeys but that of our closest relatives, based on the ninety-eight per cent similarity in DNA samples between people, chimpanzees (*Pan troglodytes*) and bonobos (*Pan paniscus*). (Bonobos, who were originally called pygmy chimpanzees, are more slender, with longer legs and more prominent genitals than their better-known sister species, but they are not too different in size [Waal, 1997].) Thanks to the research of Jane Goodall at Gombe and Toshisada Nishida in the Mahale Mountains, both in Tanzania, and their colleagues and many other researchers, we now know a great deal about the behavior of chimpanzees but far less about that of the rarer and more placid bonobos.

In her book *The Chimpanzees of Gombe*, Goodall (1986) states that aggression is common in everyday excitable chimpanzee life. Older infants' rough play may end in fights; mothers and other adults chastize young for unacceptable behavior; adult males may challenge each other for dominance; and adolescents and adults settle quarrels among males and among females with aggression and fight over who should eat a coveted food, who will take part in a consortship and who will play with a popular youngster (pp. 354-6, 321). For the first ten years of her research, this was about the extent of chimpanzee violence—lots of squabbling and screaming but few injuries.

Many years after her research began, Goodall (1986, 492ff) and her colleagues began to observe serious assaults by males. She records sixteen cases of violence from 1971 to 1982 (only two before 1975) (p. 495ff) when males attacked and killed or wounded individual females and their young from neighboring groups. More spectacular was discord among a large group of chimpanzees who regularly came to feed on up to 600 bananas a day at Goodall's feeding station (Goodall, 1986, 503ff; Ghiglieri, 2000, 172-3).[2] Sometimes they had to battle baboons as well for the food (Goodall, 2001, 74). After Goodall reduced this artificial feeding (but did not stop it), the group split into two communities which became enemies, one picking off and killing solitary individuals of the other group over a four-year period.

Some events are so momentous that they are cited by a number of authors, even though they add nothing new to the literature. Such is the report by Goodall of the combat pitting Kasakela males against lone individuals of the Kahama community. Based on her descriptions (1986, 506ff), the murders of Goliath, Sniff and other males are chronicled again in detail in at least four books by male authors who use the attacks to indicate that men have come by their aggression naturally during the course of human evolution.[3]

However, we must be careful not to treat this onslaught as the norm for two reasons. First, Goodall herself (1986, 503) notes that "Unfortunately the factors leading up to the community division are, to some extent, confused by the banana-feeding regime," so we do not know if it would have occurred under natural conditions. Second, it is the most grizzly example of chimpanzee aggression known and at the opposite extreme from normal chimpanzee life where injuries or killings are rare; nothing like it had been seen in over a dozen years of observation. Anecdotal evidence is powerful because it may resonate with one's own experience or wishful thinking, and so remain in the memory, even though one anecdotal episode is negligible compared to statistical data which reveal how uncommon the homicidal activity was.

Since human beings are about equally related to chimpanzees and to bonobos (the apes became differentiated from each other long after their and our common ancestors diverged), might we have inherited in common some of the same behavior patterns? If our ancestors were more like chimpanzees, then maybe they were aggressive too? But if they were more like bonobos, which is equally possible given our genetic similarities, one would assume they were unaggressive because bonobo society is organized around peace, not war. In addition, other behavior of bonobos is much more like that of human beings than is that of chimpanzees. For example, like women but unlike chimpanzees, bonobos copulate at any time of the year, not only when they are ovulating. In bonobos compared to chimpanzees there is more male/female bonding, more sharing of food and more toleration by males of the young (Waal, 1997).

Bonobos are female-centred and although males and females are co-dominant much of the time, the female has the upper hand when it comes to eating; a large male can't take food from females because they will band together to drive him off (Waal, 1997, 61). As in most species individuals may be annoyed with their fellows, but bonobos choose to diffuse tense situations with sex rather than with threats or conflict: "The chimpanzee resolves sexual issues with power; the bonobo resolves power issues with sex" (Waal, 1997, 32). If human beings resemble their closest relatives, why are they assumed to be more like the aggressive chimpanzees than the bonobos which share more individual behaviors with people? It is the men who publish books and articles about human aggression who have championed as our closest relative the belligerent baboon and the aggressive chimpanzee rather than the placid bonobo and thus helped shape the common belief that men are by nature violent.

But are chimpanzees themselves innately violent? Yes, they do squabble among themselves, but is the behavior more virulent than this? Margaret Power, in her book *The Egalitarians—Human and Chimpanzee* (1991), thinks not. She argues that chimpanzees aren't naturally as violent as they have been seen to be at Gombe in the past thirty years. Rather, they have been conditioned to be belligerent by the provisioning that Goodall instituted for her research in 1961 so that she would have a better chance of seeing the animals she was trying to study. The year before she had watched and followed chimpanzees in the surrounding rain forest but she was unable to approach closely to them, or differentiate between individuals, or see exactly what they were doing amidst thick foliage.

Goodall decided to feed chimpanzees by putting out bunches of bananas near her campsite and later in a feeding area. Gradually, over the years, more and more chimpanzees were attracted to the area by the food (Van Lawick-Goodall, 1971, 69ff). This enabled her to become acquainted with the various individuals she lived among, and with how each reacted to the food and to each other and herself. Without this innovation she would not have been able to study the animals as effectively as she did.

However, provisioning had a marked effect on the chimpanzees, especially when there were not enough bananas to go around (Wrangham, 1974). Goodall (Van Lawick-Goodall, 1971, 133) found that after a few years "They were beginning to move about in large groups more than they had ever done in the old days. They were sleeping near camp and arriving in noisy hordes first thing in the morning. Worst of all, the adult males were becoming increasingly aggressive. When we first offered the chimps bananas the males seldom fought over their food: they shared boxes or, at worst, chased off another individual, or threatened, without actually attacking."

Goodall describes how the new regime affected the behavior of a timid chimpanzee called Mike, judged to be one of the lowliest males because he was the last to gain access to the bananas she set out (109ff). On one occasion he was sitting by himself with five large males nearby, grooming each other. After staring at them for a while, he picked up two empty paraffin cans by their handles and rushed toward the males, giving a series of pant-hoots and hitting the two cans together in front of him, making a terrific racket. The males scattered at his clamorous charge. A moment later, he rushed toward them a second time banging his cans, and then a third time. When he finally settled down the males approached him submissively, four of them grooming him. Before long, Mike had risen to the top-ranking position in the community where he remained for six years.

Even as early as 1966, the incidence of fighting had increased more than ever before, and some individuals hung around the camp for many hours each day (p. 133). One article, "Artificial feeding of chimpanzees and baboons in their natural habitat," describes how systematically feeding bananas to the chimpanzees in Gombe resulted in a sharp increase in aggression (Wrangham, 1974). Another entitled "How wild are the Gombe chimpanzees?" agrees with this view (Reynolds, 1975). (Because of these reports, Frans de Waal [1982, 24], chief researcher of a large chimpanzee troop in the Arnhem Zoo in Holland, made a point of *not* feeding the troop all together when they would have competed and fought with each other, but supplied food in the early morning and evening to the ten cages where the ten small groups each spent the night.)

Goodall (1986, 3) concluded that the behavior of her chimpanzees was different in the first ten years during which period provisioning was attracting increasing numbers of animals; they seemed "far more peaceable than humans," compared to later when the shocking attacks and murders mentioned above were observed. However, in writing her definitive study of the animals (p. 55) she downplayed her earlier reports in which violence was described as rare, noting that "in order to present an up-to-date picture, I have drawn extensively on data collected since 1975."

Power (1991, 3) believes that at Gombe and in research at Mahale National Park in Tanzania, the competition and resentment aroused by artificial feeding when there were not enough bananas to go around "deeply frustrated the chimpanzees, which precipitated extensive, qualitative change in their behavior and organization." Her survey of the literature found that for seventeen scientific reports of nonprovisioned chimpanzee behavior based on observations at eight African field research sites, sixteen reported little or no aggressive interaction in their populations (p. 23). In only one did the author have the impression that "although the apes were rarely truly aggressive and there was no permanent leader, some extremely vague indications of a dominance hierarchy were discernible." This is in marked contrast to the later behavior of provisioned chimpanzees at Gombe and Mahale which was "aggressive, dominance-oriented, [and] fiercely territorial" (p. 23). Once (provisioned) chimpanzees were cast as fiercely aggressive, Power found that earlier data from non-provisioned groups "were summarily dismissed as yielding 'little or no data' on behavior" (p. 23).

Wildlife biologist Michael Ghiglieri set himself the difficult problem of solving whether chimpanzees were naturally aggressive, or if provisioning had made them so, as he describes in his book *East of the Mountains of the Moon: Chimpanzee Society in the African Rain Forest* (1988). He spent two years in the Kibale Forest of Uganda, waiting under fruit trees where chimpanzees came for food to study their behavior. His research was much more difficult than that of Goodall; since he did not give the animals bananas, they had no reason to depend on him. He could observe only those who stayed around because they tolerated his presence.

During his research Ghiglieri saw "surprisingly few" dominance interactions (p. 243) among individuals, and no attacking or killing of different groups. However, he notes that this could be because such attacks are never numerous, and because the forest had grassland on two sides where few chimpanzees went, perhaps precluding fights there (p. 257). He reports (p. 257) that "Not having seen active territoriality does leave the question in Kibale open" but concludes, with no evidence beyond theory, that chimpanzees are indeed territorially aggressive. Later, these males did kill other males (Ghiglieri, 2000, 174).

If aggression were an integral part of chimpanzee behavior, one would expect that the most aggressive males would be more likely than other males to mate with females and have, in turn, aggressive offspring. However, female chimpanzees in heat are eager to mate with any available male; for example, thirty-year-old Flo was so sexy that she was followed by fourteen males when she was in heat and later copulated fifty times in one day (Goodall, 1986, 446), so many males could have sired her next offspring. (Some male biologists continue to put a male-biased spin on polygamous behavior as Michael Ghiglieri does [2000, 175], stating that "males shared each other's females." Such a statement would amaze Flo.)

In the evolutionary history of human beings, anatomy indicates that our ancestors may have become less rather than more aggressive over the millennia. Male (but not female) chimpanzees have large canine teeth which tend in mammals to correlate with aggressive behavior. By contrast australopithecines, who evolved from a common ancestor of both human beings and chimpanzees/bonobos, have small canines in both males and females, as do present-day human beings.

The upshot of the recent revelations by Goodall of chimpanzee violence has been swift: baboon out and chimpanzee in. Forget, needless to say, the neglected bonobo. No need now to emphasize the violent behavior of the baboon in popular books when we have the killer chimpanzee instead, our much closer relative. Time for new books based on this new truth, including Lyall Watson's *Dark Nature: A Natural History of Evil* (1995), Richard Wrangham's and Dale Peterson's *Demonic Males: Apes and the Origins of Human Violence* (1996), Michael Ghiglieri's *The Dark Side of Man* (2000), and Neil Boyd's *The Beast Within: Why Men Are Violent* (2000). These books deal from a Darwinian perspective with hot topics such as aggression, violence, rape and war, all of which serve to keep men in control and women subservient.

Looking back on our lives, most of them have been spent living in relative harmony with others. With the possible exception of young men who are often encouraged in our society to be aggressive in sport and elsewhere, most of us live at peace with our neighbors, volunteer at food banks, make cookies for church bazaars, rally to make streets safe for our children and sing in community choirs. Why then, in the world of books, the obsession with violence rather than cooperation? With war rather than peace?

Is the hope of making a bundle of money the reason that male authors churn out books about atrocities performed largely by male animals and men, but not about cooperation and care in societies? Certainly. But there may be another hidden agenda, probably hidden even from the authors themselves. This is the cultural need reflected by the media to keep a male-defined order in society. The tenets of Darwinian psychology fit in with this political and conservative agenda. Signe Howell and Roy Willis (1989, 10) argue that if men in general are perceived as violent with limitless needs and desires, then authoritarianism is necessary to keep them in control. If conflict is inevitabe because of human nature, this justifies militarism and the production of weapons. And because it is men who are usually violent with aggression directed in part at women and at competition for women's favors, women are seen as property resulting in sexism.

The most widely touted topic of Darwinian psychology is that of aggression. Scores of books and thousands of articles have been written on this subject, some stressing the inevitability of violence and war given the aggressive nature of men, yet others pointing to the huge array of environmental factors which trigger human aggression and undercut notions of biological determinism. Most animals are aggressive if attacked, so in one sense the capacity for violence is hereditary. However, there is little evidence of genes that pass on this condition to some violent men and a few violent women in violent families as we shall see in the next chapter. In the daily course of human affairs there are many thousands of acts of compassion and cooperation for every act of physical violence. Even when a war is fought, as discussed in Chapter 5, it is caused by politicians and statesmen seeking power, resources or retribution, not individual soldiers who may or may not be aggressive in their private lives.

Notes

1. Despite Lionel Tiger's insistence in mainly comparing the behavior of people with that of baboons rather than of chimpanzees, their much closer relative, he is quoted as saying, "If I hate anything, it's self-righteous commission of empirical error. I don't like it when people get facts wrong for reasons that they're confident overwhelm any intellectual dishonesty. Can't stand it, and there's too much of it in the world." However, the bias in their book toward monkeys as opposed to apes surely leads to similar error that Tiger claims to find unacceptable (Houpt, 2002).
2. The provisioning of the chimpanzees had another negative result. Apparently because of the close contact between the animals and their feeders, a polio epidemic among the Africans was spread to the chimpanzees. Up to fifteen animals were affected of whom six died (Goodall, 2001, 16).
3. These books are: *Peacemaking among Primates* by Frans de Waal (1989, p71), *The Third Chimpanzee* by Jared Diamond (1992, p291ff), *Demonic Males* by Richard Wrangham and Dale Peterson (1996, pp16ff) and *The Beast Within* (2000, pp30ff) by Neil Boyd.

Chapter 4

How Would Inheritance Work?—Aggression

Religious feeling, territoriality, homosexuality, morality, warmongering, aggression —E.O. Wilson in his book *Sociobiology* (1975) believes that all of these behavioral traits and many more have been passed down to us genetically through evolution from our primate ancestors. Moreover, some or all of these traits are not common to all people, since not all people are homosexual, or religious, or moral, or aggressive. These traits are present in some people and not others, reflecting their personalities and experiences. This chapter will consider how a genotype, if there were one for aggression, might be possible for human beings.

One basic problem is that behavioral traits are vague and impossible to define concisely. Does the fact that you go to church or worship a deity mean that you have a "religious gene?" What if you worship every day? or every Sunday? or only on holy days? Is a moral person one who countenances abortion believing that no child should be unwanted, or one who disapproves of birth control? Is a homosexual person one who has a brief homosexual fling and then marries, one who remains celibate because of sexual confusion, or one who has never had a romantic interest in the other sex? What do we make of those who say they have no interest in either sex?

Genetic inheritance works best when it deals with discrete entities such as the size or seed coat color of sweet peas (used by monk Gregor Mendel in his pioneering work) or the presence or absence of a gene for cystic fibrosis. How would we define aggression for example, our topic here? Is it a man who hits other family members? Shoots enemies in cold blood on the street or during a war? Threatens his drinking buddies? A woman who shouts at her child and hits the dog? In the academic literature there are 250 definitions of aggression which illustrates the scope of the problem (Cadoret et al., 1997). The difficulty is compounded because at a basic level virtually *all* animals can be aggressive if the occasion warrants it. A lion is always prepared to kill for dinner. A rabbit usually freezes when in danger, but will bite if you grab it. A timid Quaker woman may become violent if someone tries to harm her young daughter.

Psychiatrist Anthony Storr in his book *Human Aggression* (1968, 2) argues that aggression is a positive force in the animal world because it ensures competition for food and mates and puts in place dominance hierarchies that reduce future combat. However, he is more pessimistic about its place in humanity, given his own dark nature. He writes (p. xi): "We know in our hearts that each one of us harbours within himself [sic] those same savage impulses which lead to murder, to torture and to war." He further states that "men enjoy the enlivening effect of being angry when they can justify it, and that they seek out opponents whom they can attack in much the same way the cichlid fish do." Surely he overstates the case?

How can we account for aggression in human beings? Proponents of Darwinian psychology believe that it is largely genetic in origin, while behaviorists who have done research on the topic know that it has an enormous environmental aspect. In this chapter we will address both these views and then consider how an inherited aggression might have been carried through six millions years of evolution to ourselves. We shall end with a discussion of sociality which answers many of the questions raised earlier.

Let's consider first the environmental aspects of aggression, meaning that a myriad of causes unrelated to inheritance can enrage people. Many thousands of psychologists, psychiatrists and biologists make a good living by doing research into the reasons for aggression and violence (Berkowitz, 1990, 316); in 1999 the academic journal *Aggressive Behavior* listed 405 newly-published articles on human aggressive behaviour appearing in 253 different journals.

A glance at such recent research results shows that any number of external factors trigger aggression. Some of them are biological (although not necessarily genetic). Women who smoke tend to have aggressive children (Conlon, 1999); children who wear hockey helmets that heat their brains are especially likely to lash out at opponents (Bailey, 2000); people who suffer from antisocial personality disorders and, to a lesser extent schizophrenia and bipolar disease, are more likely to be violent than other people (Guze, 1999, 105); and young men are more violent than older men (Baron et al., 1999).

Some triggers are related to family life. Older children are more often aggressive than are their younger siblings (Sulloway, 1996); boys born to teenage mothers with low levels of education are especially likely to be aggressive adults (Nagin and Tremblay, 2001); in China with its one-child per couple policy, offspring are now often encouraged to be aggressive by their parents with policeman, soldiers and successful businessmen especially likely to raise belligerent children (Weiping and Longquan, 1999); and a child who sees his or her father abusing their mother is the strongest risk factor for transmitting violent behavior to the next generation (APA, 1996).

Aggression is also correlated with nationhood. Homicide rates are low in Norway, China and Finland (about one per 100,000 people) but high in the United States (8.6 per 100,000) and in many simple societies (Triandis, 1994, 212). (In Chapter 5 we shall see that nations themselves may be warlike for a while, and then pacifist, or vice versa.) In Western countries murders are often correlated with laws reflecting whether or not handguns are readily available.

Religion also affects aggression: in New Delhi, Moslem children are more aggressive than Hindu children with Sikh children testing in between these groups (Österman et al., 1999); Moslems may become extreme terrorists as we have seen in al-Qaeda; Quakers and Bahai believers are usually nonviolent because of their religious beliefs.

What people drink can activate aggression: British beverages called Slush Puppies cause disruptive behavior and disobedience in school children (Jarvie, 2000) while drinking alcohol makes some men mean enough to rape (Aromäki et al., 1999).

A person's circumstances may provoke aggression. Someone with high self-esteem is especially likely to be violent if his view of himself is disputed (Baumeister et al., 1996); men who have been abused as children are more likely than others to become abusers themselves (Malinosky-Rummell and Hansen, 1994); men working in urban areas are more prone to violence than those employed in the suburbs (Baron et al., 1999); and urban violence is triggered by continuous loud noise, excessive crowding, excessive heat and poor air quality (Baron and Richardson, 1994, 166ff).

Particular situations or issues may lead to aggression: children who watch fights on television or play violent video games are more likely than other children to be aggressive toward friends and strangers (Anderson and Bushman, 2002)[1]; parents fight over child custody issues; a husband facing divorce may kill his wife and often himself too; road rage on highways; air rage in planes; and the anger felt by some people over women being allowed to have abortions which is only equalled by the anger of others if women are NOT allowed abortions. The list of situations that trigger aggression elicited by emotions such as frustration, pain or fear is almost endless.

Aggression may also be a result of a combination of factors. For example, in most societies boys are more aggressive than girls but this depends on both biology and culture. Children as they grow are taught how to control (or not) their anger: in the Western world boys are lauded for being physical among friends and in games (football, hockey), while girls are censured for acting out in what is seen as inappropriate ways.

On average, men are more violent and aggressive than women, an aggression correlated with (but not necessarily caused by) the presence of the hormone testosterone (Archer, 1991; Aromäki et al., 1999). However, in Roman times women were gladiators, Joan of Arc is famous for the battles she fought, and today in Cameroon, gangs of hefty African women roam city streets after dark, snatching the papers and money of lone men and beating up those bold enough to resist (Barley, 1983, 23). Increasingly girls and women are being convicted of violent acts, indicating that the extent of biological aggression in females is unclear (Pearson, 1997). Most cultures have repressed girls and women in the past, some of whom are only now breaking free of female stereotypes. Perhaps females have not been judged to be aggressive in part because they have practised this characteristic indirectly with verbal attacks rather than by physical acts? (Österman et al., 1999).

In his book *The Creation of Dangerous Violent Criminals* (1989), Lonnie Athens analyzes the process described to him in interviews with violent prisoners that has made them dangerous. What he calls "violentization" occurs in four distinct stages. First, the child, usually a boy, is subjected or exposed to extreme abuse, usually within the family. The child broods about the horror, then decides to attack those who provoke him to forestall future abuse. Thirdly, he carries out attacks and if his enemy capitulates, he feels himself invincible and ready for the final fourth stage, to solve all his problems with violence. The process is one of experience, not inheritance.

The coffee-growing district of Juquila in Mexico is an example of a society besieged by negative environmental factors rather than by individual inheritances. There men have killed dozens of people because of land disputes, alcohol, guns, history, political forces, witchcraft, machismo, prejudice, capitalism and class conflict (Greenberg, 1989). A popular saying in the area was "To be a man, one must drink, have passed at least one night in jail, and have been shot once." In the early 1980s the women in four towns in the region became tired of all the killing. They organized and passed ordinances prohibiting the sale and consumption of alcohol and the carrying of knives and guns which were strictly enforced. Although homicides continued in other towns, these decrees where the vigilant women lived drastically curtailed them.

Now let's consider how the inheritance of aggression might work, a process that proponents of Darwinian psychology routinely neglect, as if such a paltry detail is of little interest. We'll define aggression loosely as the tendency for a person to commit acts of violence against other people. First we must take into account that in most cultures, physical violence is practised far more often by men than women. This sexual difference implies a sexual bias in the genetic system. If a man had a gene (or genes) for aggression he could pass it on to his children who would presumably then be aggressive in turn. Would an aggressive gene be somehow muted in his daughters? Would his daughters become carriers for the trait? Would hormones be involved somehow? Would some boys have two genes for aggression and some only one, in which case would the former be twice as violent as the latter? Or might the aggression gene(s) be on the Y male chromosome?

Researchers studying the possible inheritance of specific behaviors were originally heartened by the knowledge that hundreds of human ailments such as Huntingdon's disease, hemophilia and cystic fibrosis are caused by a single gene. They tried to pinpoint single genes for behaviors linked with homosexuality, alcoholism, schizophrenia, bipolar disorder and shyness but ultimately without success. Human social behaviors are far too complex and far too intertwined with an individual's personality, development and environment to be correlated with a single gene.

Even so, in 1992 the *Los Angeles Times* published a headline announcing "Researchers Link Gene to Aggression" which reported on the study of an extended Dutch family. A school teacher in the Netherlands had noticed among his relatives a remarkable number of males with a pattern of violent behavior. This observation triggered a large research project into the genotypes of the various family members (Brunner et al., 1993). The violent individuals were found to have DNA with an abnormal gene on the X chromosome for monoamine oxidase type A (MAOA), an enzyme known for breaking down several neurotransmitters in the brain (Allen, 1996, 378). The nine researchers hypothesized that the accumulation of these chemicals could be a cause of the violence. However, they were cautious about what their findings actually meant because one man who had the abnormal gene wasn't violent, and they had no idea exactly how the relationship between the chemicals and the behavior might work. More recent research on New Zealand men indicates that those with the genetic MAOA defect *may* be more aggressive than their peers, but only if they have been severely mistreated as they grew up, indicating an environmental component to the behavior (Stokstad, 2002).

The excitement engendered by the 1992 research faded away over the next years as more and more scientists found fault with it. A major review of the subject concludes that genetic factors predisposing to aggressiveness do exist, but they will involve a number of genes and "many loci acting in concert, and will be imbedded in complex developmental pathways involving neurotransmitter systems" (Cadoret et al., 1997, 317). There is no evidence beyond anecdote that there is a human instinct for aggression that must be expressed no matter what the circumstances such as Lorenz believed existed in his aunt and in the Ute Indians with their fierce reputation (Berkowitz, 1990). (In Chapter 8, dealing with crime, we will consider another false alarm connecting genotype and aggression.) The strongest genetic marker for violence can be said to be the Y male chromosome (Stokstad, 2002).

Proponents of Darwinian psychology envision aggression present in our primate ancestors being passed down genetically during six million years of evolution to human beings. All individuals are capable of violence to some extent, but Darwinian psychology implies that some individuals have inherited through their genes a more aggressive nature than others, and that these individuals have had superior reproductive success during the past millions of years. We know that our relatives the chimpanzees can sometimes be violent, even killers, but we have only fossil bones to represent our own early forebears. Let's consider in detail the possible aggression of these ancestors, even though we can only speculate about this behavior.

Fig 4.1 Schematic Evolutionary Relationships of Apes and Human Beings

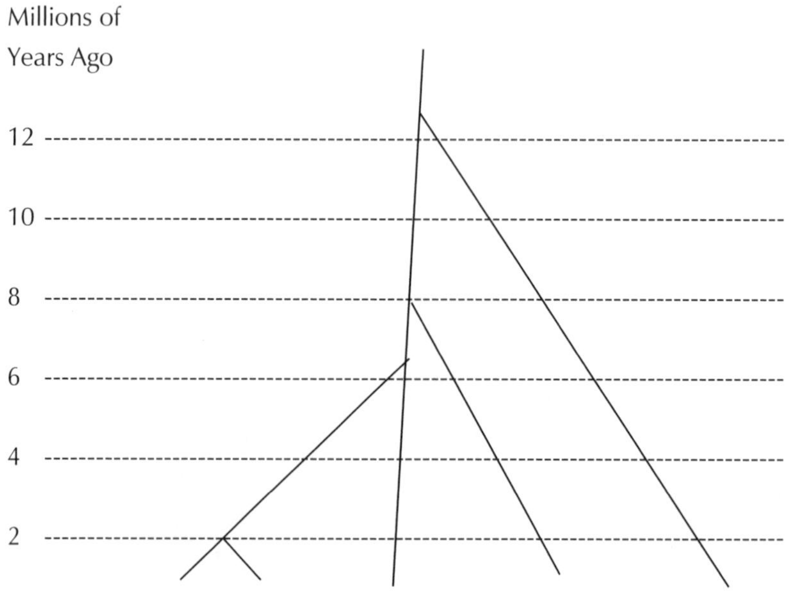

Millions of
Years Ago

12

10

8

6

4

2

Source: Data from Peterson, 2003, 6

About six million years ago our ape-like ancestors separated into two lineages, one leading to the chimpanzees and bonobos who now spend their semi-arboreal life in forests feeding on fruit, vegetation and occasionally meat, and the other leading to other hominids and to ourselves. (Human beings as a species evolved over a much shorter time period than did chimpanzees because these animals have DNA sequences almost four times as diverse as ours [Kaessmann et al., 1999].)

The story of the lineage that gave rise to human beings is incredibly important to Darwinian psychology because it comprises the Environment of Evolutionary Adaptation, EEA. It is presumed that during these millions of years our forebears developed the behaviors that eventually made them human. Such behaviors may seem dysfunctional in the modern world, but that is because the modern world is now greatly changed from the environment in which human beings evolved.

The only evidence we have to tell us about the nature of our early ancestors are a few fossil bones. What can a few bones tell us? An amazing amount. When we think about members of our ancestor *Australopithecus*, their few available bones tell us two key truths: that they were small—the fossil bones of our forebear Lucy from 3.2 million years ago show that she was only 3 feet, 7 inches (1.09 m) tall—and that unlike apes they walked on two legs judging from the anatomy of their pelvis (Cavalli-Sforza and Cavalli-Sforza, 1995). Bipedalism enabled animals to carry food and perhaps an offspring in their arms and to see farther. It kept each individual's head farther above the hot earth (humans are the only primate that sweat, especially in the head) and signalled his or her sex (Berger, 2000).

From these facts we infer that Lucy and her peers lived in open areas of Africa where, because food was much sparser than in the jungle, they had to walk long distances to find enough roots and fruit to eat and water to drink. Because of their small size they would have been in part scavengers subject themselves to predation. Because of the scarcity of food, they must have lived in small rather than large groups. Because they were nomadic, the women would only have been able to carry and nurse a new infant about every four years, or an average of fewer than five or six children in her lifetime (Howell, 1979, 128).[2]

This low birth rate, coupled with deaths from disease, famine, accidents and predation, suggests that if there had been a great deal of violence between individuals, whole groups might have perished and along with them, the genes for aggression. Were our early ancestors as violent as modern human beings? Probably not. There were far fewer of them living in small groups, with no territories that needed to be defended. Early australopithecine skulls were once thought to have been slashed with "spear wounds," but recent research shows instead that the scratches were caused by the canine teeth of a leopard dragging hapless individuals along by the head (Keeley, 1996, 36).

The australopithecines gave rise in time to the earliest hominid, *Homo habilis*, who existed from about two and a half to two million years ago (Cavalli-Sforza and Cavalli-Sforza, 1995). This species was small like the australopithecines but with a brain about fifty percent larger. This allowed it to make crude tools such as choppers and scrapers. *Homo erectus*, who evolved about two million years ago, was bigger in size with a much larger sophisticated brain used to create fire, communicate by primitive speech and eventually hunt animals; a human femur dating from 1.8 million years ago had a break, which would have incapacitated the owner but which had then healed, indicating that by that period individuals were helping each other to survive (Leakey, 2001, 263).

Members of our own species, *Homo sapiens*, appeared on the scene about half a million years ago having evolved over a period of as long as half a million years from *Homo erectus*. Journalist Robert Ardrey (1966, 261) who wrote from a Darwinian psychological perspective emphasizes human aggression by stating that as early as two million years ago *Homo habilis* was already an effective hunter of big game. He declares that meat was essential for our forebears: "Lettuce is great for diets, but not for men who have to work for a living" (Leakey and Ardrey, 1971, 14) (although members of entire cultures such as the Hindu live their whole lives as vegans or vegetarians.) Thus Ardrey believes that aggression (although not specifically aggression against fellow human beings) was present through much of our evolutionary history.

Louis Leakey, famous for facilitating the primate research of Jane Goodall, Dian Fossey and Birute Galdikas, disagreed with this view. He believed that our forebears had a far longer history of scavenging before they mastered the art of hunting effectively about 40,000 years ago when they had produced and mastered weapons such as bola balls, spears, and bow and arrows (Leakey and Ardrey, 1971). Without such weapons which could kill or wound at a distance, how could hunters hope to fell animals that ran faster than they did and were usually much stronger as well?

To illustrate the importance and feasibility of scavenging among our ancestors, Leakey and his son Richard while in the field in Africa tested their ability to scavenge as our forebears had by taking off all their clothes and grabbing giraffe leg bones to protect themselves. Approaching hyenas feeding on a zebra kill that lions had made, they were able to scare away and hold off the hyenas for about ten minutes while they hacked some meat from the zebra—the hyenas were "furious," Leakey reports.

Ardrey believed that human cooperation evolved because it was necessary for group hunting, a hypothesis that has been resurrected by the proponent of Darwinian psychology Craig Stanford in his book *The Hunting Apes* (1999). This seems highly unlikely. Nancy Makepeace Tanner (1981, 263ff) argues more persuasively that long before hunting was mastered, cooperation was essential for gathering plant foods, an activity carried out during millions of years of human evolution. Each day, members of a group had to decide where to go to look for roots or fruit, and to go together for protection against predators. Tanner believes that sharing, a behavior intrinsic to human beings, began first with mothers feeding their already-weaned young with food they had gathered. The most intelligent females, those who fashioned tools to help dig up roots and took good care of their young, were the most reproductively successful. They would tend to mate with males who were intelligent but not overtly aggressive (e.g., not with the large canine teeth present in male chimpanzees).

Martin Daly and Margo Wilson (1988, 144) suggest that violence during evolution may have selected for bigger men in foraging societies since they would win most combats and likely have more children because of this. However, the difference in size between men and women today is about the same as that in chimpanzees and bonobos, with females weighing on average about 80-85 per cent of what males weigh (Haraway, 1989, 341). As well, pygmies and !Kung are small people, but both live in nomadic societies which hunt for food.

Our early ancestors must have cooperated with each other in order to survive. However, even as early as 30,000 years ago, all was not sweetness and light among human beings. At that time some human groups were burying bodies whose bone remains show evidence of human violence (Keeley, 1996, 36ff). In one grave a projectile point was embedded in the spine of a child's skeleton and in another a skull had cut marks as if the owner had been scalped.

Aggression probably increased beginning about 10,000 years ago when tribes of people started to settle down and think in terms of protecting private property. With horticulture and farming came the need for permanent settlements where more children could be raised and used for farm work. Eventually, when conflict erupted among more or less settled groups, the winners often killed the men and enslaved the women to produce children for them; this was the beginning of patriarchy (Lerner, 1987, 212).

Since that time evidence of homicide is not uncommon. Burials in Egypt indicate that many people suffered violence both in their lifetime and at their death, with some apparently being executed. In Germany "trophy" skulls studded with axe holes from 10,000 to 5,000 years ago have been found collected in a cave and in France a pit has been unearthed containing 2000-year-old skeletons of over 100 people of all ages and both sexes, often with arrowpoints embedded in their bones.

With the rise of cities and later the industrial revolution, crowding in ghettoes became far worse with violence increasing as a result. The largely free and easy social life led by our nomadic ancestors had changed into lives organized by laws and ruled by stress and tension. These conditions continue to foster violence based on environment, not genetics.

In summary, it seems that any genes correlated with aggression have been with us since we evolved from our ape-like ancestors and long before. Human beings and individuals of most other species have the capability of aggression in their make-up, but become aggressive only if their brain tells them this is their best response to a particular situation. Whether we act out aggressively depends on our sex, our personality (which is partly inherited), our past experiences and our culture.

In Western society most people spend virtually all their lives going about their daily activities without thought of being attacked or attacking someone else. Some people have never experienced any violence in their lives although for others it is all too familiar. We know that chimpanzees (unlike bonobos, our equally close relatives) can be killers although they are usually peaceable; that men in the recent past and today can be terrifyingly aggressive or not violent at all; that people living in small preliterate societies were usually peaceable but sometimes ran amok.

How to understand all this? An explanation for human aggression should, because of evolution, connect human beings to other animals in some ways, yet also be different because human behavior is hugely affected by culture. The answer seems to be the notion of sociality which human beings share with other social animals but which they have refined to a high art (Carrithers, 1989). Instead of aggression itself being inherited, it is the capability, or inability, of socializing.

Sociality, which is present in most primates, allows young animals to observe and learn behavior from their mother or other acquaintances. Chimpanzees and bonobos (and undoubtedly our earliest ancestors) are social species. Individuals joining in groups to feed at fruiting trees, for protection against predators, or just to hang out is clear evidence of sociality. Their brilliant ability to form social alliances to gain specific ends has been the subject of recent research including three books, *Chimpanzee Politics* (1982) and *Peacemaking among Primates* (1989) by Frans de Waal and *Coalitions and Alliances in Humans and Other Animals* (1992) edited by

Alexander Harcourt and Frans de Waal. Chimpanzees have figured out that winning a fight may mean losing a friend or ally, so they reduce aggression by their tolerance of other individuals and repair damage caused by fights by practising reconciliation (Waal, 1989, 1). Such conflict resolution was surely present in the common ancestors of apes and human beings; perhaps the development of increased and more complex sociality is what separated early human beings from apes.

Along with sociality our ancestors developed divisions of labor within a group, which meant that everyone became dependent on others. Some members might scavenge while others hunted, with all joining together at night to share food and for safety; with such division of duties, individuals would become expert at a task benefitting the entire group. Those who worked best and most cooperatively in such interdependent activities would be the most intelligent, as we noted in Nancy Tanner's hypothesis for a cooperative rather than an aggressive human background. The increase in brain size and intelligence meant that eventually hominids were no longer molded by evolution, but could readily fashion their own behavior and environment to their own liking.

Does the inheritance of sociality provide answers about human aggression? First, if we think of sociality as an entity varying from cooperation at one linear extreme to violence at the other, it explains why it occurs in some people and not others. All human beings are born with the capability of being social, but those raised in a negative, combative environment may become combative themselves while those with a positive upbringing are liable to be cooperative. Secondly, great violence need not have conferred a benefit to an individual or a community as proponents of Darwinian psychology postulate, but may have been simply a dysfunctional behavior that occurred now and then. It could have arisen first with crowding and carried on to the present. Today it is correlated with depletion or degradation of renewable resources, increased demand for these resources or their unequal distribution (Homer-Dixon, 1999, 177).

Sociality also accounts for the huge variation in cultures found around the world. Each person making up a community has his or her own variation of sociality based on genetic makeup and experience; together, these people interact to build a society that best suits them given their environment. Information may be shared within and between these groups, with what seems valuable accepted and taught within a group. Quite quickly groups living in different areas will evolve into culturally different entities which go their separate ways.[3] Occasionally violence may have been valorized because it accomplished some end such as obtaining more land and workers, but it also was often a setback to a society, causing the death of autonomy and many healthy young men.

Human beings can be seen either as basically violent with aggression an "instinctive impulse which seeks discharge" (Storr, 1968, 17), or basically cooperative but given to occasional bursts of violence as the occasion warrants. These facets of their behavior can be explained by the presence of sociality in their genetic makeup. If we look out the window at the world we see contrasts everywhere: some boys are teasing cats but must children are in school learning their lessons; a few drunk women are shouting obscenities at their partners but far more women are enjoying a cold glass of beer; some young men are planning an armed robbery against a downtown bank but most are going to university or are already employed in the work world.

Notes

1. The American Psychological Association, the American Academy of Pediatrics, the American Academy of Child and Adolescent Psychiatry, the American Medical Association, the American Academy of Family Physicians and the American Psychiatric Association all agree that the data point overwhelmingly "to a causal connection between media violence and aggressive behavior in some children" (Anderson and Bushman, 2002).
2. The figure of fewer than five was calculated for sixty-two menopausal women of the foraging !Kung people of the Kalahari Desert. They had an average of 4.12 years between births, and forty-eight per cent of the girls they bore did not live to themselves have children.
3. Bhikhu Parekh (2000, 121) gives an excellent account of why and how cultures vary, noting for example: "Some cultures disjoin reason and feeling whereas others find their separation incomprehensible." "Some develop the concept of conscience and know what guilt and remorse mean; others find these emotions incomprehensible." "Some others lack a sense of tradition and cannot make sense of the desire to be worthy of one's ancestors, loyal to their memories, or to cherish their heritage."

Chapter 5

Groups As Such Don't Have Genes —Gang Violence And War

When Jane Goodall visited a private girls' school in Toronto in 2002, she made a point of telling the girls that chimpanzees engage in war (Barker, 2002). She said that this fact had been fiercely contested by other scientists:

> It was ridiculous. I had carefully observed seven incidents [of assaults and killings]. They said it would give people the impression that aggression was innate and therefore war was innate...But I knew I was right.

Goodall was right that chimpanzees can be very violent as we saw in Chapter 3, but the animals she referred to included those fed up to 600 bananas a day; when the number of bananas was reduced, the large group split into two which became enemies. The attacks mentioned by Goodall were spread over at least four years, from 1974 to 1977. Can one really apply the word "war" to such sporadic violence?

In her book about the Gombe chimpanzees, Goodall (1986, 530, 533) has sections entitled "The Precursors of Warfare" and "On the Threshold of War?" which conjure up human conflict in the Middle East or in central Africa rather than sporadic assaults among chimpanzees. Nevertheless, Goodall writes about the Kasakela males that "If they had had firearms and had been taught to use them, I suspect they would have used them to kill" (p. 530). Goodall insists that chimpanzees engage in "war," even though her stated evidence is seven occasions over a long period of time when a chimpanzee group attacked usually a single animal from the neighboring troop. She believes that the chimpanzee has reached a stage "where he stands at the very threshold of human achievement in destruction, cruelty, and planned intergroup conflict. If ever he develops the power of language—and, as we have seen, he stands close to that threshold, too—might he not push open the door and wage war with the best of us?" (p. 534).

Despite Goodall's opinion, intergroup fighting on such an insignificant scale cannot be deemed war. She insists (1999, 118ff), despite the extensive criticism noted earlier, that her provisioning of chimpanzees with bananas (which over the years evoked orgies of feeding and intense competition) did not make them territorially aggressive. She feels that, in line with the tenets of Darwinian psychology, the "warring" behavior of these males means that people have inherited their propensity to go to war because of their common ancestry with chimpanzees.

Is her compelling scenario of chimpanzees waging war (surely unlikely considering the reality that they are in danger of becoming extinct) based on natural aggression in chimpanzees? Or from data skewed because of human interference (giving them mountains of bananas to fight over among themselves and sometimes against baboons) which has made these animals seem on rare occasions far more aggressive than they are naturally? And once such aggression is accepted, does wishful thinking about aggressive human origins keep it alive and well, especially in the minds of male authors who relish the macho idea of male aggression?

It is aggression, and their large brain that enables men to use it for their own ends, that has been their weapon against the world. Because men are larger than women and in a patriarchal society fashioned for men's benefit, they can beat women up and force them to accept what they are given, whether it be domestic drudgery, low paid service jobs or sexual slavery. Our male ancestors figured out (even as chimpanzees have) that a large number of aggressive individuals can defeat a smaller number of individuals and grab what they want for themselves.

By definition of how evolution and heredity work, aggression that is inherited must be inherited by individuals, not groups. When we think of group aggression such as ghetto battles or warfare itself, we imagine individuals with a propensity for aggression acting together to attain some common goal by violent means. We might imagine Goodall's chimpanzees joining together on infrequent occasions to kill neighboring chimpanzees or young men belonging to motorcycle gangs attacking rival gangs. But only the humans wage wars; other animals (luckily for them) are intellectually incapable of sustained major conflicts using weapons against members of their own species.

It would seem ridiculous to compare chimpanzee wrangles with world politics, but this is what the eminent scholar Francis Fukuyama has done in a 1998 issue of the prestigious journal *Foreign Affairs* in an article entitled "Women and the evolution of world politics." He begins the article by telling the story of two attacks. The first is about captive chimpanzees in a Dutch zoo. Two males seeking power joined together to slaughter a third male, "his toes and testicles littering the floor of the cage." It is hardly strange that three large chimpanzee males cooped together in a small enclosure should come to blows, even fatal blows.

Fukuyama either does not tell, or does not know, the early history of this chimpanzee group or of Yeroen, the male who murdered his cagemate as told by Frans de Waal (1982, 56ff). When the troop was first established in 1971, a large female chimpanzee called Mama who was about forty years old became the group leader, dominant to all the other animals including the adult males. When three more adult males were added to the group in 1973, she and her female friend Gorilla spent much of their time harassing the newcomers. Yereon and the other two males would huddle on top of a tall drum to fend off Mamma and Gorilla and other females who bit their feet and pulled their hair. The males showed their fear of the females by screaming, vomiting and having diarrhea. Two weeks of this tension was too much for the staff who removed Mama and Gorilla from the group after which the males at last became dominant. Fukuyama's story would have been less exciting if the reader had known that a dominant female had had to be removed before the males were able to assume positions of power. The second story is that of the fighting between two communities of chimpanzees observed at Goodall's Gombe research area and recounted so often in the literature, as we have seen in Chapter 3.

These incidents wouldn't seem to most of us to be the stuff of legend, but Fukuyama disagrees. He claims that the victorious group of Gombe chimps "have done, in effect, what Rome did to Carthage in 146 B.C.: extinguished its rival without a trace." (Actually this is only true for the males in this male-oriented saga; some females survived to carry on their lives.)

Fukuyama draws from these tales three generalizations, assuming (although this is not known) that human beings descended from chimpanzee-like ancestors rather than the more serene bonobo-like ancestors. The first is violence. He states that "Only chimpanzees and humans seem to have a proclivity for routinely murdering peers." This is untrue because chimpanzees do not *routinely* kill their peers—other species such as lions kill their peers more often. The second is the importance of coalitions which are common, because of their intelligence, among monkeys, apes and humans.

The third is that it is men, not women, who form aggressive coalitions, bonding together as they have done for millions of years as hunters to carry out violent projects. (Except, as we have seen in Chapter 4, our small forebears did not have the weapons necessary to become effective hunters until fairly recently.) He states that "male bonding is in fact genetic," a claim with no scientific basis; he does not give any reference for this because the article is entirely unreferenced—all the facts and inferences flow unimpeded from Fukuyama's brain, trained and steeped not in biology or psychology but in the history of public policy. (His article was surely published not because of his research into Darwinian evolution, but because of his fame in the public policy area.)

These three concepts meld together, in Fukuyama's mind, to produce male societies throughout human history that wage wars and keep women subservient. He writes that when he thinks about the wars in Bosnia, in Rwanda and in Afghanistan, he thinks of the chimpanzees of Gombe. He believes that if some societies become feminized with more women in positions of power, these less aggressive societies will be more at the mercy of societies in which males remain bonded together for war, meaning that women should never be allowed into combat armies because they undermine the male bonding of the real soldiers. Fukuyama opts for the status quo: "Liberal democracy and market economies work well because, unlike socialism, radical feminism, and other utopian schemes, they do not try to change human nature." By accepting the inherent violent nature of men, they can constrain it with institutions and laws. "It does not always work, but it is better than living like animals"—although even Fukuyama has admitted that few nonhuman animals actually kill their peers.

Irenäus Eibl-Eibesfeldt (1979, 240) in his book *The Biology of Peace and War* concludes that since early in their evolution, protohumans formed into groups which fought each other for space and raw materials. Despite the obvious risk of losing, they had a variety of reasons for going to war including the promise of new wealth, an increase in food and resources, an expansion of territory, and an enlarged pool of workers and sexual partners. However, the biological imperative to kill, if such it be, must be countered by the need to have enough time and peace for one's children to grow to maturity. Eibl-Eibesfeldt sees war not as a pathological phenomenon but as an inherent part of human nature, believing that peace can only be attained if society supplies other means than war by which to extinguish men's natural aggression.

More recent proponents of Darwinian psychology also believe that war is inevitable, given men's alleged aggressive nature. Christian Mesquida and Neil Wiener (1996) correlate the possibility of war with the number of unemployed young men in a society. Their Darwinian theory is that because young men have fewer material goods than their elders, they have a harder time attracting women. It is worth it to them to risk their lives in combat to obtain women and other possessions. However, this doesn't make much sense. Young men willing to fight are certainly essential for war, but there is no assurance that the men themselves will benefit personally even if a war is won; if it is lost, they may be worse off than before, if not dead. Young men fight for any number of reasons that have nothing to do with evolution—they have no job, they are roused by emotional rhetoric, they are given a uniform and food, they enjoy fooling around with guns, they love to show off to women, they like the feeling of power that a uniform brings.

In his book *The Code of Man: Love Courage Pride Family Country* (2004), Waller Newell stresses not only that war is correlated with human nature, but that it is a worthy endeavor. Before the 2001 attack on New York's twin towers, he believes that Americans had become unscrupulous, shiftless, self-indulgent, hedonistic, lacking in conviction in their way of life and unwilling to defend it. The recent wars in Afghanistan and Iraq show, for him, that war can spark a period of moral uplift, stock-taking, and soul-searching, reflecting the ennobling virtues of the battlefield.

By contrast, Thomas Homer-Dixon in his book *Environment, Scarcity, and Violence* (1999) argues that large scale violence, including insurgencies and ethnic clashes, is largely caused not by human nature or a need for renewal but by a scarcity of renewable resources such as arable land, fresh water and forests. This "environmental scarcity" is caused by degradation and depletion of renewable resources, an increased demand for them, and/or their unequal distribution. He predicts that violence in the future will increase, especially in the developing world, because of increase in population pressure on the environment.

War is not determined by individuals, but by governments. The correlation between going to war and large numbers of unemployed young men reflects not the inheritance of individual men, but the decision of a government to put these men to use to try to obtain more land or other resources, often for the benefit of the leaders themselves.

Evidence discounts a Darwinian psychological explanation for war. Certainly there are cultures such as the Yanomamö and the Masai which raise young men to be warriors, but other cultures focus on peace such as the Arapesh of New Guinea, the Lepchas of Sikkim, the Ituri of the Congo rain forest, the Mardudjara of Australia, the Semai of Malaya, small societies in Tibet and Pueblo Indians of America (Glad, 1990, 19; Keeley, 1996, 30). Many nomadic groups simply flee if they are attacked; they have nothing to lose since what they own they can carry with them. These peace-loving peoples have much in common including few stereotypical roles for men and women, no ideal of a macho male and a great gusto for physical pleasures such as eating, drinking, laughing and sex (Glad, 1990, 19). Could these traits also help those of us in the modern world transcend the possibility of war?

Because war is a rational way to win resources and power, it has been all too common in human history, involving at some point in their existence ninety-five per cent of societies (Keeley, 1996, 28). Despite this, warfare does not tie in with genetics. For cultural reasons a society can change from being war-like to being pacific, or vice versa, in a short period of time (Keeley, 1996, 32). Both Sweden and Switzerland have been at peace for almost 200 years, but before that time Sweden especially, home of fierce Vikings, was considered one of the most belligerent nations in Europe. Or a nation can suddenly become war-like in adapting to specific circumstances; when horses and guns were introduced into mid-west America, the Ute and Snake Indians transformed themselves into warriors while the neighboring Diggers became fearful refugees. With the emergence of the slave trade in Africa, coastal tribes became slavers selling members of interior tribes into slavery.

War is fostered within a nation by state propaganda and emotional rhetoric. The Jews were described continually as filth in Nazi Germany, until ordinary people began to think that such subhumans should indeed be destroyed. Aryan Germans and German Jews who had lived peacefully side by side for centuries quickly became adversaries because of such cultural pressure. (Speaking of propaganda conjures up for me the ridiculous picture of myself as a small child earnestly discussing with small friends whether it would be worse to be attacked by a yellow-bellied slant-eyed Jap or by a goose-stepping, leering German.)

Germany gives an example of how ordinary men, presumably no more or less aggressive than anyone else, were transformed into inhuman killing machines. During World War II Germany, which didn't believe that women should take an active part in war, ran out of men to carry out the work that Hitler believed had to be done. The young men had been enlisted into the army, so it was often left to their seniors to carry out the job of murdering Jews, a horrific experience for family men such as those from Hamburg drafted into the Order Police because they were too old for the regular German army (Browning, 1992). Their first mission was to shoot in cold blood women, children and old men from a Jewish population of 1800 in a Polish village. Their superior officer cried as he gave his men the orders and none wanted to carry them out (the officer couldn't even bear to go to the scene of the slaughter), but they did as they were told. Before long, inured to atrocities, they formed an efficient killing squad.

War is quite different from innate aggression. It is an instrument of policy, mounted not by aggressive young men but by politicians, chiefs and statesmen who have political or historical or even personal reasons for engaging their nation in war—(perhaps the bombing of Kosovo by United Nations' forces in 1999 helped deflect attention from President Clinton's sexual/ethical problems?) Young men are often swept up in the patriotic fervour for war (although usually less eager when they find out what it is really like). War is a cultural institution which many men and a few women revere; for my uncle, the best years of his life were his military service in the second World War because of the excitement, the status of serving his country, the bonding among his mates and their idealistic goal of making a better world safe for democracy. Ethologists have stated that we are adapted for war by our inborn aggression and our inborn rejection of strangers (Eibl-Eibesfeldt, 1979, 124), but individual adaptation may as likely reflect the positive experiences of my uncle.

Has group violence been a positive force in human evolution? Let's consider aggression as it evolved along with humanity itself, with first feuding, then tribal warfare, and finally modern wars. We have already considered in Chapter 3 that four million years ago our ancestors would surely have survived as a social species only if they formed cooperative rather than pugnacious groups.

In the Yanomamö, feuding among men triggered by such things as malicious gossip, accusations of stinginess, or cowardice involves either contests of chest pounding, side slapping, or club fighting. In each of these encounters the rules are strict so that no one is badly injured—a man will try to hurt his opponent enough to force him to accept defeat, but not to shed his blood. In this way men get rid of their anger but continue to remain on fairly good terms with each other (Chagnon, 1968, 118). Such feuding is usually considered to be a local affair between men of the same community or from nearby villages who likely have relatives in common. It makes evolutionary sense for conflicts between relatives to be diffused in such a way that no one is maimed or killed.

In contrast to feuding, tribal warfare occurs mostly between more distant groups that have few or no relatives in common; if there are brothers or cousins involved on opposite sides of a conflict, their political allegiance proves greater than their kinship ties. Among the Yanomamö, the men who take part in tribal warfare tend not to be young unmarried men (despite Mesquida and Wiener's [1996] surmise that the occurrence of warfare is correlated with the large number of men in this age group), but middle-aged men with children (Ferguson, 2001). The goal of these men was often to kill a member of a rival tribe, usually in revenge for past wrongs. It was not, as Wilson surmised, to obtain territory, although Wilson writes in his book *Consilience* that "territorial expansion and defense by tribes…is a cultural universal" (1998, 170). Nor were the tribal wars started to capture women (Ferguson, 2001). The number of men killed in tribal warfare is small, but even one or two dead is a significant loss to a group which itself is small.

Killing non-relatives in such armed encounters makes some evolutionary sense because it benefits in general the successful raiders who are related and disadvantages their usually unrelated opponents. However, if aggression is an inherited trait, then the most violent men will have the most children who will in turn be violent because of their inheritance. This trait will have been passed down over many generations. Napoleon Chagnon, who as an anthropologist lived for years with the Yanomamö Indians in the headwater area of the Orinoco River in South America, claimed (1988) that those warriors who were responsible for killing other Indians did indeed have more children than did other tribal men. However, a close analysis of his data shows that this is not so, in part because Chagnon included headmen who had many children because of their position not their violence, and omitted warriors who were dead, often because of revenge killings, with fewer children than they would have had had they remained alive (Ferguson, 1989).

Unlike the above examples, modern wars not only account for thousands or millions of times more deaths, but they are largely without evolutionary rationale. Men killed in battle may or may not have superior genes, but in any case they are unable to pass them on to the next generation. Women who remain at home must look after their children by themselves, living often on rationed food. Soldiers fight side by side with men to whom they are not related, often risking their lives for each other, while men who are related to each other, sometimes brothers, may be on opposite sides of a conflict, as in the American civil war or some Yanomamö conflicts.

Until the advent of farming, intertribal warfare served to drive groups apart. With the spread of agriculture, such warfare acted instead to join tribes together, with losing factions undergoing subjugation and becoming incorporated into winning factions, often as slaves. Because of warfare or threat of warfare small villages were gradually amalgamated into multi-village units, then chiefdoms, and then states with the result that most individuals lost the autonomy they had held in small foraging groups. Whereas in 1000 BC there were 600,000 autonomous units of human population, there are now fewer than 200 (Carneiro, 1994). Societal culture in the form of capitalism and communism rather than biology has come to govern people's lives which does not fit with Darwinian psychological theory.

Although there were more "wars" long ago (preindustrial states had 10.6 per decade), weapons were primitive and few people were actually killed (although they represented a significant percentage of the male population) (Beer, 1974; Carneiro, 1994; Keeley, 1996). Recently, for various societies there are now only 2.7 wars per decade with sometimes long periods of peace (Carneiro, 1994, 20). This doesn't jibe with Darwinian psychological theory as Lorenz saw it; because inhibitions on what individuals can do goes along with an increase in civilization, if there were a need for outlets of aggression among young men one would expect *more* rather than fewer conflicts recently.

The reasons for war are often illogical. Who would have thought that the murder of an Austrian noble would lead to an armed conflict, the first World War, which would leave nine million men dead? Causes of war are as various as politics, an arms race, power imbalance, economic and resource development, imperialism and religious fanaticism. What have these entities to do with the genetic inheritance of individuals?

The division remains between those who believe war exists because of people's inborn aggression, and those who believe it is caused by culture and the desire and greed of a group to have more. Lawrence Keeley, in his book *War before Civilization* (1996, 158), describes in detail the large legacy of war in human history but believes that there are two major stumbling blocks toward correlating such conflicts with Darwinian psychology. First is humanity's innate aptitude for social cooperation, possible because of language. Many animal species are aggressive but only human beings, even those who live in bellicose societies, have extensive social devices which most of the time preserve harmony and collaboration between individuals. If millions of people can virtually eliminate killing within their groups, there is no reason why this can't be managed for the whole of humanity. It is far more difficult to explain war than peace if we keep in mind the inborn capacities of human beings based on their evolution.

The second and even more important problem for a biological explanation of war is the incredible plasticity of human behavior. Our conduct is shaped by experience and education to a remarkable extent. As we have seen, some societies are war-like while others are pacific. Some, such as Sweden, can be war-like for centuries, yet then become peaceable. Some cultures welcome strangers, some are reserved toward them, while others treat them with hostility. Human societies are capable of either opting for war or creating peace, depending on their culture, history and circumstances. It is curious that, since far more nations at any one time are at peace rather than at war, proponents of Darwinian psychology focus far more on aggression than cooperation.[1]

Note

1. If we have the intelligence to make war, we should equally have the intelligence to prevent it. Maybe Robert Morris's (1918) tongue-in-cheek theory about why we engage in mass conflict is worth considering: he states that because we walk upright unlike our very early ancestors our brains, which can't readily adapt to this position, are mechanically faulty leading us to carry out absurd activities such as war.

Chapter 6

A Never-Ending Stereotype—Male Dominance

This chapter will discuss dominance in social non-human animals and two features that theoretically (from our human perspective) correlate with it: leadership and protection. Dominance, the ability to inflict one's will on other individuals, has been studied extensively in zoos or laboratories where an animal can be classed as dominant to others if it grabs the most food, demands the best resting sites and cuffs or threatens individuals who annoy it. Such transactions are easily observed and quantified in captivity. But does dominance correlate in the wild with having more progeny than subordinate animals? If so, it becomes a central issue for Darwinian psychology.

Dominance in a social context in the wild is far more difficult to investigate than in the lab. In human society one thinks of men as dominant to women: Men earn more money; religion, politics and man-made laws (needless to say) have always heavily favored men; women perform much more unpaid labor in the home; and as a bottom line men, who are stronger, can have their own way by threatening or delivering physical abuse. Male scientists in the past have decided that because men are dominant to women, then males in all social species must also be dominant to females (Dagg, 1983). Does this make the dominant animal a leader and a protector? Male animals don't have religion or politics or laws to confirm their superiority. Why should a female consider a male dominant if he has no male culture to back up his right? Obviously if he is stronger he can demand the best resources, but what if he is the same size as the female or smaller? These are questions we shall consider in this chapter.

To return to the fractious captive female chimpanzees Mama and Gorilla described by Frans de Waal (1982) in the last chapter, they were kept separated from the other chimpanzees for three months until one of the males became accepted as the new head of the group and "was firmly in the saddle." When Mama and Gorilla were reintroduced into the colony there was terrific fighting among them and the introduced males, but the alliance between the females and the other chimpanzees had been broken; a few weeks later, Mama was dethroned as the dominant animal.

Waal admits that feminists questioned his manipulation of the individuals included in the large colony. Why was the zoo so anxious to have males in control? Why was Mama not considered good enough? Surely Mama with her forceful personality had earned the right to be the dominant animal? Waal's answer illustrates the power of stereotype. He writes (p. 59) that Mama was removed for two reasons: first because "It is known that in the wild the adult males are dominant" (even though, as will be discussed shortly, Goodall had already shown that this was not true); and second because Mama was so aggressive that a number of the chimpanzees had been injured by her. (One wonders why he didn't notice the discrepancy here.) Waal admitted that the males could never have subdued the females in the oppressive indoor winter quarters of the colony, but perhaps they could have outside. "In the extensive open-air enclosure the males would have been able to keep their distance from Mama and the other females. Perhaps then they could have gained courage, and slowly, week by week, they might have given increasingly provocative bluff performances. Outdoors they would also have had the opportunity to isolate Mama from her supporters in order to fight with her separately. Adults males are stronger than females, and faster."

Because Waal insisted (incorrectly) that male chimpanzees were dominant in the wild, he felt it was fair to do everything he could to cripple the power of the combatant females in order to support the frightened males. In the battle of the sexes he was determined the males should win. Unfortunately, Waal was merely replaying the sexism that has plagued much of the long history of dominance research in primates.

The early famous primate researcher, Abraham Maslow (1936), was able with a series of strange experiments to discover that size, not sex, was the best predictor of dominance. Maslow's methods were highly original because at the zoo in Madison, Wisconsin, he studied not the behavior of one species, but groups made up of several species, something unknown in the wild. His thirteen cages included sooty mangabeys, java monkeys, pigtail and rhesus macaques, mandrills, hamadryas baboons, mona guenons and a moustached guenon. The dominant animal in each cage was usually easily recognized by its aggressive and confident air. It strutted while subordinate animals slunk. It stared fixedly at other animals while they avoided its gaze. It came to the front of the cage and initiated group actions, while they retired discretely to the rear of the cage or followed its lead. If the dominance was not clearcut, Maslow threw bits of food into a cage and watched to see which animals grabbed the booty, snarling at the others, and which relinquished any right to it.

Maslow concluded that if there were a marked difference in the size of a pair of animals, the larger was dominant, whether male or female. Changes in dominance only occurred with changes in conditions. For example, an agile sooty mangabey female found that when she whirled about on a chain fastened to the center of the top of the cage, the heavy wooden block attached to its lower end frequently struck her companion, the large dominant male who usually sat on the floor. Although he tried to catch and punish her for her behavior, she was too fast for him. Soon, to avoid being hit by the block, he retired to a corner of the cage. Later he greeted her whirling efforts, now seemingly done deliberately to annoy him, with squeals of fear. Within a month, when the experiment ended, she was noticeably more dominant than before and was able to grab more food. Her small size had been compensated for by her ingenuity, speed and agility, allowing her sometimes to triumph over the larger male; dominance was again shown not to depend on sex.

Unlike Maslow, Robert Yerkes, another pioneer scientist studying behavior in captive primates, chose not to report the results of actual experiments as Maslow had done, but what he felt to be true. Whenever possible he kept male-female pairs together in a cage to emulate what he believed must be their monogamous nature (Haraway, 2000, 410). After years of observing his apes in captivity, he claimed that he "knew" the larger males were dominant to females not only in the laboratory, but also in the wild. Yerkes wrote (1939, 135): "The prevalent and characteristic cultural pattern of chimpanzee life (for instance, the patriarchal family group), as presumably has been true also of man, tends to favor the development of capacity for dominance, leadership, originality, and creativeness in the male, and, correspondingly, of subordination, imitativeness, and conventionality in the female." Yeah, right. Yerkes fabricated for chimpanzees the patriarchal family with a dominant male, then surmised that this fabrication also applied to human beings.[1] Thanks to decades spent researching chimpanzee behavior in the wild, Jane Goodall and other later biologists have found that Yerkes' information was largely fictitious and biased against females. Goodall discovered that:

a) The stable group among chimpanzees is a mother and her offspring. Thus the "patriarchal family group" referred to by Yerkes does not exist. He housed adult males with one or more female chimpanzees which must have given him the (forced) illusion of patriarchy.

b) Natural foods (leaves, fruit, blossoms, seeds, insects, rarely meat) and resting sites for chimpanzees are spread widely and not limited, so there is little need for competition in everyday life. As we have seen, though, when chimpanzees were fed bananas, they began to fight for them when there were not enough to go around. This unnatural competition did give rise to dominance struggles (Goodall, 1986, 245).

c) Dominance is not a prerogative of either sex but is usually correlated with size. For any two animals, the larger is usually dominant. (Did Yerkes arrive at his contrary opinion by purposely omitting observations for Lia and Patti, two chimpanzee females known to be highly dominant? To have included them would have invalidated his sweeping and sexist conclusions.)

d) Groups, because of their changing composition, cannot be said to have leaders. If anything, the females with offspring act more often in leading than do other animals.

e) It is difficult to know what Yerkes had in mind by "originality and creativeness," but these are not prerogatives of males. Goodall discusses the use of objects as tools at length, which seems creative, but more females than males were involved: for example females (watched by their young) spent more time than males "fishing" with grass or twigs for termites to eat from their mounds; more young females than males poked sticks into possible insect holes, perhaps searching for food; and more females than males used leaves like sponges to collect drinking water. It seems that in chimpanzees, as in Japanese monkeys, it is often the young animals, especially females, who discover new techniques and that these activities pass quickly to the mothers who keep in close touch with the young, but slowly to the adult males who are more divorced from the communal life of the troop. Once a male does take up a new invention, it is quickly spread to all the monkeys who watch him, but his actions can hardly be called original or creative (Itani and Nishimura, 1973).

Yerkes claimed that female chimpanzees are subordinate, imitative and conventional, but since he was obviously listing these qualities because they are the antithesis of what he presumed males to be, and because it's obvious from the foregoing that males are not as he described them, there is no need to deal separately with these traits. Suffice it to say that the females are no more as Yerkes surmised than are the males.

Biased reports of primates such as that of Yerkes were common fifty years ago. A.J. Haddow (1952), for example, who observed small groups of male and female red-tailed guenons moving through the trees, decided on the basis of no evidence but his own intuition that a male must be the head of each group. Although he had no data to support his view, he wrote that "The existence of such small family parties [of monkeys] seems, in turn, to lead definitely to the conclusion that some form of male dominance must be exercised, in order that each male may hold together his small group of females. The difficult question—and it is one which cannot as yet be answered—is how and when such dominance is brought to bear, and what form it takes."

As another example, Michael Chance (1956) who studied captive rhesus monkeys in the London Zoo devised an experiment in dominance that was itself sexist. For his methodology he identified the adult males in the colony "by the letters D1, D2 and D3 etc., indicating their position in the male hierarchy. The adult females were not similarly identified, but are mentioned as and when they were observed in association with particular males." Not surprisingly, Chance concluded that the social life of these monkeys revolved around the dominant males, something that has not necessarily been found in wild groups. What other conclusion could he make, when the research focused exclusively on the males and the females were nameless?

It was generally accepted fifty years ago that male must be dominant to female monkeys and apes, despite the lack of evidence, because men were dominant over women. Dominance was considered an important behavioral concept by which an individual, male or female, obtained what they wanted by aggression, or threat of aggression, or a subordinate's memory of past aggression. Best of all from an evolutionary point of view, dominant animals were assumed to have the best reproductive success—dominant females would willingly mate with dominant males to produce superior offspring. Every individual would strive during its lifetime to become dominant and therefore able to produce as many fit progeny as possible.

The experiments of Maslow with monkeys had shown that males were not necessarily dominant to females, but his results were largely ignored; similarly despite Goodall's discovery that wild male chimpanzees weren't the dominant sex, Waal also disregarded this fact. In reality if dominance exists, it is size, not sex, that largely determines it. Which animal is large enough to defeat another in battle? In species such as hawks, hares, hamsters, and hyenas (I remember them as the four Hs) in which the female is larger than the male, it is the females who are dominant (Dagg, 1983). Sometimes even size isn't important in social species smart enough to form coalitions to defend their rights, as many primates have been seen to do including the female chimpanzees in the early stages of the Arnhem Zoo colony described above. Goodall's chimpanzee Mike was clever enough to gain dominance when he had the brilliant idea of banging together empty cans to terrorize his snobbish peers.

Recently the concept of dominance has lost favor in biology because it leaves so many problems of social life in wild animals unexplained. In the abnormal, stressful conditions of captivity, linear hierarchies may be obvious and dominance easily tested, but this is not true for wild populations in the field where food, water and resting sites are spread out and competition usually unnecessary. Different types of dominance have also been defined: are territorial dominance, sexual dominance, aggressive dominance and dominance causing dispersal related? Some individuals are dominant in some types of interactions but not in others. Thelma Rowell (1974, 139) further maintains that a hierarchy is set up and maintained largely by the subordinate rather than the dominant animals. She writes: "Reflection will make it clear that in the majority of cases it is the movement of the subordinate animal which turns the interaction into an approach-retreat, 'dominance' interaction. You cannot chase someone who doesn't flee."

It took sometime for researchers to accept this. In the 1970s, Shirley Strum (1987, 78,114,160ff) discovered that male baboons do not have a traditional dominance hierarchy (although the females may have) and so male dominance couldn't determine reproductive success. When she presented her extensive data at an exclusive primate conference, however, most of her peers refused to accept her conclusions since they went against conventional wisdom. It was only later and gradually that she was acknowledged to be right.

That the most dominant (big/strong/forceful/intelligent) males produce the most progeny is a central tenet of Darwinian evolution, yet there is no strict correlation between reproduction and dominance in most species (Hinde, 1974, 298). Dominant animals don't do all the mating as we have seen in many primates and other species (Bercovitch, 1991). For example, sometimes non-alpha rhesus monkey males who hang out with females and young have more offspring than alpha males who focus not on sex but on defending their status (Angier, 1995). And often females in estrus mate with as many males as possible, as did the sexy chimpanzee Flo. Indeed for chimpanzees studied in the Ivory Coast, females often became pregnant not by males of their community, dominant or otherwise, but by males outside their group entirely (Wrangham, 1997).

Nor is dominance necessarily correlated with aggression and hormone level; in free-ranging baboons it is the subadults, not the dominant males, who have the most testosterone and start the most fights (Sapolsky, 2001). In lions as we have seen, pride males share mating opportunities: this makes some Darwinian sense if the males are brothers, but not if they are unrelated which is fairly common (Schaller, 1972a). Dominant Soay rams sire many young early on in the rutting period, but later their sperm supply is depleted so that subordinate males become increasingly successful in producing lambs (Preston et al., 2001). We shall see in Chapter 10 on sperm competition that dominant males aren't necessarily reproductively successful in this area either.

In social species where there is noticeable dominance, there is likely also a dominance hierarchy; this is especially obvious in captive or domestic animals but is also present in some wild populations. Females and males challenge or fight with all the other members of their sex and/or the other sex to determine their place in a hierarchy or "pecking order." The latter name derived from the rough treatment hens, females, mete out to each other when in stressful captivity; many hens have died from loss of blood because of vicious pecks given them by their colleagues. The presence of a pecking order ensures relative peace because it allows animals to interact with others without fighting. An individual will not generally risk confrontation with animals dominant to it, while animals subordinate to it will know enough to give way. As we have seen with single dominance interactions, dominance depends mostly on size in both single sex and mixed sex hierarchies.

As an example of such a dominance hierarchy, A.M. Woodbury (1941) related how in his herd of cows the top ranking individual, A, invariably got to eat at the first pile of hay thrown over the corral fence at feeding time. When she had picked over this pile she turned to the second pile at which cow B had been munching and drove her away so she again could have the best. Since no two cows fed at the same pile, B in turn usurped C's pile, and so on down the line. When A started this chain-reaction she might have hooked B with her horns if B did not move away fast enough. Depending on her mood, this could be a gentle toss of the head, a goring bunt or a short run followed by a vicious head thrust. Such an assault was also passed down the line as each cow took over the hay pile of the cow ranked just below her.

Because men in our society seem to be dominant to women and children, males are also assumed to be the natural leaders of animal groups. Children are brainwashed to believe this from infancy as they listen to or read books describing the omnipotent Bambi's father, Kipling's head wolf in the *Just So Stories*, the male pigs in Orwell's *Animal Farm*, and Adam's rabbit Hazel in *Watership Down*. This seems to make Darwinian sense because the best leaders will presumably mate with the best females to produce superior young.

Yet the idea of a male leader is strange for social animals where the leaders are far more likely to be females. The main reason for this is that most social species comprise a core of adult females with their young. In many species males, when they reach adulthood, emigrate to other troops where they live among strangers in a foreign territory, conditions not conducive to effective leadership.

The reality of female leadership has been recognized for domestic species for many years. In a flock of sheep a lamb is trained to follow its mother because when it does so it is rewarded by being allowed to nurse. The leader of the flock is not the strongest animal, but rather an old ewe who is weaker than most of the other adults; she has cared for and fed many of the rest of the flock who are her direct descendants. The tendency of lambs to follow their mothers, of younger sheep to follow older ones, and of males to follow ewes in heat culminates in the oldest ewe leading a flock (Scott, 1945). This scenario also holds true for the desert bighorn where old ewes lead groups even when rams of all ages are present (Simmons, 1980). Because of their age, these females are likely to remember such things as where water is to be found in periods of drought and where the best pastureland exists.

Among lions, another well-studied social animal, the youngest cubs are unable to follow their mothers at first, but they do so as they grow larger. A lion pride core consists of females and young known as a mother-lineage group which perhaps consists of an old female, her mature daughters and their offspring comprising both male and female infants and juveniles (Schaller, 1972a). As the juvenile sons become subadults and then adults, they move away to live on their own, or to join other males, or to become attached to another mother-lineage pride as the pride males. It is the females who lead and do the hunting for prey to feed the pride. The pride males stay with the pride for only a few years before being driven off by younger males. When the old leading female dies, her pride may split into several groups, each led by one of her daughters. The members of these new prides will continue to share an affinity for each other if they meet in the future.

Extensive research in the wild shows that female leaders are most likely in the majority of social species in which the females are closely related to each other—elephants, hyenas, many monkey species and members of cattle, sheep, antelope and deer families. Males of these species follow the females, especially if one is in estrus, or go off by themselves or in male groups. Other species may have either a male or a female or both as leaders, including gibbons, wolves and wild dogs (Dagg, 1983).

Of course, one must be careful about designating who is a leader. Rowell (1969, 250) reports that for the olive baboon,

> The position at the front of the group does not necessarily imply leadership in any fundamental sense...Adult males would be seen to move out a hundred yards or more from the main group and then to sit facing back towards the group and wait. We learned that there was no point in starting a

> count until some of the old females rose and started to move after such a male. If they ignored him he returned to the troop after a while.

In Western culture until recently, children were taught through their schools, books and movies that a man's role, as well as being dominant and a leader to his wife and children, was to protect them from harm. This makes Darwinian sense because his protection helps ensure that a male's young will survive to adulthood. Anyone who has read *Bambi* by Felix Salter, or seen the Walt Disney movie, is well aware of the protective aura emanating from Bambi's Father which encompasses the young Bambi and his mother. He may not be seen, but He is always nearby, watching for danger to His family and ready to spring into action against predators and other perils. All of which is nonsense, given the actual behavior of white-tailed deer. In this species the sexes come together during the fall rutting season to mate and also, in the north, in winter to form yarding groups where there is food and some escape from deep snow. The rest of the time, however, the sexes remain separate and usually solitary. Even when males and females are together, none protects other deer except for a mother who looks after her young.

The concept of protector is equally puzzling when used for hamadryas baboons, the murdering animals whose behavior Zuckerman researched at the London Zoo. Hans Kummer (1967), who studied this species both in the Zurich Zoo and in Ethiopia, found that females from their early infant days are taught by the male who comes to "own" them to obey his every wish:

> In the strongly cohesive one-male groups of hamadryas baboons, several females are conditioned to follow one male at all times. Females wandering away are brought back by the group leader's neck bite. For each female, thus, there exists but one protector, and seeking out another male would lead to severe fights in which the female would be physically torn back and forth between the two males. *This protector, however, is also her main potential aggressor* (p. 65, my emphasis).

"Protector" is a strange word to use for a male who would not hesitate to mutilate his charge if she disobeyed him.

A controversy began in the 1960s about whether adult male non-hamadryas baboons position themselves at the front, rear and sides of a troop as it moves along to shield the females and young from possible predators. This is how one might imagine evolutionarily correct animals would behave. Irven DeVore and Sherwood Washburn (1963), who started the debate by asserting that they do so, were quoted by many other authors who frequently copied an illustration of how a baboon troop arranged itself during travel and even applied it to populations of early hominids moving onto savannahs from the forest. Their version of baboon processions was backed up by Rhine and Westlund (1981). However, other biologists later refuted this arrangement (Altmann, 1979; Sapolsky, 2001, 170). Robert Harding (1977) reported that he had never seen the protective formation in which males were said to shield females and young in his year's study of wild olive baboons in Kenya, nor had it been reported by other field workers since its original description. Anyway, if males were seen in the front of the troop, this may have meant that they were subordinate in that they were forced to occupy the most hazardous position.

Whatever the order of baboons on the march, Thelma Rowell (1972) was not impressed with male olive baboons as protectors. She writes (p. 44):

> Baboon males are often described as defending their troop, but this I never saw and find difficult to imagine, since Ishasha baboons always reacted to any potential danger by flight. If the threat is very small adult males may walk slowly away while juveniles run, so that they do walk between the danger and the rest of the troop. But the whole troop flees from any major threat, the males with their longer legs at the front, with the females carrying the heaviest infants coming last.

Indris from Madagascar offer another example. The fact that these male primates sat near the base of trees while the rest of the indri troop foraged high up in the canopy at first led observers to conclude that indri males acted as lookouts against terrestrial predators, as do patas monkey males. J.I. Pollock (1979), who studied various indri groups in depth, however, found that only dominant individuals, all females, were free to move about in the trees and feed at will. Fear of predation for indris comes far more from eagles and hawks than from ground-living animals, so the males were not acting as sentinels or protectors; rather, they had been forced out of the canopy by the aggression and threats of the females who didn't want male competition. The enforcement of her dominance by the female for herself and her young was probably vital for them during conditions of food shortage.

Nor is such behavior limited to primates. For example the meerkat, a small species of mongoose that lives in colonies in underground burrows, notable because of the way individuals stand erect to watch for danger from predators, has been used as a good example of kin selection—a member possibly sacrificing his or her own life by calling out to all members of the colony when danger threatens and possibly being killed for this heroic example of selflessness. However, Tim Clutton-Brock and his colleagues (1999) who studied meerkats in the Kalahari Gemsbok Park, South Africa, found that this wasn't true. Solitary meerkats as well as group members spend part of the day standing on guard on a raised site such as a stump, barking now and then to let others know they are on the job, and giving a loud alarm call when they spot a predator which often sends other meerkats scurrying for cover. However, when the predator such as an eagle or jackal approaches closely, the guards are among the first to disappear underground. During over 2,000 hours of observation no guard was ever caught by a predator; since they were the first to spot it, they had the most time to rush for cover.

The next chapter will consider dominance in human beings. Males are larger than females on average, so are they dominant for this reason? Many females are the same size as their mates or sometimes bigger. Does that make these women dominant? Is dominance even important in human society when few of us actually threaten or fight each other to determine our place in the hierarchy of our friends and acquaintances?

Note

1. The primate quarters in Atlanta now known as the Yerkes Regional Primate Research Center continue to discomfit primates. Although funded by the National Institutes of Health, it has recently been fined for violations of the Animal Welfare Act and censured for negligence and ill-treatment of animals (News release of July 11, 2001).

Chapter 7

Silly Assumptions—Dominant Men And Other "Universals"

> At night, after they had both as usual been drinking, Caitlin Thomas would savagely attack her husband, the poet Dylan Thomas, grabbing his hair so that some came out by the roots and banging his head against the wooden floorboards as she held him down. "It was a wonder there were any brains left in it," she wrote. They were about the same size, but she was stronger and violent. Many Welsh wives in their neighborhood, "swarthy brawny-armed cockle women," regularly beat their husbands if they came home late and drunk from the pub. After Dylan died, Caitlin expressed her grief by hurling herself at anybody who mentioned his name, pushing him crashing to the ground and punching and pummeling him with all her grief-stricken strength (Thomas, 1997, 26,168,180)

That men are alleged to be dominant to women is one of the most important of the "human universals" (defined in anthropology as behavioral phenomena alleged to be present in every human society) held dear by Darwinian psychologists (although, as the above quotation indicates, male dominance isn't *completely* ubiquitous). If men weren't the more important sex, anthropologists Bill Divale and Marvin Harris (1976) insist, why would male dominance be so widespread? After all, three-quarters of societies studied by anthropologists are patrilocal, meaning that upon marriage a couple moves into the man's community; a man having several wives is a much more common arrangement than a woman having several husbands; male work is less like drudgery than female work which often includes hauling water to the home, cleaning, cooking and childcare; chiefs are usually men rather than women; male gods generally outnumber and outpower female goddesses; weapons of the hunt and for war are monopolized by men; and if infanticide is practised, it is usually girl babies rather than boy babies who are killed as we saw in Chapter 2.[1] Divale and Harris argue that women are subordinate to men *not* because they are usually smaller (which is the situation in most mammal pairs as we have seen), but because male aggression which ensures domination (inclining them to violence and even warfare) is embedded in men's genes.

Steven Goldberg mentions in his book *The Inevitability of Patriarchy* (1973) the absolute universality of "the *feeling* [his italics] of both men and women that the male's will dominates the female's." He continues later, "The ethnographic studies of every society that has ever been observed," meaning some 1200 societies studied by anthropologists, "explicitly state that these feelings were present, there is literally no variation at all" (Leacock, 1981, 264). Did anthropologists really meet with women from 1200 societies, with no men present to inhibit their free speech, to collect such personal information? I think not.

Men are stronger and more aggressive than women, but this does not mean they are necessarily dominant, any more than the large aggressive chimpanzee males are dominant to the smaller females in the (unprovisioned) wild. They aren't. Rather, ever since our ancestors evolved beyond nomadism and began settling down into an agrarian lifestyle, the condition of patriarchy has slowly evolved over 2500 years (Lerner, 1987, 212). The labor of children became important to increase production of crops, so women began to be seen as a reproductive resource which brought wealth into a family; this could be accomplished by marriage exchange between groups or, if there were conflict, the winning side killing the men of the losing side and enslaving the women to become child-bearers. Men used their large brain, greater strength and possibility of being violent toward women eventually to found and organize for their own benefit religions, governments, military forces, and institutions of higher education. It is culture backed by the possibility of aggression, not inheritance, that has enabled men to be dominant.

Nomadic groups living today are egalitarian, with neither men nor women dominant (Power, 1991). Social groups work best through cooperation, not violence. For example in order to survive, hunting was imperative for Inuit men in the olden days, but equally important was women's work of preparing warm clothing without which the men would have been unable to venture outdoors in winter. Because our ancestors were also nomads living in small groups, there is every reason to believe that they were also egalitarian, even if men and women had different tasks. This makes sense because in a small group living hand to mouth year after year, every person knows the strengths and failings of every other person. There is no reason for anyone to allow others to take power over them; the diverse labour of all is needed for the group to survive. Most aboriginal nomadic societies that have been forced by Europeans to settle down in one place are now male-dominated. Why is this so? Following the time of first contact between preliterate societies and European explorers, adventurers and missionaries, sexual equality of native groups was subconsciously or deliberately destroyed. Invariably the European men, who all came from male-dominated societies, met first with the native men. They traded goods with the men and made treaties and arrangements that benefitted these men rather than the native women in the background. As settlement progressed, the colonizers solidified this male-bias into laws and attitudes which are only recently being addressed because of their bias.

In her book *Chain Her by One Foot* (1991), Karen Anderson gives an example of how women of the Huron and Montagnais Nations in Canada were physically subdued during a period of thirty years, to the mid-1640s, by Jesuit priests. These men came from a French society in which Christian doctrine proclaimed that women were worth far less than men and needed men's guidance. When they first arrived in New France, now eastern Canada, the native women cursed them as sorcerers because they brought with them disease and death. The women at first continued to do as they pleased, having sex with any man who attracted them and ostracizing their Christian spouses; in the matrilineal, matrifocal Huron nation men needed women more than women needed men so a man could easily find himself homeless if no woman would take him in.

The priests set out to destroy the equality between the sexes and make aboriginal women subservient to their menfolk, as the Bible stated should be the case. Under the new Christian regime, one woman who ran away from her husband was caught, tied up and put into a canoe to be carried to a dungeon in Quebec City. When she realized her predicament, she agreed to return home (p. 220). Another woman who tried to leave her husband "without just cause" was put into a prison built for her at Sillery, Quebec. She spent a January day and night in midwinter, without fire, food or water, before being chastened and released.

"Human universals" are social behaviors or attributes common to all human societies. In the past, anthropologists have spread out all over the world collecting information on preliterate communities. Their data have been analyzed en masse to determine what features are present in all human cultures that could therefore be said to be part of human nature. Proponents of Darwinian psychology presume that these universal features have become embedded in human genes which is why they are present everywhere; they perhaps promote "human universals" as biologically determined because they fit in with their wishful hypothesis of human evolution.

Opponents of Darwinian psychology argue instead that human social behavior is now so plastic because of our large brain that we develop traits that suit our environments; if some characteristics are present world-wide, it is because they have proven to be successful everywhere.

Human beings are born with far too many connections between brain cells for efficiency. As youngsters live through various experiences involving constant feedback from their environment, some pathways between neural cells are reinforced while others, unused, wither away: the brain is being turned from a general into a specific device that makes us who we are. This process continues well into the teen years (Strauch, 2003). For Darwinian psychologists this process is organized mainly by genetics, while for their critics it is guided largely by adaptation of the individual to his or her environment.

Many of our social behaviors we share with our primate ancestors from over six million years ago—for example aggression, sociality, inquisitiveness and a fair level of intelligence; these are "primate universals" rather than "human universals," our subject here. "Human universals" evolved in our ancestors since that time and are indeed present in all human societies. Most importantly, human beings are born with the ability to speak in a grammatically correct way, the language depending on the language the child hears spoken around him or her. Chimpanzees and gorillas can learn to communicate using hand signals, but the anatomy of their mouths and throats makes it impossible for them to articulate a large variety of sounds.

Second, for most people a sexual and affectionate nuclear bond exists between a man and one or more women which may last a short or long time and involves caring for each other and sharing food, shelter and experiences; when the mating systems of 862 cultures were analyzed, sixteen per cent had exclusive nuclear pair bonds although eighty-three per cent practised polygyny at least some of the time (Sussman, 2000, 97). Both arrangements may be advantageous. When the Jesuit priest Paul Le Jeune first lived among the Montagnais natives in eastern Canada in the 1630s, he found it was the women who resisted monogamy, in part because each had to work harder to support one man than they did in a polygynous household. There was another reason as well: he wrote, "Since I have been preaching among them that a man should not have more than one wife, I have not been well received by the women; for, since they are more numerous than the men, if a man can only marry one of them, the others will have to suffer. Therefore this doctrine is not according to their liking" (Leacock, 1980). Such strong nuclear bonds are extremely rare among other primate species who are generally promiscuous; even white-handed gibbons, who until recently were thought to be models of monogamy, are now known to mate with other animals when their partners aren't looking (Reichard and Sommer, 1997).

Third, a man in such a union who fathers a child usually cares for that child (as does the mother) by providing him or her with food, protection and education. Most modern human groups live in patriarchal societies; only sixteen of 179 hunting and gathering societies were found to be matrilineal (Sussman, 2000, 97). By contrast, nonhuman males probably never know for sure if they are the father or not of an infant, so that parental care from male mammals is relatively uncommon. Most mammal species are matrilineal, with biological descent traced from a common ancestor only through females and the mother passing on to her young cultural advantages such as status.

Fourth, parents rear their children for many years until they reach sexual maturity, far longer than any other species; during this time they are taught a vast amount about relationships within their family and their group and about their environment, information that enables them to succeed as adults.

E.O. Wilson postulated in 1975 that many other characteristics in human beings beyond these four are "human universals," governed by our genetic inheritance. Since then many armchair psychologists have added to the number—religion, spite, risk taking, flattery, mathematical superiority in males (although factually untrue [Kimball, 1989]), rape, selfishness, kin selection, altruism, reciprocal altruism, cooperation and especially notable, the inheritance of intelligence (IQ) which will be discussed in Chapter 15. As mentioned earlier, it is easy to think up some means by which a behavioral trait could have evolved and then write a paper about it to be presented at a conference or accepted for publication. What better way for an academic to advance his or her career? After all, it is impossible to *prove* these hypothetical genes exist, and equally impossible to *disprove* their existence.

Some anthropologists have joined the group, agreeing that since many behaviors are found in most or all human societies that have been studied, they must be universal and genetic in nature. Joseph Shepher (1983,9) writes that "if we find uniformity of behavior throughout an entire species, we can hardly ascribe this uniformity to culture, for *culture is variability par excellence; it cannot cause universals*. Universals exist *in spite of culture*. The logical conclusion must be that genes are the ultimate source of universal behaviors."

Despite Shepher's emphasis, uniformity of "universals" only means that certain behaviors are present in all human societies. It does not mean that they must be genetic in character. They can come equally well from societies thinking about their basic needs and using the brain power of individuals to solve them; our large brain ensures that we are better able than any of our ancestors to make decisions depending on our circumstances.

Donald Brown mentions well over 300 "human universals" in his book *Human Universals* (1991), describing much of what people do as reflecting "human nature" and our genotype,[2] but few of these behaviors, although often universal, have a genetic origin (Sussman, 1995). For one thing, the projected relationship between genetics and behavior is extremely vague. What specific genes could govern the expertise to practise magic, attempts to control the weather, or the ability to use fire? (p. 135). How would the inheritance work of such items as hairstyles, folklore, synonyms, cooking, personal names and false beliefs (note ironically the last item)?

For another, many of the "universals" mentioned aren't found in all cultures, so aren't universal at all. For example, the Oedipus complex (which is itself non-Darwinian because a family's genes would not benefit if boys killed their fathers) is not universal if it even exists, and the ability to recognize "abnormal mental states" can hardly be a "universal" when different ethnic groups use varied criteria to determine what is abnormal.

Finally, Brown's grab-bag of "universals" includes traits of different levels of abstraction, some constrained for example by the organization of the human brain (e.g., that we are bipedal and mostly right-handed), with no attempt to organize them in any meaningful way. Making an unorganized inventory of human "universals" is a fruitless exercise (Sussman, 1995).

Brown (1991,69,134) includes human gestures used for communication as one of his likely "universals." However, Desmond Morris in his book *Bodytalk: A World Guide to Gestures* (1994) describes 380 different gestures, many restricted to a geographical region, of which twenty-seven per cent actually convey different messages within different groups. For example, the holding up of a hand with thumb and forefinger tips joined to form a circle can mean six different things: the widespread symbol for okay or good, a sexual insult (in Germany, Russia, some of the Mediterranean area and parts of South America), zero (in Belgium, France and Tunisia), money (in Japan), perfection (in South America), and What are you talking about? (in Italy). Obviously if you are visiting in Germany and give the circle gesture to show the native guide that everything is fine, it won't be fine for long. Nor will a Japanese tourist who makes the gesture for money be amused if her Belgian host treats her as if she has none.

"Universals" have been said to include war and xenophobia (the opposite of ethnocentrism), words which reflect the feelings of people against strangers and for their own group (Wilson, 1975, 565); the Darwinian explanation is that human beings are most empathetic to those like themselves because of the many genes they share in common—an example of expanded kin selection. If a sister or friend dies we are devastated, but if a thousand people perish in an earthquake on the other side of the world, we feel only momentary sorrow. But is this impulse genetic?

We have already seen in Chapter 5 that war does not reflect Darwinian theory. Although there are far too many nations at war, many more are at peace. In World War II, diverse nations with relatively little in common fought together to defeat Germany and Japan. In North Ireland and the Punjab, fighting was/is based primarily on religious grounds. In the American Civil War, genetic brothers fought against and killed each other over the historical principle of secession. E.O. Wilson (1975, 562b) argues that the genetic foundation for war may mean some warriors will die, but victory will be beneficial enough for the survivors to make war genetically worthwhile. If this were true, wouldn't we already have suffered through more wars, or even a nuclear war?

What about xenophobia, the apprehension of strangers? History shows us that when a new human race was discovered by Europeans, often members of it were at first treated by the Europeans as objects of curiosity and interest. It was only after large numbers of these people, say, migrated into a country and people began to fear for their jobs that interest turned to anger and fear. Much of tourism (but certainly not all) is based on the wish of people to visit countries where people are different than they are, the reverse of xenophobia.

In relation to xenophobia do we share and help our close relatives? Is blood thicker than water? Usually yes. But there are large numbers of individuals who turn away from their birth families when they reach adulthood, and most people as adults share their lives far more with unrelated friends than with relatives. (The number of books and plays about suitably apprehensive adult children going back home for a family reunion are legion.) How many people would rather spend their time with relatives than with the members of their garden clubs, reading groups, senior hockey leagues and/or choral singing choirs?

Wilson (1975, 562) wants ethics to be "biologicized" by which he means, for one thing, correlating a sense of morality with heredity to explain how parents pass on standards to their young who have greater reproductive fitness because of this. However, morality is relative. In the Pleistocene, infanticide would be the moral solution for a nomad woman unable to carry or care for a second infant. To another group who had a high death rate, infanticide would be seen as immoral. Which morality would be coded in early *Homo* genes?

In his book *The Dangerous Passion* (2000), David Buss argues that jealousy, another "universal," evolved in human beings because of its benefits. Our ape-like ancestors probably weren't much into jealousy, since they were polygamous, so a gene or genes must have mutated for this behavior during more recent human evolution. Those who possessed it would have had more reproductive fitness than their peers and would have produced more offspring. Buss provides many titillating anecdotes about jealous couples illustrating two evolutionary attributes: it is a way a person tests his or her partner to determine if he or she is truly committed to their relationship, and once a couple has transcended a bout of jealousy, the pair have great sex.

Does this make sense as an evolutionary theory? I don't think so. For one thing, many human societies today (as well as chimpanzees) are polygamous, as we have seen, so undoubtedly many of our ancestors were, too. As well, some early groups of people did not even know that the male had a part to play in pregnancy and birth. Buss doesn't elaborate on the down side of jealousy—that it can destroy an otherwise satisfactory relationship and that many people are killed by a jealous mate, the aggressor spending many years or life in exile or in prison as a result. Such behavior doesn't enhance either parent's ability to have children. Besides, Darwinian theory pushes the concept of men bedding as many women as possible in the subconscious hope that some of these affairs will lead to children to carry on their genetic inheritance. This theory is the exact opposite of a man being jealous of and obsessed with an individual woman to the exclusion of all others. Both theories can't be right.

Recent research in the wild of various animal species shows that groups living in isolation develop customs not present in other peer groups, an example of learning and culture passed along within a community which has nothing to do with genetics. So many observations have been made of chimpanzees in Africa that Andrew Whiten and his colleagues (1999) have been able to compare the presence or absence of thirty-eight different activities in seven different populations. For example in four of these groups most chimpanzees dance when it rains, but in two only several individuals do this while the activity is unknown in the seventh group. When it comes to using a stick as a club, two groups have individuals who do this repeatedly although members of the rest of the group do not, it occurs inconsistently in members of three other groups and is unknown in two populations. From these examples it is evident that inventive individual chimpanzees have dreamed up new customs or technologies and, depending on his or her community, some have caught on to become virtually "universal" while others have not. How reminiscent of the erratic spread of baseball or soccer in countries around the world.

Nor are chimpanzees, who we like to think of as the most intelligent animals after ourselves because of our close genetic links, the only animals with culture. Orangutans in different populations have other diverse social behaviors (Yoon, 2003), songbirds invent melodies that are specific to their geographic areas (as Warren, 2002) and each pod of killer whales has underwater noises that contain a unique dialect (Yurk et al., 2002). Undoubtedly members of other species as yet understudied have a variety of different customs too. If such social behaviors are variable and arise spontaneously rather than through inheritance in these animals, why would we believe that similar behaviors are genetically based in people?

In summary, there are "human universals" not found in other primates that are almost certainly genetically based, but they are few in number: spoken language, the presence of close male-female bonds, extended paternal care of young and many years of child-raising by both parents. Other social behaviors, present to a lesser or greater extent in the vast number of human societies, seem rather to have their basis in learning and culture, attributes present also in many "lower" animals.

Notes

1. In their paper "Population, warfare, and the male supremacist complex," William Divale and Marvis Harris (1976) argue that male dominance in early cultures was virtually universal; however, some of the data on which they base their research are inaccurate, as a variety of experts point out in volume 80 of *American Anthropologist* (1978, 110-115, 115-117, 665-667 and 671-673, with replies by Divale and Harris 117-118 and 668-671.)
2. Steven Pinker (2002, 435-439) includes a list of Brown's human universals in his book *The Blank Slate*. The items include characteristics common to other primates and other mammals (incest taboo, pain, daily routines, feasting, ambivalence, group living, weaning) as well as those peculiar to human beings.

Chapter 8

Blaming The Victim—Criminality

- **Theft:** A dog learned to go to the store to buy a cookie by depositing a sou on the store counter. One day she put down a metal button instead, grabbed a cookie with her mouth and fled.
- **Selfishness:** A dove who wasn't hungry sometimes hid food under her wings so that the other doves couldn't have it.
- **Adultery:** While the male of a pair of nesting storks was away hunting for food, a younger male visited his mate. She pushed him away at first, then tolerated him and finally welcomed him. The two adulterers fled together but the cuckolded male chased them and killed his rival with blows from his beak.
- **Revenge:** A dog, abused by a guard dog, collected bones for several days in a cellar, then invited a number of neighborhood mongrels to a feast. When they were full, their host urged them to help him avenge his mistreatment by the guard dog.
- **Murder:** Three beaver built and lived in a house near a solitary beaver. One day the three visited their neighbor who received them hospitably. When this beaver returned the visit, however, the trio fell upon him and killed him.

The first person to study crime "scientifically" was Cesare Lombroso, an Italian doctor and psychiatrist. For centuries people had worried about crime and how it could be reduced. Should poor people who might steal be shut up in work houses? Should rich people defend themselves with bigger dogs and better locks on their doors? But it was Lombroso who, in a sudden inspiration, decided not to concentrate on the environment in which crime took place, but to look at the criminals themselves. He was performing an autopsy on the brain of a notorious Italian "Jack the Ripper" when he noticed the enlarged size of the *vermis*, the central lobe of the cerebellum lying beneath the cerebral hemispheres. He realized that it almost resembled this lobe found in the lower apes, rodents, and birds (Lombroso, 1911, 6). "At the sight of that skull," he rhapsodized, "I seemed to see all at once, standing out clearly illumined as in a vast plain under a flaming sky, the problem of the nature of the criminal, who reproduces in civilised times characteristics, not only of primitive savages, but of still lower types as far back as the carnivore." Thus began one of the earliest foreshadowings of Darwinian psychology.

To prove that criminal behavior was a result of Darwinian psychology (although he would not have called it that), Lombroso (1887) hunted for evidence that "lower" animals, presumably from whom human beings had evolved, could also be criminal in nature. He hunted through accounts of the behavior of various species until he found what he was looking for—individuals who had committed a whole range of crimes, as we can see from the above examples (Lombroso, 1887). Strange as it may seem, in Europe in the Middle Ages and into the nineteenth century all manner of animals were accused of wrong-doing and tried with due ceremony before courts of justice—including insects for damaging crops and sparrows for chattering in church (Humphrey, 2002, 237f). What an unending bonanza for state-supported lawyers who represented these animals and argued their cases in court!

Aggression often leads to crime, a subject easier to research than the more vague concept of aggression because there are statistics available denoting who was and is in jail and why, and what research has found out about these criminals. Or are we fooling ourselves? The concept of crime is unique to each country, varying widely for the practice of such things as female genital mutilation, abortion, marital rape and driving while drunk. How can we come up with a theory that satisfactorily encompasses all such possibilities?

Crime does not apply to animals (although Lombroso insisted that it did) because it is a human construct involving the breaking of human rules of behavior. Nor does it apply as much to women as to men. It particularly involves poor people, especially black men, who are often victims as well as offenders. The right-wing proponents of Darwinian psychology seem happy to publicize their science which views black people and the poor as more likely to be criminals than other human beings. Is criminality inherited as some Darwinian psychologists believe? Are blacks and poor people especially likely to have genes that cause criminal behavior?

Lombroso's brainstorm, which would become the substance of his new discipline of Criminal Anthropology, was that criminals were a throwback to their forebears, a theory called atavism. Their anatomy and behavior, inherited in some unknown manner, reflected evolution in that their "stigmata" resembled anatomical features in animals such as apes and monkeys, in depraved savages or "inferior" people who weren't Europeans, and in children. In other words their bad traits, including criminality, were those already present in forms thought to be lower in the evolutionary scale.

For "savage" people, Lombroso described sickening fantasies of depravity including the detail that idiots and savages did not know how to blush because they were not only criminals but shameless. For children, who were assumed to be raw delinquents before they became civilized, he attributed other excesses and misbehavior, including their predilection for alcohol: "It is only too common a thing to see even suckling babes drink wine and liquors with wonderful delight." Since he was writing for the middle and upper classes, he added that they only believed in the innocence of young children because they were unaware of the bad behavior that confronted maids and nannies (Gould 1981, 127).

Lombroso's "Eureka!" would be a curse to the many poor people whose basic shortcoming was having a large jaw, the fleshy protruding lips of a rapist or the thin straight lips of a swindler. (Did he wonder what a swindling rapist looked like? Would his lips be straight or protruding?) Lombroso's life work became the analysis of about 7000 criminals focusing on what they looked like and how they behaved. The results of his research were that one-third of convicts were Born Criminals who committed monstrous crimes such as murders. The other two-thirds, Criminaloids, whose crimes were less serious, did not have an inheritance of criminality, but had fallen into a life of villainy because of environmental conditions or because they had a disease such as epilepsy.

The Born Criminals of interest to Darwinian psychology were, of course, not responsible for their sins. They were born that way because of their genetic inheritance, with many of their characteristics reflecting more "primitive" life forms. Lombroso stated that Born Criminals were likely to have extra teeth as snakes have, a thick skull like those of "savage peoples," a flattened negroid nose in thieves, or an aquiline nose like the beak of a bird of prey in murderers. (What about the nose of a thieving murderer?) Some criminal men had no nipples which reminded him of the primitive condition of the egg-laying duck-billed platypus or echidna, or flabby breasts like those of Hottentot women. He declared that Born Criminals were likely to be left-handed, hairy, keen of vision, with dark hair (murderers) or curly and woolly hair (swindlers). They were cynical, treacherous, impulsive, idle and given to orgies, gambling, using slang and wearing tattoos.

One of the major crimes for women was prostitution, as Lombroso and William Ferrero describe in their book *The Female Offender* (1915). Prostitutes were depicted as frequently having moles, hairy bodies, prehensile feet, a virile larynx, large jaws and cheek-bones and anomalous teeth. They are not actually called ugly, because that would have been unlikely given their occupation; instead, most of their negative attributes were hidden under the dresses and petticoats worn over 100 years ago. The book includes many photographs of criminal women but none of them Italian because, as the authors state querulously, Italy foolishly forbade the measuring and photographing of the worst criminals once they had been condemned so that their shame would be respected (p. 88). (To me, all the women in the photographs look quite ordinary if not prim, given the high necklines of their dresses [Fig 8.1].)

Fig 8.1 Photographs of a Born Prostitute and a Born Criminal

Margherita

Louise

Source: Lombroso and Ferrero, 1915

The photograph of twelve-year-old Margherita, an example of a Born Prostitute, looks to my untutored eye like that of a pleasant young girl, but the authors know better. They describe with distaste her strong jaw and cheek-bones, sessile ears, hypertrophy of the middle incisors, and dullness of her sense of touch (p. 98). She apparently had a violent temper (she liked to invite her brother to kiss her as she held a pin between her teeth), and was so given to masturbation that her clitoris was removed when she was eleven years old.

The photo of Louise, aged nine although she looks older, is said to represent that of a typical Born Criminal with a Mongolian caste to her face, immense jaw and cheek-bones, strong frontal sinuses, flat nose, asymmetry of features "and, above all, precocity and virility of expression" (p. 99), apparently a very bad thing. She was said to have bad instincts, weak intellect, turbulent conduct and, like Margherita, to be always in a condition of sexual excitement. She stole things from the age of three, resisted arrest by the police at age five, shrieked, tore off her stockings and threw her dolls into the gutter, all ostensibly attributes of the Born Criminal.

Lombroso's work, focusing on the biological basis of criminal nature in men and women, was unappreciated in Europe. As we have seen, his own country refused to facilitate his research and Europeans from other countries complained not only that his methodology was faulty, but that it demonstrated that not all criminals should be punished. Conservative judges and lawyers refused to go along with Lombroso's ideas not because they were pseudo-scientific and fraudulent, but because they trespassed on the judges' ancient domain of deciding who was guilty (Gould 1981, 139). Fortunately for Lombroso, however, the United States gave his ideas a "warm and sympathetic reception" (Lombroso, 1887, xix) which resulted in translations of his books being published there well into the twentieth century. His ideas percolated through society for many years but fortunately had little influence in courts of law.[1]

Most people no longer believe with Lombroso that people are born with inherited anatomical "stigmata" that destine them to be criminals or prostitutes, or that these occupations are held by people with specific genetic traits. However, the concept lingers. Psychologist Philippe Rushton (1990) argues that Lombroso was correct in some of his beliefs about the biological basis of crime, while James Wilson and Richard Herrnstein in their book *Crime and Human Nature* (1985) present many photos and charts indicating that people of mesomorphic body type (usually shorter than normal with heavy-boned muscularity [p. 81]) are more likely than those of other body types to be criminals. Their data are from fifty years ago with more modern studies contradicting them ignored. For example, recent surveys showed Princeton students, bus and truck drivers, California children and 400 Army recruits were *more* mesomorphic than a sample of Boston delinquents (Kamin, 1986).

The huge variation in number of prisoners held in different Western nations is also telling:

Number of prisoners per 100,000 inhabitants in 2002 (Hoge, 2003):

Finland	52
Germany	97
Britain	126
Russia	664
United States	702

Even if prison policies among these nations were harmonized, it remains difficult to believe that a genetic explanation could account for the vastly different numbers of criminals in these countries.

Although he was a proponent of what would become Darwinian psychology, Lombroso did not study or postulate exactly how criminality would be inherited. Did Margherita or Louise have mothers who were prostitutes or fathers who were murderers? We have no way of knowing. If criminal behavior were inherited by a dominant gene, the children of criminals could inherit the trait directly. If it were recessive or a new mutation, it would arise in a population more sporadically. But how would it confer a benefit on its possessor? According to Darwinian psychological theory, a genetic characteristic becomes embedded in a group only if people carrying it have relatively more offspring than other people. How would this work for criminals?

In our evolutionary history, one would imagine that individuals who broke social codes would be shunned by their peers and even perhaps expelled from the group, implying that they had fewer offspring than others. For people today, some must break the law and get away with it, perhaps making money that enables them to successfully raise children. The individuals we know as criminals, however, have been convicted in a court of justice and probably spent time in jail where they would be unable to reproduce. When they are freed, they are less likely than average to settle down with a spouse and raise a family. Indeed, because they have the alleged gene, they would probably break the law again. These facts do not fit with a theory of Darwinian psychology.

In 1965 a scientific breakthrough claimed a specific genetic connection for criminality. There was widespread excitement when Patricia Jacobs and four colleagues (1965) reported that they had discovered not one gene but an entire chromosome for this condition. A criminal chromosome could make a judge's job easy. These researchers studied the chromosomes of 197 men "with dangerous, violent or criminal propensities" imprisoned in a Scottish institution. They discovered eight inmates, nearly four per cent of that population, who not only had the rare XYY (instead of the usual XY) sex chromosomes, but who were, on average, abnormally tall with subnormal intelligence. Four per cent was far higher than the percentage of XYY genes in the rest of the population, although at that time this exact statistic was unknown.

This study triggered the usual bonanza of media hoopla targeted at newly discovered correlations between genetics and social behavior, and a flurry of related studies supporting the finding of a criminal chromosome. One high school text reported the XYY male as usually over six feet tall and *very aggressive*; the *Georgetown Law Journal* described XYY men as "walking `powder kegs' "; a *Newsweek* article was headed "Congenital Criminals"; magazine articles talked about the excessive violence of XYY men and "the gene for criminality;" and in several states prisoners with an extra Y chromosome were treated with female sex hormones to counteract their supposedly extra maleness/violence (Beckwith and Miller, 1976).

In 1976, however, Herman Witkin and eleven colleagues from the United States and Denmark produced a little-publicized article which counteracted most of the original 1965 paper. They found that indeed tall men were especially likely to have an XYY chromosome, that such XYY men were below normal in intelligence, and that they were especially likely to commit crimes. However, their crimes had been against property, not people, and they were in fact *less* violent on average than the majority XY prisoners. The crime rate of the XYY men was deemed to be most likely related to their low intelligence; such men are more liable to think that they can get away with crimes and to be apprehended for them, so that the XYY group probably reflected a higher detection rate rather than a higher rate of carrying out crimes. The authors (most of them men) stress that it is NOT the extra Y chromosome itself that is implicated in low intelligence and crime, but that its presence somehow upsets the overall organization of the affected men's genetic material.

In 1975, a year before this paper was published, Stanley Walzer and Park Gerald had set up a program at the Harvard Medical School whereby all baby boys born at the Boston Hospital for Women would be tested to see if they had an unusual sex chromosome (Davis, 1976). Of the first 15,000 newborns, 45 were either XYY or XXY. The aim of the program was to compare the behavior of these boys as they grew up with that of XY boys, and to help them cope with any problems that might arise because of their unusual genotype.

This program soon revealed the deep split among scientists working in genetics. Whereas the Harvard faculty en masse saw the program as benign at best, and possibly of great use to the boys and their families, it appalled the dissidents. Dr Walzer and his family received abusive and threatening phone calls which eventually convinced him to stop the screening.

In their protest against the program, Jim Beckwith and Larry Miller (1976) pointed out that there was no concrete evidence that an XYY syndrome even existed, let alone that it was correlated with criminality, and that the vast majority of XYY men lived perfectly normal lives. They queried how one defined criminality, stating that "one person's criminal is another's revered ex-President," and noted that the proposed program was biased in that both ends of the double-blind approach were violated—the doctors knew which boys were XYY and so did most of their families. Ideally, neither should have known so that the boys would have been treated as normal children. This lack of proper experimental design meant that the results of the program would always be suspect. Perhaps most importantly, if a boy is labeled and his parents are told that he may grow up to have a problem, he may easily meet their expectation (Culliton, 1975).

Philippe Rushton, a staunch Darwinian psychologist, believes that criminal behavior is not caused by a specific criminal gene but by the absence of a gene that encourages social responsibility. He speculates that when scientists find the social responsibility gene, they will be able to rehabilitate the criminals who lack it by means of gene therapy rather than imprisonment (Chwialkowska, 1999). However, he has no DNA evidence that such a gene exists or that its non-existence matters. Rather, his theory is based on questionnaires, answered by twins, focused on issues related to social responsibility.

Rushton found from the questionnaires that the responses of monozygotic (MZ) identical twin pairs were twice as similar to each other as were those of fraternal twin pairs. However, he assumes that the responses are caused by the respondents' genotype, rather than by their past experiences. MZ twins are more likely to be close and to share similar ideas because they have often been treated alike by their family and schools. By contrast dizygotic (DZ) twins, who do not look as alike and are often of both sexes, are usually less close.

Another source of error in Rushton's work is that he assumed a person would act in the same way that he or she answered questions. The questionnaire involved statements such as "It is always important to finish anything that you have started"; "In school my behavior has gotten me into trouble"; "I have been in trouble with the law or police"; "I am the kind of person people can count on"; and "Every person should give some of his or her time for the good of his or her town or city." The responses would raise more questions than they answer. Was "trouble in school" because a girl wore a short skirt? or a boy skipped a class? or a senior brought a gun to school? If a person is the kind that one can count on, would this include the stereotypical honor among thieves? Might not a person be willing to give time to a good cause but never do so? Or be unwilling in theory but do so anyway?

One of the tenets of Darwinian psychology is that human social behavior is largely inherited rather than learned. To determine if this is true, Sheldon and Eleanor Glueck (1950, 1960, 1968) tackled the problem in an enormous research project optimistically called Unravelling Juvenile Delinquency (UJD). This project addressed the age-old conundrum: What makes one person a delinquent while another from next door, immersed in similar living conditions, becomes a respected adult? The Gluecks in 1939 began a longitudinal study in the Boston area of 500 boys aged ten to seventeen who had been involved in crime. They paired each of these lads with a boy of the same age from the public school system who had never been in trouble with police (the controls). Each pair shared the same ethnicity (whether they had an Irish, Polish or Spanish background for example), race (white), intelligence level (IQs averaging 92 to 94), and neighborhood, so that any differences between the groups of delinquents and non-delinquents could not be blamed on these variables.

The Gluecks' investigators were incredibly thorough. They interviewed the boys, their parents or guardians and their teachers. They combed through records and reports kept about the boys and their families by social workers, public welfare agencies, police officers and judges. And if they couldn't get the information they needed at an agency the first time, they went back a second time.

The facts they gathered were incorporated into data sheets focused on the boy's family, his other associations and himself. Family data included family size, whether the household was crowded, whether the family moved often, and whether it was often disrupted. Parental data included if and where the parents worked, if they drank a great deal and if they had criminal records. Information centering on the boy himself encompassed whether his parents were erratic or harsh toward him, whether they rejected him, how the mother supervised him, how attached he was to those around him (his parents, siblings, school and peers), how difficult he had been while a young child and the marks he got in school.

This was just the beginning. Since the experiment was set up to find out what happened to these boys as they grew older, the Gluecks and their many helpers had to keep in touch with them which they did when they were aged twenty-five and thirty-two; their follow-up success rate was ninety-two per cent, an amazingly high rate reflecting their persistence and the relative lack of mobility of Americans in the 1940s and 1950s compared to today.

The Gluecks' data have been reanalyzed (along with a third census of the targets as forty-five-year-olds) by Robert Sampson and John Laub who published their findings in their book *Crime in the Making: Pathways and Turning Points through Life* (1993). They emphasize that the collection of such voluminous data will likely never again be possible, given current ideas about the rights of privacy of families and individuals (p. 29). The results did indeed begin to unravel the mystery of juvenile delinquency.

Why do some boys become delinquents? The UJD study found that delinquency was not correlated with a boy's family and therefore with his inheritance. It correlated best with poor parental supervision, erratic, threatening and harsh discipline and weak parental attachment. Less important were a boy's dislike of school and his having delinquent friends (p. 247).

What factors affected their behavior when these boys became adults? A simplified conclusion was that for both the delinquents and the controls, the stronger a man's ties to work and family, the less likely he was to be involved in crime (p. 248), although one limitation was that for some men, heavy drinking (at that time drugs were virtually unknown) undermined their ability to hold a job or have a strong marriage. Marriage by itself didn't turn a delinquent's life around, but did so indirectly by disrupting or ending the husband's friendships with criminals that had existed earlier (Warr, 1998).

Since the publication of *Crime in the Making* further research studies, listed chronologically, have confirmed and expanded the analysis of criminals:

- Taking into account factors of sex, age, poverty and race, the only consistent correlation for the violent behavior of criminals is with poverty (Markowitz and Felson, 1998).
- Membership in street gangs increases the criminal activity of young men and women (Battin et al., 1998).
- The lower the social and economic status of men, the more likely they are to be violent and to consider a display of courage during confrontations paramount. For many young men in urban communities there is no legitimate employment which will earn them respect among their peers. Some are willing to steal or kill in hopes of improving their status, even if this only increases their chance of obtaining drugs (Kovandzic et al., 1998).
- Women who smoke during a pregnancy are more likely to have sons who become criminals (Brennan et al., 1999).
- Babies born with complications such as breech presentation, umbilical cords wrapped around their necks or birth injuries are more likely than other babies to have prefrontal brain injury which sometimes leads to extreme violence by the person when he is grown (Raine et al., 2000).
- Poor parenting, based on child welfare worker reports, is correlated with criminal behavior in children (Hodgins et al., 2001).

- Safe and legal abortions are statistically correlated with lower crime rates because they prevent the birth of unwanted children who are especially likely to become criminals (Donohue and Levitt, 2001).

There is no real evidence that a tendency for crime is inherited. There is no evidence of gene(s) for criminality and it is impossible even to imagine how there could be for the huge number of Nazis who implemented the holocaust, for example, or for members of the Klu Klux Klan who murdered blacks or for white collar embezzlers greedy for money. Violent crimes are strongly correlated with poverty which isn't a genetic condition. A person who has a genetic mental or physical defect may be forced to live in poverty, but so are single parents who can't leave their children to take a job, people who have been in accidents that prevent employment, people with crippling addictions and those with other private disasters in their lives.

The Glueck's data were published extensively in 1950, 1960 and 1968, and given much publicity; two of their books were published by the prestigious Harvard University Press. It is therefore difficult to understand why proponents of Darwinian psychology such as Philippe Rushton, whose biased research will also be discussed in detail in Chapters 14 and 15, insist on claiming that the criminal behavior of one group (black men) is in large part genetic (Rushton, 1990). Because such opinions, no matter how ill-founded, are certain to inflame racism, Julian Roberts and Thomas Gabor (1990) in their article "Lombrosian wine in a new bottle: Research on crime and race" present a devastating critique of Rushton's work which he is largely unable to refute except with inaccurate and irrelevant data (Rushton, 1990). Roberts and Gabor note that it is impossible to define race: most black Americans have some "white" blood and some people who are black have more white than black ancestors. They point out that there is no causal connection between black men and crime, only correlations which are readily explained by the poverty in which many blacks are forced to live owing to past and present discrimination.

The crime statistics cited by Rushton, a major player on the topic of criminality as an inherited trait, are often incorrect or biased. He states that blacks commit fifty per cent of crimes in Britain and the United States, but in America it is only twenty-nine per cent. For violent crimes in the United States, FBI data claim that forty-seven per cent are committed by blacks, but victimization surveys indicate that the rate should be about twenty-four per cent. Which is correct? Probably neither, since most crime goes unreported; in Britain a Crime Survey found that only eight per cent of robberies were recorded. Racial stereotypes ensure that black men are more likely than white to be stopped by police, questioned and picked up. Homicide rates vary by state, with Delaware having a homicide rate for blacks of seventeen per 100,000 inhabitants and Michigan a rate four times higher. Other studies have found that virtually *everyone* has committed many crimes in their lifetime including shoplifting, running a red light, jay walking and cheating on their taxes.

Rushton also errs in treating crime as a single entity, even though for fraud and embezzlement blacks are under- rather than over-represented. Are blacks genetically predisposed toward violent crimes while whites are programmed to commit white-collar crimes? A more sensible reason for this difference is surely that many blacks live in ghettoes where drugs, guns and violence are endemic while whites are more likely to have white-collar jobs where fraud is feasible.

If blacks are genetically more likely than other "races" to commit crimes, why does the crime rate vary in the same place in different decades? Why is the homicide rate in the African country of Mali .01 for every 100,000 inhabitants while in Jamaica it is 22.05? Are genes involved with crime two hundred times more potent in one country than the other, both of which have predominantly black inhabitants?

The data used by Rushton and other proponents of Darwinian psychology to link black men and a genetic propensity to crime are extremely questionable and their conclusions highly suspect. One can only assume their research was undertaken not as a scientific endeavor but to pursue, in missionary spirit, a right wing agenda that finds black people to blame for their own difficulties with the law. If crime were indeed largely correlated with one's genotype, the solution would be to punish the criminals (however unfairly because presumably they could not help themselves) rather than rectify with billions of dollars the terrible conditions in which many live.

Note

1. The industrious Lombroso continued to collect statistics throughout his life on such bizarre characteristics as: the ears of Born Criminals (often very large, sometimes very small, twenty-eight per cent standing out like those of chimpanzees); the sense of smell of prostitutes (normal in eighty-two per cent of moral women, seventy-seven per cent of thieves and sixty-six per cent of prostitutes); and the sometime stump of a tail, maybe tufted with hair, in a murderer.

Chapter 9

False References And Other Academic Booboos—Rape

> The male longear sunfish busily shoves aside sand and pebbles to fashion a small excavation, a nest, on the river bed near the bank. A female fish stout with roe swims there to lay her eggs. The two fish circle slowly over the nest. Periodically, the female tilts sideways so that her vent is near the male, then releases a batch of eggs. The male immediately sheds sperm over them as they settle into the nest below. Suddenly another male darts into the nest area trying to secrete his own sperm near the eggs, hoping to fertilize some of them. The resident male chases him away, then returns to the female (Keenleyside, 1972). This incident doesn't sound too traumatic for the fish, and hardly forced, but Randy Thornhill and Craig Palmer designate it as an example of rape.

Sometimes whole books are written to bolster hypotheses that are weak or nonexistent. This happens all too often in Darwinian psychology as acolytes strive to further their subdiscipline—and, of course, let's not forget the profit from book sales. This chapter will consider *The Natural History of Rape: Biological Bases of Sexual Coercion* (2000a) by entomologist Thornhill and anthropologist Palmer, a book redolent of the macho, misogynist aura prevalent in Darwinian psychology.

The authors' thesis is that rape, forced copulation, is an evolutionary strategy by which males ensure their sperm produce as many young as possible—more than they could manage if they had to wait for their female victims to agree to have sex. Some of the book deals with rape in non-human animals, but most focuses on people. The hypothesis is that males in our evolutionary past who had a mutation to rape females had more offspring than other males; those who raped produced male young who also raped because of a genetic inheritance to do so. Evolution thus ensured that for men, like their male forebears, rape is an evolutionary strategy.

Those of us who don't believe this read *The Natural History of Rape* with a critical eye. After all, in general if a female animal wants to avoid rape, she need only keep her tail down and fly, walk or swim away from the male rather than stay still; most males can't do anything about this as they don't have hands with which to grab her and hold her in a fruitful position.

First, as a biologist, I studied the animal data provided by Thornhill and Palmer. They devote an entire section to "Cross-Species Evidence" (p. 143-6). In this section there are paragraphs containing a huge number of references of articles about rape in a variety of animals—a total of eighty-one to be exact.

'Oh no,' was my first thought. 'Rape must be far more widespread than I'd realized.' My feminist heart sank although it was not supposed to; scientists theoretically look at facts with dispassion even if they show that one's heart-felt beliefs are wrong. Truth is supposed to be the only thing that matters.

I decided to make a list of the references so I could check them out to determine if indeed scores of species besides human beings were known to rape, as the list seemed to indicate. The first and earliest (Severinghaus 1955) was about deer, which surprised me. Some of my students have studied the behavior of deer for graduate degrees, but none had mentioned rape or forced copulation. The article reported on white-tailed does in New York State penned with bucks during the fall mating season. The bucks were insistent on mating, but the females who were not yet in estrus refused to be involved. One buck became so angry after chasing a doe who would not stand still so he could mount her, that several days later he attacked, killed and disemboweled her. Severinghaus writes, "This act apparently did not satiate his madness because he also killed a second doe for which he previously had shown no serious interest." In all, Severinghaus reports on six captive does killed by captive bucks, all of the animals confined in small areas rather than free. He notes that such abnormal mayhem does not occur in the wild "because the doe manages to elude her pursuers." Why would Thornhill and Palmer have included in their book on rape a reference for this article which is about murder rather than rape? If the does *had* succumbed to rape, they might have survived.

Another article also deals with animals in captivity. Rape among gorillas doesn't occur in the wild, but has been observed under laboratory conditions (Nadler and Miller, 1982). Male and female gorillas were put together in pairs for tests. Even though the females were not in estrus and would not in the wild have allowed mating, they did so as a response to the level of aggression in the males—the more violent the male, the more likely he was to force copulation; the researchers report, however, that such mating "is unlikely to contribute to reproduction." (I hope I am right in thinking that such unethical research producing such irrelevant results would not at present be allowed.) Because the rapes occurred under highly abnormal conditions and would not have taken place in the wild, reference to the article should not have been included in the book's list.

Among the insect references cited were five on scorpionflies, species new to me whose behavior the senior author, Randy Thornhill, has made one focus of his life's research. A scorpionfly male approaches copulation in two different ways (Thornhill, 1980). He may send out a long-distance smell or pheromone while he is waiting beside a hardened mass of saliva he has secreted for her on the ground or in the vicinity of a dead insect. The aroma attracts a female who feeds on the mass or the insect while he copulates with her. The second way is to grab a passing female by her leg or her wing with his genital claspers located at the end of his abdomen; then he doesn't have to bother with a nuptial offering. Although the female fights to escape and bends her abdomen tip away from her attacker as they struggle, he is usually able to force copulation on her.

Rape is defined as coerced rather than willing copulation by the two authors but this concept is tricky to apply to non-human females because we don't know what they are thinking. It is especially tricky for female insects with whom it is difficult for people to empathize because of our differences. Maybe they like their sex rough? Certainly this example and examples in some other invertebrates seem like rape.

After the insect references in the book comes a list of articles reputedly about birds who rape. The concept of rape is highly unlikely in most birds which mate in a second or two by merely touching their cloacas together in a "cloacal kiss"; it is possible in primitive species such as waterfowl which, during the breeding season, develop a type of erectile grooved penis on the ventral wall of the cloaca (Welty, 1982, 160).

Rape does indeed seem to occur in some primitive and colonial birds such as some ducks, gulls, herons and egrets, as the citations indicate (Gladstone, 1979). I first found one on mallard ducks which made sense, because I myself have seen males in the spring chasing females, sometimes almost seeming to drown them in their determination to copulate. But then I came to a second citation of rape in mallards, and then six more.[1] It seemed as if the authors were padding the list. There were also individual papers on rape in white-cheeked pintail, green-winged teal, blue-winged teal and lesser scaup. However, one paper based on a three-year study in a Nova Scotia marsh of the black duck, a close relative of the mallard, showed that the males did not attempt to rape females (Seymour and Titman, 1979). I couldn't help thinking that if rape really were a widespread successful evolutionary strategy as the authors imply, why would it be present in primitive birds such as some waterfowl but not in more advanced species? Why wouldn't the more advanced species have taken this new adaptation and run, flown, with it? The authors do not address this possibility.

For evolutionarily advanced birds, rape is rare or unknown. Thornhill and Palmer seem to make the mistake, widespread until recently, of believing that paired birds are monogamous, so that if a female mates with a male other than her partner this must be rape. However, as we shall see in Chapter 10 on sperm competition, a huge number of females and males both seek additional sexual partners for good evolutionary reasons despite their presumed monogamy. The authors cite in their book an article that they claim shows the English magpie has rape behavior in its repertoire. In this species even a mated male may keep an eye on a mated female other than his partner, waiting for her to be unguarded. Tim Birkhead (1979) reports watching one pair of magpies for most of a day, with the female foraging while her mate sat on a wall watching/guarding her. Because it was a warm afternoon the male eventually dozed off, at which instant a neighboring mated male flew over and mounted her. Before they could touch cloacas however, her partner woke up and attacked "the raping male" as they call him, who flew off. Birkhead noted that the female did not resist this "raping" male, nor did this male's partner interfere.

A similar situation exists for bank swallows which have been well studied by a number of researchers. They have focused on the males who share parental duties of nest-building, incubation and feeding of the young with one mate to whom a male is paired, while at the same time he is seeking to have sex with other females in the colony. In their study, Michael and Inger Beecher (1979) saw males apparently trying to copulate with females but never actually doing so, a behavior they nevertheless called a "rape" reaction. They, as well as Thornhill and Palmer, assume that the female would not want to mate with a second male. Yet for evolutionary reasons the female is probably as willing as the male to have sex outside her partnership, if only to ensure she produces young in case her mate is impotent.

Next in the book came the list of citations for fish articles. Most species of fish have external fertilization in which females lay eggs and males cover them with sperm, called milt or spawn, as described above. How could this be rape? How indeed. However, a few species such as the poeciliid fish do have internal fertilization where what we think of as rape becomes a possibility. The anal fin of the sailfin mollie male found in Florida develops into a copulatory organ, the gonopodium, when he reaches maturity (Farr et al., 1986). In the breeding season, a willing female remains still in the water to allow the male to copulate with her. However, a male may try to force insemination apparently without the female's consent, which allegedly constitutes rape. However, James Farr and his colleagues report that "Successful inseminations following forced copulations were rare."

Amphibians are defined as such because they have evolved to some extent to live on land rather than in water, but few have the internal fertilization which would make them into a completely terrestrial group. They must return to water to reproduce using external fertilization, as do frog and toads. So again, as for most fish, how could a female be raped? For bullfrogs, a female is attracted to the booming calls of a male each spring during the mating season (Howard, 1978). When she enters a male's territory, the male fastens himself to her back in what is called amplexus, so that he can deposit sperm over the eggs as the female lays them. Rarely, a male (called a parasitizing male) other than the territorial male will attach himself to the female; it is this phenomenon that is considered rape. However, amplexus is how frogs copulate. We have no way of really knowing if the female objects to any one male. How can this be called rape?

Few species of mammals rape, but this is not evident from the list provided by Thornhill and Palmer. The one primate species in which rape is well documented, the usually solitary orangutan, is given six citations. In all other primates the use of force during copulation is nonexistent or rare (Smuts, 1992, 5). The few cases of chimpanzee rape reported by Goodall were of individuals closely related to each other involving incest, with the female trying to avoid sexual intercourse with a close relative. If anything, chimpanzee females are over-sexed compared to most species, with those in estrus demanding copulation from as many males as they can vamp; female Flo mated fifty times in one day with a number of consorts (Goodall, 1986, 468, 446).

In their book Thornhill and Palmer claim that rape is present in the mantled howler monkey citing work by Clara Jones (1985), but Jones specifically states that although forced copulations are attempted by males, they are apparently unsuccessful. Similarly the authors claim that Japanese macaque males rape, but the evidence they cite applies only to captive monkeys living in artificial conditions in an enclosure in Kyoto University (Soltis et al., 1997).

Another animal for which rape is cited by the two authors is the northern elephant seal (Mesnick and Le Boeuf, 1991). In the North Atlantic Ocean dominant male elephant seals, four times as heavy as the females, space themselves out on beaches where females are nursing their young. At the end of the lactation period the male mates with the females near him, biting each female's neck to hold her still and resting his heavy head and neck on the female's back to facilitate intromission. When the females leave this male's territory to reach the sea, they have to run the gauntlet of smaller males who attack them to demand copulation as well. Most females do copulate with a male pursuing them before they reach deep water and safety.

What can we conclude about rape in animals? Thornhill and Palmer claim that it is widespread by citing eighty-one citations which the reader readily assumes refers to a large number of species. They state later (p. 197) that "rape is not universal across animal species. It is, however, common" which is certainly not true. In reality, rape is absent in far more species than it is present; in the wild it occurs in some insects, extremely rarely in those few fish species with internal fertilization, in some primitive but not in advanced birds and in a few mammals including orangutans, chimpanzee relatives, sea lions and other seals. If it were a successful evolutionary strategy, it would be far more widespread.

What about rape in human beings? Many of the reasons given by Thornhill and Palmer for claiming that rape is an evolutionary strategy for men are simply untrue. This may not be evident at first, because they are accompanied by reference citations implying solid scientific research. But even fellow Darwinian psychologist Craig Stanford (2000) finds the sources for human rape in *The Natural History of Rape* wanting. He complains that the authors cite a 1979 book eight times in two pages, even though the book is an early "think piece" rather than a compendium of actual behavior. He states that the first data pertinent to their argument appear only on page 100, half way through the text. Many of the articles cited are by Thornhill himself and these, like the citations for non-human animals, also have credibility problems.

As an example, Thornhill and Palmer claim (2000a, 72) that rapists largely choose women who are fertile to rape so that they may make the woman pregnant, but this ignores the large number of young girls and postmenopausal women who are also raped (Coyne and Berry, 2000). (Rape statistics are estimates only, given that most women do not go to the police after being raped. The authors give recent estimated reporting rates of sixteen to thirty-three percent [p. 89].) A 1992 survey in the United States found that twenty-nine per cent of rape victims were under eleven years of age, even though this age group represents about fifteen per cent of the female population. Young premenstrual girls were therefore twice as likely to be raped as other females, even though there would be no possibility of them producing babies. Nor would postmenstrual women produce young. This clearly demonstrates that rape is not necessarily about reproduction.

The authors claim (p. 88) that young girls and older women aren't as upset as their fertile sisters about being raped because they know they won't get pregnant. The Darwinian rationale is that only the fertile women grieve at not having themselves chosen the father of their possible future child. The data they consider were for 790 sexual assault victims (primarily of rape) from Philadelphia, aged two months to eighty-eight years, who were assessed or interviewed about the psychological trauma they suffered. However, the data cited, from Thornhill himself, indicate that the older women were equally as traumatized as their fertile sisters. The young girls were *assumed* to be less traumatized, but this would be almost impossible to prove, especially when "a caretaker sometimes helped the child respond to the interview questions." The apparent trauma suffered by the two-month-old baby and other very young children as evaluated by a caretaker hardly provide valid and worthwhile data. Children are often unable to express themselves and indeed may not even be aware of shock and changes in their feelings because of what happened to them.

Thornhill and Palmer note (p. 91) that women of reproductive age fight harder against a rapist and suffer more injury in the process than do girls or women over forty-five (although we are also told on the next page that the harder a woman fought against a rapist, the less psychological trauma she suffered). They relate this violence to Darwinian theory—the men are especially eager to rape women who might produce their children and these women are especially eager not to be inseminated by a rapist. This is one possibility, but a much more reasonable one is that children and older women are far less powerful than a rapist and unlikely to be able to put up strong resistance. It is as difficult to imagine a two-month-old baby or a child of eight fighting courageously against a rapist as it is a woman in her eighties.

The basic idea behind Thornhill and Palmer's theory is that when a woman is raped, she is likely to produce the rapist's child; if this is not true, then the theory is undermined because the behavior of the rapist has costs as well as benefits. If he rapes a woman within his community, the police or her men friends may punish or kill him. If she spreads the word among her women friends, his future chances of mating with women will tend to be frustrated.

Moreover, for every hundred females raped, only one or two will become pregnant (Thornhill and Palmer, 2000a, 100): most rapes involve activity other than vaginal intercourse such as anal intercourse or fellatio, the male may suffer from premature ejaculation or failure to retain an erection, the female may be too young or too old, the woman will usually not be in a fertile period of her menstrual cycle or may not become pregnant even if she is, and pregnancy, if achieved, may be spontaneously aborted as about one-fifth are (Harding, 1985).

The authors boast that between them they have over forty years of research on matters of rape (2000b) which makes one wonder why they have left so many major questions unanswered and usually unaddressed. Why is rape involved in so many non-evolutionary situations—bestiality, necrophilia, pedophilia, incest, homosexual rape? Why do societies with greater gender inequality have more rapes? Why are rape victims often physiologically or psychologically damaged or even killed following a rape, if the object is to have a healthy child produced? Why are there gang rapes? Why may rapists be able to perform only if the woman is passive or instead, only if she resists?

The biggest unaddressed question of all is that if rape is caused by a rape gene, as is stated may be the case (Thornhill and Palmer, 2000b), how exactly might that work? We evolved from ape-like animals, relations of chimpanzees and bonobos who do not practise rape as a strategy. If rape proved a superior method of reproduction for our ancestors, rape genes would have had millions or thousands of years to spread to all males. Why then would only some men have rape genes since most men don't rape? Would a rape gene be on the X chromosome so that a man need only have one to rape (since the Y chromosome would not have a comparable gene to mask its effects)? Would it be on the Y chromosome? In times of war all soldiers may be required to rape enemy women—would those without rape genes be unable to comply?

Scorpionflies have a great deal to answer for. Entomologist Randy Thornhill spent his early career studying them in depth. Because he witnessed what he called rape by scorpionfly males, he postulated a theory of this behavior which led him to consider the possibility of rape in other species including human beings. Soon he began writing papers on Darwinian psychological aspects of many human behaviors such as beauty in women, the cry of babies, women's orgasms, and the symmetry of men as judged by the size of their right and left ears and wrists, most of which are regarded with disbelief by critics of Darwinian psychology. He has published dozens of articles and books from a Darwinian perspective on these and related subjects, thirty-five of which, authored or coauthored by Thornhill, are cited in his book on rape. By distinguishing himself as an active Darwinian psychologist, he has had a well-paid and successful career.

Craig Palmer, an anthropologist who is younger than Thornhill, wrote his 1988 doctoral thesis on evolution and rape for Arizona State University and has continued to publish research on this topic. In an interview on National Radio (May 28, 2000), when questioned about the many scientific criticisms of his coauthored book on rape, Palmer indicated twice that such questions were irrelevant because he and Thornhill had based their work on the 600 scientific articles cited in the book. However, as we have seen, when citations do not show what they are said to show, and when they refer to articles which themselves are faulty, they create only the illusion of authenticity.

Jerry Coyne and Andrew Berry state that "Thornhill and Palmer cloak themselves in the authority of science, implying that the controversy over their ideas is purely political, and that the underlying biology is unimpeachable. This is a serious misrepresentation." In an interview for the University of New Mexico newspaper *Daily Lobo* (posted on the WWW 2/4/00), Thornhill declares that opposition to his new theory comes not from fellow scientists but from two specific camps: right-wing creationists and certain feminist groups, ignoring the large number of academic critics who actively dispute it. He claims that because the opposition comes from an ideological basis, it is socially irresponsible.

Without apparently realizing the irony of his position, Thornhill then goes on to explain how he and Palmer have a plan to manipulate the "media disco" so that their important new message (he does not claim *his* work is ideological)—that rape is about reproduction not violence and that it is an inherited condition—will reach as large an audience as possible. First, he spoke briefly to newspapers and TV stations in the United States about his controversial theory of rape to pique their interest. Then he and Palmer agreed to be interviewed only on radio and TV shows that allowed them enough time to explain their views in depth. Next he planned to visit the United Kingdom and Europe with his new message that rape must be considered from an evolutionary perspective so that there can be better prevention against it. What sort of prevention do these men advocate? Rape should be severely punished by law. As well (p. 199), women should be told about men's propensity to rape and warned about the risk factors for rape such as wearing short skirts and being alone outside at night. This is a new message?

Note

1. Female mallards retaliate against rapists in an unlikely way. Cunningham and Russell (2000) found that if a female is attracted to a male (rather than one who forces copulation on her), she will lay larger than average eggs which will develop into superior ducklings better able than most to survive.

Chapter 10

How Evolution Really Works —Sperm Competition In Animals

> It's 1630 hours on a May day in Madagascar and the central male (number 10) in a small troop of male, female and young ring-tailed lemurs (*Lemur catta*) approaches female 53 to see if she is interested in sex. She isn't. She gives him an angry cuff that drives him away. Researcher Michelle Sauther (1991) is taking careful notes on 53's behavior because she also noticed her enlarged reddish rump which indicates she is approaching her fertile period of estrus; luckily the lemurs have become so used to human beings that Sauther can watch what they do from as little as a meter or two away without disturbing them.
>
> At 1700 hours, half an hour later, female 53's hormones have kicked in. With a 180 degree change in her sexual appetite she comes looking for number 10, presents her hindquarters in his direction with her long black-and-white-striped tail raised and looks expectantly at him over her shoulder. He immediately takes the hint and copulates with her in a series of brief mounts ending with a long mount lasting about one and a half minutes; this last involves several deep thrusts ending with ejaculation. Then he dismounts. Once is enough.

Their sexual activity galvanizes the rest of the lemur males. Howling and sporting erections, they crowd around the couple: they also want to mate with 53. For the next little while the central male chases one and then another male away from 53 as best he can. The longer he can prevent her from mating a second time, the more likelihood there is that his ejaculate will have hardened into a copulatory plug in her reproductive tract. This will make impregnation difficult for her next partners; nine such periods of guarding timed by Sauther ranged from four minutes to just over an hour.

The males fight constantly not only when a female is receptive, but during the entire mating season which leaves many with deep wounds and all of them underweight shadows of their former selves. They battle not only on the ground but in the trees; one struggling pair fell eight meters into dense brush, extricated themselves and rushed up the tree again to continue brawling.

In the week preceding her period of estrus, as each day 53's vulva grew more prominent, the central male had hovered around her in a display of precopulatory guarding. She herself hit and chased away other males who attempted to sniff or lick her genitals or to mount her. The central male, after joining her in chastising these rivals, stayed near her, grooming her and sometimes remaining in physical contact with her during rest periods and while they slept. Such close attention was worthwhile. Females are in estrus and willing to copulate with males only once or at most twice a year for a period of less than twenty-four hours, so to the central male it is important that he be at hand when this happens.

So far in this book we have considered the many ways Darwinian psychologists have fudged and massaged data to make a number of social behavioral characteristics seem to have evolved in human beings. In this chapter we shall see how beautifully evolution *really* shapes animal behavior in nature, in this case using the example of the phenomenon of sperm competition. In the following chapter we shall contrast this phenomenon in animals with the putative evolution of sperm competition in human beings.

The evolutionary importance of animal males, including men, resides in their ability to produce fertile offspring who will in turn have numerous progeny. To do this, a male will sire a number of young, the more the better, and therefore copulate with as many females as possible depending on the species' way of life. Ideally he wants to be the only one to mate with each female so that he will be the father of all her offspring. However, the female has another agenda. She wants to mate with more than one male because the first one may be infertile; if he is sterile and she is a seasonal breeder like the ring-tailed lemur, unless she accepts one or more other males during her brief period of estrus she will have missed out having offspring for an entire year, a large portion of her reproductive life.

Males of species with internal fertilization (that which takes place within the reproductive tract of the female rather than externally with a male releasing sperm over eggs laid in water such as by most fish or frogs) have been amazingly creative in evolving new ways to increase the chance that their sperm will be more likely than those of other males to fertilize females' eggs. A new effective mating adaptation arising by mutation will quickly spread throughout a population; the male with the adaptation will mate more successfully than will other males, and since this new adaptation will be present in his more numerous sons, they too will have superior reproductive success. Of course, once all males have the adaptation, it will give no one individual an advantage.

One of the most intriguing adaptations has been that of pregnancy block, whereby some male mice and voles have evolved a personal odor so potent to a female that it will prevent her eggs, fertilized by the sperm of another male, from being implanted in her uterus. Hilda Bruce discovered this "Bruce Effect" in the 1950s in mice (*Mus musculus*) housed in her research laboratory (Whitten, 1966, 164). She found that if stud males who had recently mated with females were replaced in the females' cages for several days by males of a different strain, seventy to eighty percent of the females did not become pregnant as one would expect, but returned to estrus within a week. It was as if the first matings had never taken place. If the females were allowed to mate with this second male in a second mating, their offspring were all sired by him rather than the first male. What was going on? The Bruce Effect also occurred if newly-mated females were put alone in a cage previously occupied by alien males so that the males' scent, not they themselves, was present; the causative agent for the pregnancy block was obviously some smell emitted by the second males that affected the females' physiology.

Further research found that, as expected, females who had their sense of smell destroyed (even the study of behavior can cause pain to animals) did not have their pregnancies blocked, nor were pregnancies prevented when the second males belonged to the same strain or even to a closely related strain as the first; apparently the sense of smell of the females was not discriminating enough to distinguish between closely-related individual males. The Bruce Effect could occur on any of the first four days of a mouse's pregnancy, but by the sixth day, when the fertilized eggs had been implanted in her uterus, it was no longer present. The ability to block a pregnancy develops in a male at puberty and disappears if he is later castrated.

The Bruce Effect, which occurs in at least five species of small rodents, is relevant to evolution (Stehn and Jannett, 1981). Male mice have evolved a method whereby they can negate the activity of a rival's sperm even if the rival has already mated with a female. After their smell has done its work, they themselves will mate with the female to become a father (unless, of course, a third male comes forward in turn to negate his sperm.) Often several female mice have home ranges that are overlapped by that of a single male, and in that case there might be little chance of the females smelling a male previously unknown to them. At times of instability in the environment, however, and the death of the single male, pregnancy block could kick into effect and allow a new male to father her young, perhaps making their survival less precarious.

(My students always enjoyed this topic when we discussed it in class because we fantasize what life would be like if the same thing happened in human beings—women begging other men to come over with their dirty laundry after a bad date, women seeking seclusion after a good one, and the potential power of men who smell bad.)

At least three species of voles (pine vole, montane vole and prairie vole) have evolved an even more potent method of combatting a rival's capacity for fatherhood—that of embryocide. Females who are pregnant with young fathered by one male abort their embryos about halfway through their pregnancy if they have been exposed to the smell of a second male for about five days (Stehn and Jannett, 1981). For prairie voles this was true both for strains bred in laboratories for many years as well as for animals whose forebears had been recently trapped in the wild, so embryocide is not merely an artificial response of long-time laboratory-bred individuals.

Would there be a benefit to the female prairie vole in aborting her young? Because this species is monogamous, with the male helping to build a nest for the young and care for them after birth, there might be an advantage in the female bearing the second male's young rather than those of a male who had left her; if the second male knew somehow that he was their father, he would presumably be willing to put effort into raising them (Stehn and Jannett, 1981). However, the researchers found that some prairie vole males did help care for young they did not sire, which does not support this hypothesis.

These two examples of male breeding strategies, pregnancy block and embryocide, are advantageous from the perspective of the second male who will become a father, but not for the first male whose genetic heritage has been wasted. Does this mean that the second male and his progeny will be better able to survive in a changing environment? Maybe yes and maybe no. It was just luck that enabled one male rather than another to be a close second in line to sire the female's young. Evolution has not been better served in any major way because one male became a father and another did not. Even when the mutation that resulted in a male developing the ability to stop a pregnancy by his smell first appeared, there is no reason to believe that this ability was coupled with genetic qualities that made this male superior to others.

A far more widespread example of sperm competition is that of the copulatory plug mentioned earlier in the account of the ring-tailed lemurs. By contrast with pregnancy block and embryocide, the copulatory plug benefits the first male who mates with a female rather than later males. Again, there is no evidence that the successful male is superior genetically to later males although this could be so; the first male is more likely a settled individual known to the female because they share the same home range rather than a male passing through the area.

Copulatory plugs, sometimes called with reason chastity plugs, are made of a mixture of sperm and seminal fluids which, following copulation, hardens to form a plug that prevents or impedes the forward movement of sperm in subsequent copulations. The copulatory plug was first described in 1847 but no one knew exactly what it was for. Was it to prevent sperm from flowing back out of the vagina after mating? To facilitate sperm transport from the vagina to the uterus? To serve as a reservoir for the gradual release of sperm? (Martan and Shepherd, 1976). At Southern Illinois University, Jan Martan and Benjamin Shepherd (1976) were able to prove that it acted as an obstruction to the sperm of a second male. They took albino guinea pig females, copulatory plugs in place because they had newly mated with albino males, and put them in the same cages as colored males. Although they mated with these males too, their young were all albinos. In a second group of albino females who had also mated with albino males the researchers removed their copulatory plugs before putting them together with colored males. This time, the coat colors of the young showed that they were sired by either male or by a combination of both in one litter.

Copulatory plugs, varying in composition from soft to hard, must be effective because they have evolved in many different classes and species of animals although not in birds; birds lay their eggs not all at once, but at intervals of a day or more so that each egg, as it is produced, would dislodge any plug.

Among invertebrates, copulatory plugs are particularly common and variable in insects; at one extreme, in the honey bee, the drone's genitalia may be wrenched off at mating, leaving it inserted in the female to act as a barrier to the sperm of other males (Parker, 1970). For snakes, plugs may be especially effective. In garter snakes a female with a copulatory plug gives off an odor that inhibits other males from even trying to mate with her (Ross and Crews, 1977); this is a boon for both sexes because, since copulation is prolonged and conspicuous, the individuals involved are vulnerable to predation. Plugs are present also in many mammals including some primates. The evolution of plugs makes evolutionary sense for the males of many species.

After copulatory plugs evolved and spread throughout many species, other mechanisms evolved to counteract this innovation. In the much-studied female rat, where a hard copulatory plug forms after mating, the male has a sharp penis with backward pointing spines which can sometimes loosen a plug. In one study in which copulatory plugs were already present in females, new males mounted them and gave a number of rapid thrusts with their penis which removed the plugs in sixty-nine percent of the females; then the successful males examined and groomed their own penises before mounting the females again and ejaculating (Mosig and Dewsbury, 1970 in Baker and Bellis, 1995, 170). Now their own sperm had a good chance of fertilizing the females' eggs unless, of course, other males succeeded them in gaining the females' favor.

Copulatory plugs that harden some time after mating are found in some primate species such as macaques, mangabeys and chimpanzees that have societies in which each estrus female mates with many males, and therefore in which sperm competition likely occurs (Baker and Bellis, 1995, 172); however, these species do not have penises with spines such as are present in rats and in some lemurs and monkeys (but not great apes [Dixson, 1987]). Although human beings evolved from the same ancestors as did chimpanzees, women do not have copulatory plugs; rather, excess sperm and seminal fluid, after ejaculation, leak out of a female's vagina in what has been called a "flowback."

Another form of sperm competition, this time one that on occasion includes human beings as we shall see in the next chapter, is that of guarding the female. Males do this to try to ensure that no rival mates with "his" female and that she will bear his offspring. This is a prime male strategy, but a female who mates with only one male will not become pregnant if he happens to be infertile, as mentioned earlier. Her best strategy is to mate with more than one male to ensure her eggs are fertilized.

Many males such as the ring-tailed lemur do what they can to keep females to themselves, but they have a hard time of it as we have seen. As another example, let's consider the large Hamadryas baboon troops (*Papio hamadryas*) studied in Ethiopia by Hans Kummer (1968) in which guardianship is almost total. Each large adult male in a troop has one or a few females with their infants whom he considers his property, ruling them with force and intimidation. He makes sure that the members of this unit walk near him when the troop moves daily, from the cliffs where they sleep beside him to the savannas where they forage together. If a female, who weighs only half as much as the male, gets out of line, he threatens her or gives her a bite on the neck. He never mates with females outside his unit and he tries to ensure that the females are equally constrained.

When one of his unit's females enters estrus, her swollen rump advertizing her condition, the male becomes even more vigilant toward her than usual. He mates with her either by initiating mounting by pulling her to a suitable standing position or by accepting her invitation for sex when she presents her hindquarters to him. Estrus females copulate not only with the unit male, but also, when he isn't looking, with subadult males who hang around the troop unconnected with any unit. On one occasion when following the adult male from their sleeping rock, an estrus female paused briefly to present her swelling to a subadult male who quickly mounted her. As they were copulating the unit male glanced back, scaring the subadult so that he leapt off the female and fled. The unit male rushed to the female and bit her on the back, then mounted her himself.

One of the most inventive types of sperm competition connected with that of guarding the female is that of the rather drab dunnock or hedge sparrow (*Prunella modularis*), a common small bird studied in the Botanic Gardens of Cambridge University in England. There are more males than females in the population because more of the smaller females die during the winter when food is scarce, so some of the dunnocks live on territories as pairs and some as trios, with two males and one female (Davies, 1983). In the trios, the larger alpha male who is dominant to the other spends much of his time during the mating season guarding the female so that she can't mate with other males including the beta male, the third trio member. He is often successful in this, but the beta male has some success too, because the female solicits mating from him when the alpha male isn't around.

The unusual feature of mating in the dunnock involves both the length of time it takes and the cloacal peck. During the ceremony, far more elaborate than in most birds, the female crouches, fluffs her body feathers, shivers her wings and raises her quivering tail to expose her cloaca. The mating male, whether from a monogamous pair or trio group, hops about behind her for about two minutes, pecking at her cloaca with his bill. Her cloaca responds by becoming pink and giving periodic strong pumping movements after which she may eject a small mass of sperm onto the ground. When she has done this the male mounts her and ejaculates; his "foreplay" actions have resulted in the removal of some of a rival's sperm and their replacement with his own. The female puts up with this ritual presumably because it increases the likelihood that her eggs will be fertilized by more than one male. When only one male mates with a female, he alone helps to raise the young, but when both the alpha and beta males mate with the trio female and her chicks hatch successfully, both males feed the brood. Since young fed by two males are stronger and survive better than those fed by only one, a female is willing to have both males mate with her so that they can both think they had some paternity invested in the offspring.

Researchers must study "their" species for many years to become completely familiar with its patterns of reproductive behavior. Some behavior which seems to be that of guarding to a human observer, with one male keeping a female for himself during her estrus so that rivals cannot compete with him, may not be so. In lions, for example, females in estrus and males will form couples that mate exclusively with each other for a day and night or more. This would seem to be a good example of mate guarding because the female receives the sperm of only one male over a long time period. However, when that male is finally depleted, the female may trot over to another male and begin mating with him, without any attempt from her earlier partner to stop her (Schaller, 1972a; Bertram, 1978).

As far as actual (or possible) competition between the sperm of two or more males goes, this theoretically happens when two male fish excrete milt to cover the roe of a female during external fertilization. However, sperm competition is generally defined as occurring in species with internal fertilization which takes place inside the female where sperm from two or more males mingle.

For direct sperm competition to occur, sperm introduced into a female's reproductive tract is often stored. In some species storage is essential if the season when males and females are together and mating occurs too far removed from the optimal time of the year for birth of the young. In northern bats sperm are stored for up to six months, during hibernation, so that the young can be born in the springtime when their mothers have quantities of insects on which to feed. In insects, sperm may be retained for years: in the red harvester ant, a queen mates for the only time in her life before founding a new colony which lasts, thanks to her fertility, from fifteen to twenty years until she dies (Gordon, 1999). For reptiles, a few species can store sperm for up to three years, for birds for up to a month or more, and for mammals (with the exception of bats) usually at most fifteen days (Birkhead and Moller, 1992, 7,63).

In mammals mating usually takes place only during the female's estrus period when sperm from one or more males quickly fertilize the eggs shed into her reproductive tract. When a male mammal copulates with a female, his millions of sperm (A) swim about randomly in her reproductive tract. There are so many of them that a few are sure to swim up an oviduct by way of the female's vagina, cervix and uterus where, if they encounter an egg newly released from an ovary, one fuses with and fertilizes it, beginning the creation of a new individual. If a second male mates with the female shortly afterward, a few of his sperm (B) follow the same route. Depending on the species as discussed briefly earlier, the B sperm may, or may not, also have a chance of fertilizing her eggs.

Sperm competition may be why sperm are so small, comprising only the haploid nucleus that will fuse with that of the egg and a long tail to propel this DNA bundle forward. If sperm were larger they could swim faster up the reproductive tract and reach an egg sooner, but they equally well could arrive too soon (or too late) to fertilize it. By having tiny sperm, a male can produce far more of them, enough to inseminate one female and have many left over for other females as well, especially if their testes are large like those of the chimpanzee.

Perhaps internal fertilization evolved, as it has in a number of unrelated groups such as some insects, some fish, sharks, some amphibians and land animals (reptiles, birds and mammals) so that the sperm are released as close as possible to the females' eggs: the closer the male's sperm-releasing apparatus come to the female's reproductive tract, the more likely his sperm is to fertilize her eggs and the more likely this trait of closeness will be carried on and improved upon in his progeny (Parker, 1984, 47).

How do we know that sperm competition can actually work beyond that of a simple lottery system, that females can actually choose one individual's sperm to fertilize her eggs over those of another? The most persuasive evidence is in the extremely bizarre shapes of penises in insects; they are so peculiar that they are often used to identify a species—endless combinations of long, short, thin, fat, spined, leaf-like, bulbous and pointed characteristics. No such elaborate structures are found in species with external fertilization. Therefore, they must be connected with internal fertilization, either the male's ability to remove or supersede a rival's sperm or, by far the more important choice, some sort of an "internal courtship device" which the female fancies and chooses (Eberhard, 1990).

In the past, chance mutations have produced insect penises that stimulate the female in various ways; in addition, the male may enhance his copulation with positive behavior such as stroking, tapping, rubbing, biting, rocking, buzzing or singing to the female. If a female finds these new innovations attractive enough, they will prosper because of her assistance in the reproductive process. She will stay still so mating can occur, her reproductive tract's peristalsis or other movements will help transport the sperm, glands may be stimulated to keep the sperm healthy, and sometimes the sperm itself will be "activated" by her to ensure fertilization. With enough female supporters the beneficial innovations will soon sweep through a population, producing male young in the next generation with the same penis type and behavior as their fathers. Of course, once all males have added these new features to their mating repertoire, they will all be on an equal footing again as breeders. If this hypothesis for genital evolution is correct, it means that the females choose their partners not because of their "good genes" (a term we will consider in detail in Chapter 16), but because of their genital and behavioral proficiencies.

Besides insects, the only other zoological class in which sperm competition has been researched in a large number of species is that of birds (Birkhead and Moller, 1992). This is surprising, because it has only been for the past few decades that many zoologists have even realized that the over ninety percent of birds classified as monogamous are not necessarily monogamous at all; often both males and females mate with birds other than their partner as circumstances allow. Zoologists found this out after painstakingly watching the behavior of individual birds of many species, an ongoing process. Patricia Gowaty and Jonathan Plissner (1998) report, for example, that for what we used to think of as contentedly-monogamous eastern bluebird pairs, twenty-five to thirty percent of nestling broods are actually sired by more than one male, a sure indication of sperm competition.

The importance of sperm competition in birds is correlated with their ability to fly and the consequent necessity of keeping their weight as low as possible. To accomplish this, birds produce their eggs one at a time, usually every day or so rather than all at once as other animals do. Some sperm stored by the female travels regularly to the top of the oviduct where fertilization takes place during the fifteen to thirty minutes the egg is in that part of its assembly-line production. Then the albumin layers, shell membranes and calcified shell are added as it slowly travels along the oviduct to the cloaca (p. 49-50). Sperm storage is essential because of the unlikelihood that a female would have a male ready to mate with her each day during such a short specific time period.

Most birds live in pairs because two parents can do a more effective job than one in the onerous work of feeding and raising offspring. The sperm stored by the egg-laying female could all belong to her mate; however, many females choose to copulate with more than one male which improves their chance of circumventing an impotent male and of having offspring with a large variety of genes. This gives their young a better chance of adapting to a possibly changing environment.

It is easy for birds to be promiscuous because they are so mobile and copulation is so quick. A female can flit behind a bush, mate with a neighboring male by touching cloacas, the "cloacal kiss" during which sperm is passed from the male into the female's reproductive tract, and be back at her nest in a matter of seconds. Possibly what monogamy there is in birds and the associated care of young by both their parents arose because of sperm competition (p. 11). Males may have evolved the behavior pattern of spending most of their time close to a fertile female to prevent rivals from inseminating her. If a male guarded her until she was no longer fertile, he could be relatively sure that his sperm fertilized her eggs. Because the male was present when the eggs were laid, he was available to help raise the young; those that did so produced heavier and healthier fledglings which gave this behavior pattern an evolutionary advantage.

In summary, male animals have evolved a number of ways to try to keep a female from mating with males other than themselves, while females are equally inventive in circumventing this male goal. In insects the evidence suggests that female choice has dictated the various shapes of male penises, implying that the females have chosen the shape that most appeals to them. Has female choice been equally important in shaping vertebrate evolution? Sperm competition as it occurs in animals gives us an exquisite example of evolution in action. Whether or not it is present in human beings is the subject of the next chapter.

Chapter 11

Irrelevant Nonsense—Sperm Competition In Women

> Seven young people sprawl relaxed on the nude beach, passing around a bottle of wine and sharing a joint. Most drift into sleep. The two women who have been lying together, stroking each other's bodies occasionally, rouse up when they notice that their guide, asleep on his back, has an erection. They crawl over to him and the younger one mounts his penis while the other kisses his nipple, her breast resting on his face as she does so. This position raises her rump into the air so that the man behind her can take advantage of the situation to enter her, not that she minds. After the guide ejaculates, the younger woman shifts off him and in a single continuous movement sits astride the erect penis of the man lying next to her. By the time the sun has gone down, all five men have had sex with each of the two women. One of the women subsequently becomes pregnant.

This isn't a description from a porn magazine but a scene from a book by Dr. Robin Baker, PhD, entitled *Sperm Wars: The Science of Sex* (1996, 148). He ends this scenario by noting (p. 151) about the pregnant woman that "The sperm war among five different armies that had taken place inside her had produced a winner." This is science? In a book that doesn't even have a bibliography? Each chapter begins with a long fantasy of some sexual adventure featuring nameless women and men longing for sex and nameless men and women eager to provide it. The author obviously wants to show the reader that women having sex at about the same time with more than one man is so common that this Darwinian behavior of sperm competition has affected human evolution. Does this seem plausible for most working women, single mothers on welfare and stay-at-home moms who make up our population? Hardly.

Much of Darwinian psychology, as we have seen, focuses on such things as infanticide, aggression, dominance and rape which demonstrate men's superior power over women. Sperm competition is a new way to flaunt the importance of machoism—have a war between men continue even inside a woman's body, emphasizing her inability to control her fate.

That sperm competition might occur in women as well as in other animals was first suggested in 1984 by Robert Smith in his article "Human sperm competition." Robin Baker and Mark Bellis expanded on this idea in their 1995 book of the same title, as does Baker in his fanciful book *Sperm Wars* referred to above. Do large numbers of women have sex with several men during the few days a month that they are ovulating? Does sperm competition make evolutionary sense for human beings?

Of all the forms of sperm competition discussed in the last chapter, only those of female guarding and of direct sperm competition have been proposed for human beings. Baker and Bellis (1995) believe that the presence of guarding of females in human societies is fundamental in proving that sperm competition exists; if there were no sperm competition, there would be no need to guard females. Certainly females have been guarded in historic times, with harems overseen by eunuchs in the Near East and medieval European women locked into chastity belts during their husbands' absence. It continues to be important today in Muslim societies that insist on strict segregation of the sexes, but not in Western society in general.

The importance of spouse guarding in preliterate societies is impossible to gauge. For 186 small societies studied by anthropologists, those at one extreme (sixty-one per cent) allowed "no wife lending or exchange" while in those at the other (four per cent) women had the option of unlimited extramarital sex (Broude and Greene, 1976). There are a myriad of possibilities between these extremes, especially because nominally disallowing the "lending" of wives does not prevent sexual liaisons. Baker and Bellis (1995,21) describe the former group of women (sixty-one per cent) as being guarded by their mates, not as being lent or exchanged, which misrepresents the information they cite; this feeds into their own theory of sperm competition in human beings.

As an example of guarding, for the Dobu peoples living in the south west Pacific Baker and Bellis (1995, 21) state that men were so jealous of their wives that they timed them when they excused themselves to defecate or urinate (Fortune, 1932, 7), thus indicating that guarding of women was very important and therefore sperm competition could occur and was feared. However, Baker and Bellis are wrong again because they misrepresent the information they cite in Reo Fortune's study of the Dobu. In Dobu society each marital grouping had two house sites, one in the woman's village and one in the man's, with the couple and their children living alternate years in either location (p. 5). When they were in the women's village, the wife did what she liked in secret to the annoyance of her husband who, if he objected and fought with her, was banished from the village by her and her kin. It was only when the couple lived in the husband's village that he was able to watch her carefully and perhaps circumvent any sexual liaisons.

Most simple preliterate societies are egalitarian, so that the men do not control the women any more than the women control the men (Boehm, 1999). For example among the bushmen or !Kung peoples a woman such as Nisa, described in a book by that name, had many serial relationships during her lifetime (Shostak, 1981). Similarly, in the arctic an Inuit man might encourage his wife to sleep with a visitor or a woman might make arrangements unbeknownst to her husband to have sex with a man she fancied (Balikci, 1970, 142). In Western society as well, many women apparently living in a monogamous relationship have extramarital affairs but as we shall see later, this does not necessarily mean a woman has sex with two men within a day or two of the time she is ovulating, the prerequisite for sperm competition.

In animal species, a female allows a male to copulate with her once she enters estrus and her eggs are ready to be fertilized. Depending on the species, the first male to mate with her after that time may have an advantage because he is the first (for example if there is a copulatory plug). Or the last may be favored because he is last (in small rodents when there has been a pregnancy block or embryocide). By contrast for women, whose period of fertility and ovulation is hidden, there is no way for a man to know when is the best time to mate with her to produce a child. There can't be a first man with A sperm or a second with B sperm because the terms first and second are meaningless. Either man's sperm could fertilize her egg: the A sperm may have a better chance because there happen to be more of them and they have a head start, but perhaps they arrive too soon, before an egg is released from the ovary. B sperm may win because by chance they arrive at an egg just at the right time for fertilization.

Some women do now and then have sex with several men in a short time period, a reality on which Baker and Bellis's book *Human Sperm Competition* is based. They argue that for women in a heterosexual relationship, "cheating" on their partner which allows sperm competition to occur is the cornerstone around which the human reproductive system has developed. However, how common was and is such "cheating?"

Sperm competition is probably applicable to a few preliterate societies which have sexual organizations based on the concept of partible paternity, meaning that to produce a baby, it is generally believed that a number of men must have sex with a woman just before or during her pregnancy in order to ensure its biological development. (Was this a rite invented by women?) If sexual intercourse with several men occurs before pregnancy and within a day or two of each other, sperm competition becomes relevant.

Among the Ache people in Paraguay studied recently, the man or men who have been having sex with a woman after her last menstrual period are named the primary father(s) of her next child (Hill and Hurtado, 1996). Those who have sex with her before and after this time including during her pregnancy, are designated secondary fathers. Their male presence is important to the existence of a child because children without "fathers" are far more likely to die young, often as a result of homicide.

A similar structure was present in the Bari people of Venezuela who plant crops as well as hunt and fish (Beckerman et al., 1998). Sometimes the women took lovers, usually when they were already pregnant, pronouncing these men when the baby was born as secondary fathers who were expected when possible to give their new relative food. This was a good idea. The survival rate to age fifteen for children who had at least one secondary father (and therefore sometimes received extra food) was eighty percent while for those who had no such father it was sixty-four percent, so women who had sex with men other than their husband during their pregnancy had a higher success rate in raising their children. (However, for a hundred years before 1960, Bari people, especially the men, were hunted and shot down ruthlessly by landowners, oil company employees and homesteaders who wanted to exterminate them, so these circumstances may have affected the data for secondary fathers.)

In both the Ache and Bari societies the importance of women having a hidden estrus compared to the advertized estrus in other animals (by smell, enlarged rump patches, presenting behaviors etc.) is emphasized. If a man knew when a woman was in a fertile stage of her menstrual cycle, he would presumably know that if he alone mated with her at this time, the resulting child would be his. By not knowing when she was ovulating, any men who slept with her might think themselves the possible father of the child and make him willing, at least to some extent, to help in the child's rearing.

Today the vast majority of humanity lives in monogamous relationships, either permanent or serial, which on the surface precludes the possibility of sperm competition. However, in the past and also today, sperm competition can occur in other ways beside that of partible paternity including rape, prostitution, communal sex, courtship and, by far the most important, a woman "cheating" on her mate.

Rape, as we saw in Chapter 9, rarely results in pregnancy, nor was it likely at all common during human evolution when men and women lived in small groups and knew each other well. If a man raped a woman of his own small community, all the women in the group would be in a good position to see that he suffered for this. Rape may have occurred during periods of aggression between preliterate groups as discussed in Chapter 5, but the possibility of resultant pregnancy then was also unlikely, given that women's fertility was inhibited by their nursing their children for about four years. Currently, as a result of mass rape in times of war and as a spoil of war, many children have been born, but aggression on this scale was inconceivable among our nomad ancestors.

Prostitution is obviously a job that could foster sperm competition, but pregnancy interrupts the working possibilities for prostitutes and the financial return for pimps for some months so prostitutes practise birth control. Prostitution was not a feature of early nomadic groups. Rather, it arose following the agricultural and industrial revolutions when social rules began to govern marriage and some men were able to corner more resources, including women, than others. This left the losers with no women of their own.

Communal sex has been a much remarked-on feature of hippy-type communes and swinging people who like variety in their sex lives. However, there is little or no evidence that it was frequent in our nomadic ancestors. Recently, except for hippies, it has resulted in the production of few children.

Courtship behavior is defined as that which takes place among adolescents eager to experiment with sex before they choose a partner with whom to settle down and raise a family. It is probably rare nowadays for sperm competition to occur in young Western women who usually are involved in serial rather than simultaneous relationships (Gomendio et al., 1998, 729). Few want children at this time in their lives so they practise birth control or have abortions if necessary. Children born from courtship behavior involving sperm competition were probably more common in our ancestors. Even so, such intercourse often involved young women who had not yet begun ovulating, so that pregnancy was impossible; women in traditional societies begin to menstruate later than their Western peers and remain sterile for a longer period after menarche (p. 729). In some societies such as that of the Trobriand Islanders young women had complete freedom in sex until they decided to marry which involved an improved status. With such status, however, and with the arrival of children standards changed and adultery was no longer tolerated; various women committed suicide because their affairs were discovered (Malinowski, 1929, 56,101). At best, then, sperm competition may occur in courtship behavior but this concerns at most only the first child of a few women.

"Cheating" is by far the most likely behavior in which sperm competition could be involved. With the exceptions noted above, virtually all women who engage in regular sex have one main partner. Sperm competition enters the picture if a married or cohabiting woman in her fertile period cheats on her partner and has sex with another man within a few days of having sex with her mate. Those who claim that sperm competition is an important function of human sexuality believe that such a condition is common; others doubt that women often carry the active sperm of two men in their bodies at the time they become pregnant.

There is good reason for their skepticism. Proponents of sperm competition Baker and Bellis (1995, 201) report from blood-group studies and their own survey that a conservative four per cent of children born in Britain have a father other than the one to whom their mother has been married.[1] In other words, the mother has "cheated" on her husband and through sperm competition her lover's sperm has sired "his" children. However, if sperm competition were really a central feature of human reproduction, why wouldn't the percentage of "illegitimate" children be far higher?

The assumption of Baker and Bellis is that while the woman was having sex with her lover, she was also having sex with her husband at about the same time which would result in sperm competition. However, many women look outside their marriage because their husbands aren't interested in sex or in having sex with them, or because they themselves are no longer interested in their husband. In movies such as *The Thornbirds* there is great theatrical possibility in a woman having sex with her lover and then, when she is sure she is pregnant, coercing her husband with all her wiles to have sex with her so that he won't know, when she produces a "premature" baby, that she has been unfaithful. However, this scenario does not include sperm competition because the woman doesn't know for some weeks that she is indeed pregnant; by the time she has wrestled her husband into bed, one of her lover's sperm has done its work and the remainder are long since dead and gone.

Baker and Bellis assert from their survey that women are likely to have sex with men other than their main partner in their highly fertile period just before ovulation rather than after it. However, the same chart that illustrates this (p. 161) shows that even more extra-pair copulations occurred during their menstrual period when there was no danger at all that they would become pregnant.

Let's consider other features that Darwinian psychologists Baker and Bellis believe help prove that sperm competition was and is an important part of human evolution, namely testes size, penis size, sperm characteristics and female orgasm.

Testes Size

If sperm competition is a basic component of human reproduction, it must have evolved during the millions of years of human evolution. Male hominids who inseminated more sperm than normal into females could on average have more young including juvenile males growing to adulthood who had inherited this same attribute of inseminating large amounts of sperm. Do men have large testes to produce the large amounts of sperm which are presumably correlated with sperm competition?

We know from DNA evidence that human beings evolved from the same ancestors as chimpanzees. It seems possible that since chimpanzees have large testes like many other primates in which many males mate with many females, our ancestors also had them. However, when these ancestors moved out of the forests of Africa onto the savannas about five or six million years ago, they had to change their lifestyle. They became nomads who travelled constantly over long distances in small groups of adult males and females with their young to find food. Over time, they evolved relationships that were more monogamous than those of the great apes because it was more effective to have both a male and a female raising offspring. Such a relationship was possible because of the development of a female fertility cycle which was hidden from the male. Males couldn't see when a female was nearing her fertile period because she had no bright pink swollen rump like those of chimpanzees. Along with this development females began to copulate with males at any time in their menstrual cycle. This behavior, agreeable to both sexes, presumably kept the males relatively faithful to their partners and willing to help in protecting and feeding their mate and their children.

Did these changes in lifestyle affect our ancestors' anatomy? Did they retain the large testes which facilitate sperm competition found in chimpanzees? The average body weights of chimpanzees, orangutans, gorillas and human beings can be compared with the size (weights) of their respective testes to determine possible correlations (data from Short, 1979):

	testes weight in grams A	**body weight in kgs B**	**A/B**
Chimpanzee	119	44	2.7
Human being	41	66	.62
Orangutan	35	75	.47
Gorilla	30	169	.18

The proportion of testes weight to male body weight is over four times greater in the chimpanzee than in any of the other three species, presumably because the chimpanzee alone has a mating system that involves many males mating with each receptive female—the ideal battle ground for sperm competition. In the gorilla, females often mate only with the group leader. In the orangutan the adults are largely solitary so the female also will have few mating opportunities. In human beings monogamous relationships are predominant (although as we shall discuss later, this does not mean that females then or now restrict themselves to one partner even if married.) The testes of men are larger than those of the monandrous (usually one male per female) orangutans or gorillas, but this is likely because the vagina of women is also larger owing to the large head of the babies that must be accommodated during childbirth. The larger the vagina, the more sperm must be introduced because some will be lost before entering the cervix.

Looked at in another way, the average testes weight of a male of a species could be compared with the average body weight of the female rather than the male, which perhaps makes more sense. After all, it is the female's body in which the sperm perform. When this is done, the testes weight to body weight ratio for human beings is the same as for orangutans and only larger than that of gorillas (Dahl et al., 1993); these data cast further doubt on the supposed largeness of human testes which would imply sperm competition.

Baker and Bellis argue that men produce more sperm the longer a man has been away from his main partner (p. 206), even taking into account the time since his last ejaculation. They feel that this indicates an adaptive reaction to the possibility that the sperm will be needed because the female has been cheating on him. However, a male may interpret past absence as indicating possible future absence, and may inseminate more sperm to try to make up for this (Gomendio et al., 1998, 733).

Penis Size

Average length of erect penis (data from Short, 1979)

Human Beings	13 cm
Chimpanzee	8 cm
Orangutan	4 cm
Gorilla	3 cm

Baker and Bellis (1995, 167ff) believe that the long and large penis of men evolved because of sperm competition. They argue that other reasons that have been suggested are unrealistic, such as that a large penis size evolved for aggressive display

—a large hominid with a small penis was unlikely to be intimidated by a small hominid with a large penis. Today women are far more likely to be sexually aroused by a man's buttocks than by the size of his penis, and penis size has little to do with a woman's satisfaction with intercourse or with orgasm (p. 168).

The authors argue that a large penis evolved so that during intercourse its piston-like action of repeatedly thrusting and retreating in the vagina served to remove by suction sperm and seminal fluid placed in the reproductive tract by an earlier male. However, if this were so, where does the dislodged material go? It would presumably still be moving forward and back with the movement of the penis rather than being discarded outside the vagina, and would still be present to compete with the copulating male's sperm after he ejaculated. Instead, thrusting may stimulate movement in the vagina which encourages the suction inward of sperm (Eberhard, 1990).

A more mundane theory to explain man's large penis is that since the female has had to evolve a large vagina to enable her to give birth to a child with a large head, the male in turn had to evolve a large penis to enable him to ejaculate near the cervix. Moreover in a further deflation of Baker and Bellis's argument, although the human penis seems long and large, it is not any longer than that of the chimpanzee when the respective body weights of males are taken into account (Gomendio et al., 1998, 733).

Sperm Characteristics

In mammals, sperm are present in enormous numbers in each male ejaculate. Most of them are normal in shape and function, they swim efficiently along the female tract, and they are ready at the right time and place to fertilize an egg should they meet one. However, unlike in birds and other non-mammals, sperm have a short lifespan except in bats, so that few mammals have sperm storage organs in females (although sperm can congregate in cervical crypts [Birkhead, 2000, 67]). For most mammals timing is everything. There may be sperm competition, but it must occur when several fertile males mate with an ovulating female within a few hours or days.

Most authors believe that when sperm competition occurs in mammals, it acts like a lottery system, with on average the male who inseminates the most sperm most likely to fertilize the most eggs. Baker and Bellis argue at great length and with many charts and figures that sperm competition in human beings is far more sophisticated than this. Since a large proportion of sperm in human beings is abnormal in shape (about twenty-five per cent), they hypothesize that this is not because of errors in their production as is commonly believed, but because different types of sperm have evolved to perform different functions. Baker and Bellis and their helpers obtained ejaculates of 132 men, then studied the sperm of these men in pairs, one slide for each man and one slide for a mixture of their sperm. By watching through a microscope, observers reported that they could see sperm on the mixed slide stuck together in the process of killing each other (p. 273). The authors write (p. 276) about "head-to-head combat" and "seek-and-destroy" sperm. However, they couldn't tell if the sperm apparently in combat belonged to different men. They called their speculation the kamikaze sperm hypothesis, reflecting their belief that some of a man's sperm selflessly give up their chance of fertilizing an egg in order to increase the opportunity for one of their "peers."

Baker and Bellis (1995) define three types of combatants that make up the attacking force: Blocker sperm are large and double-headed with coiled tails that are programmed to try to block the sperm of other males from entering the uterus. Seek and destroy sperm are those which roam about the female reproductive tract hunting for "foreign" sperm which they then destroy with chemicals. Egg-getter sperm are those which race single-mindedly onward to try to locate and fertilize an egg.

These are interesting speculations, but are they valid? In a much more sophisticated experiment to see if they could replicate the work of Baker and Bellis, Harry Moore and his colleagues (1999) had fifteen fertile men after three days of sexual abstinence ejaculate into containers. The sperm were then examined in various ways including mixing fluorochrome-labelling sperm from one man with unmarked sperm from another so that it would be clear, if warfare occurred, which sperm were attacking which other sperm. Their results showed that, compared to pure ejaculates, mixing ejaculates from two men didn't slow up the sperm, didn't cause more aggregations of sperm and didn't result in more sperm being killed. The researchers concluded that there was no evidence from their work to support the kamikaze sperm hypothesis.

Animals who practise sperm competition have large numbers of sperm produced and ejaculated. In human beings, the number in an ejaculate ranges between forty-eight and 134 million while in chimpanzees it is over 650 million (Gomendio et al., 1998, 732). Similarly, human sperm are shorter and therefore slower than in the apes, indicating again that human beings have apparently evolved to be monandrous (one male mating with a female).

Baker and Bellis (1995, 189) and Smith (1984) claim that sperm from two men can coexist, causing sperm competition, for as long as a week in a woman's reproductive tract, but this is far longer than is believed to be true by other scientists (Birkhead, 2000, 67). Gomendio and his colleagues (1998, 730) state that although sperm may live for six days, their average lifetime is 1.4 days (while the average lifetime of an ovum shed from the ovary is less than a day). They calculate that for sperm competition to be possible, double matings would have to occur within two or three days of one another, with the first being three days before ovulation (p. 731). Because this time constraint is much narrower than that of Baker and Bellis, it excludes many of their examples in which they claim sperm competition would occur.

Female Orgasm

Traditionally, female orgasms have been considered important from a Darwinian perspective for several reasons. Some authors think they relax a woman who will then be less likely to leap to her feet after intercourse to try to rid herself of the ejaculate while urinating (although there is no evidence that this works). Others believe that the orgasmic muscle contractions in the uterus help suck up sperm into the cervix (Pollard, 1994, 129) although the lack of an orgasm does not preclude conception. The widest held belief is that orgasm is so pleasurable that women are anxious to copulate, a reaction among animal species climaxing in bonobos, although orgasms occur in other primates too (Wallen, 1995, 73). During human evolution the pleasure of orgasms for women doubtless helped to maintain long-term relationships which in turn provided optimal care for their children (Pollard, 1994, 51).

Baker and Bellis (1995, 243ff) valorize female orgasms, claiming that by their use, a woman can organize the sperm in her reproductive tract to her own reproductive advantage. They state that a woman's decision to have an orgasm or not, and its timing with regard to copulations before and after, enables her to manipulate sperm retention and determine which male will fertilize her egg. Although they supply many charts, graphs and tables to justify their belief, there are serious problems with their findings as will be discussed below. If such power were within the grasp of women, one wonders why so many have unwanted children with their lovers.

Problematics of Human Sperm Competition

It is very difficult to prove whether or not sperm competition occurs in women. Robert Smith (1984) addressed the problem first, but he had no real data on which to base his hypothesis that it did. Baker and Bellis (1995, 309) set out to collect such data. They convinced themselves not only that sperm competition was pivotal in the evolution of human reproduction, but that it remains so today. They studied the everyday behavior of men and women as if any copulation might be expected to produce offspring, although there are about four million copulations around the world every hour (Yu, 1994). In reality, Western couples have sexual intercourse thousands of times in their life (most of which they hope won't result in pregnancy) and only a few of them produce children. It is only the behavior of couples at the time of conception that matters in evolution, and the authors have not focused on that, if indeed this would be possible given that self-scrutiny would certainly affect the couples' activity.

Many authors disagree with Baker and Bellis's hypothesis (as Gomendio et al., 1998). Some points of contention have been raised in the chapter already, but others remain. The major difficulty, of course, is that of obtaining accurate information about people's sex lives. Many people are too uptight to take part in research dealing with their sexuality, while those who do volunteer are unusually uninhibited and not representative of the population at large. For Baker and Bellis's (1995, 12) survey of sexual behavior in British women, an extensive questionnaire about this topic was completed by 3587 sexually experienced women aged between thirteen and seventy-two years, with a mode of twenty-one years. This represented 0.84 percent of the readership of *Company* magazine which sent out the questionnaires, which itself represented about five percent of the United Kingdom population of women of reproductive age. Although the authors emphasize that by nature men are "urgent" about sex and woman are "coy" (p. 13), their methodology by necessity highlights the experiences of women who are not at all coy.

Some women were asked by Baker and Bellis to take an active part in their research. Those who agreed collected, fifteen minutes to two hours after intercourse, their "flowback" (consisting of seminal fluid containing sperm and cervical fluid) which leaked out of their vaginas. Nine women recorded flowback by the crude criteria of heavier than normal, normal, lighter than normal, or none (p. 46). The authors claim that the composition of the flowback shows that the women usually retain one of three possibilities: almost none of the sperm, forty to fifty percent of the sperm, or sixty to seventy percent of the sperm (p. 233). How could they be sure of this when the retained sperm remain within the woman and when the volume of an ejaculate can vary by a factor of 120, from 0.1 to 12.0 ml (Smith, 1984, 620)?

The research subjects were asked to think back over the details of their sex life covering many years, a difficult assignment if accuracy is important. One in every 200 women who had taken part in 500 lifetime copulations claimed that she had been inseminated by two different males within thirty minutes of each other. Is anyone's memory that accurate? Were these women prostitutes? There is also discrepancy about frequency of sexual intercourse. The women said that they had had three sex partners, but the men said they had had ten (p. 9). Why this huge difference? Granted many men visit prostitutes, but even so this is a large variance.

Might men and women both be lying—the women so they won't seem promiscuous and the men to enhance their macho image? This would not be unusual. In a study carried out with undergraduates at the University of California at Los Angeles for a course credit, heterosexual students were assumed to be fudging details of their sexual behavior in their self-reports (Berk et al., 1995, 380). About fifty percent of women reported giving oral sex but only twenty percent of men said they received it. Conversely forty percent of the women said that they were getting oral sex, but only twenty-five per cent of men reported giving it. Since it is likely that the men and women were dating each other or people like them, it seems that some or all of the respondents were not telling the truth.

Another problem is that Baker and Bellis misrepresent data about anthropology from the literature to the advantage of their hypothesis: they emphasize that early societies closely guarded their women because of the possibility of sperm competition. As mentioned earlier, they claim that the Dobu women are always watched by their husbands, which is not true, and that most societies guard their wives when in fact they were only reported as not allowing wife lending or exchange. Our ancestors belonged to nomadic groups in which the men largely foraged or hunted while the women gathered plant foods. There would be no possibility of men guarding women closely when they were apart for much of each day.

In their book, Baker and Bellis emphasize that sperm competition in human beings has a history going back many millions of years (p. 133), implying that it has a worthy inheritance and, of course, that it is still present. However, if our ancestors of five or six millions years ago had a jungle lifestyle similar to that of chimpanzees, since then they have evolved into human beings who have smaller testes and a much greater tendency toward monogamy. These changes do not jibe with the presence of sperm competition.

Proponents of human sperm competition in a Darwinian psychological context argue that it has always been an integral part of human evolution. Baker and Bellis (1995, 309) write: "Even in the modern sexual world of efficient contraceptives and lethal sexually transmitted diseases, sperm competition is still as ruthless a force as ever." Yet it is highly unlikely that sperm competition was significant in the past few millions years of human evolution or that it is important today.

In a few individual lives, sperm competition may matter a great deal—an ovulating white woman who has unprotected sex with a black man the night after sex with her white husband is asking for trouble. On the big canvas of evolution, however, even if there were much sperm competition in human beings the result would still be insignificant. It would only become meaningful if the men who won sperm competitions also had some other heritable attributes, good or bad, that significantly affected their progeny. Say we have two couples who decided to switch partners one steamy night. So what? Instead of children with their husbands, they may have them with their lovers. Both men's genetic heritage is passed down to the next generation, albeit combined with different female genes than expected.

The hypothesis that because of sperm competition a woman is primed to want to mate with men other than her husband doesn't make sense. Why would another man be better genetically than the one she chose to marry? Do we have to assume pessimistically that after one gets to know a man well in marriage, other men seem better as potential fathers? And if the woman knew this lover better, might she not also find him lacking in potential? He is surely as likely as her husband to prove a disappointment as a father. The lover may be handsome and seductive, but does the possibility that her son will inherit the trait to cheat on his mate really appeal to most women? If cheating on his wife enables a man to father more children, why isn't this trait, if inherited, more widespread in the world? Darwinian psychology may predict that sperm competition is an important part of human behavior, but hard data and common sense indicate that this is completely implausible.

Note

1. Other sources believe that about ten per cent of people have biological fathers other than whom they believe to be their fathers, an average that can rise to thirty per cent in some areas. (Abraham, 2002). By contrast, in Muslim cultures where women are strictly guarded, false paternity is very low.

Chapter 12

Denying Reality—Homosexual Behavior In Animals

I'm sitting in a car on a South African ranch watching two male giraffe. One of the males swings his long neck at the other's trunk, landing a heavy blow with his horns. The second retaliates, hitting his head against the other's neck. The first male, Star, then aims his horns at the other's right front leg, knocking it off the ground. His opponent rocks back at the impact of the blow, then swings his head in an awkward arc, missing Star entirely. They pause, glancing at the group of five female and young giraffe that has stopped browsing to watch them.

Folded into my small Ford Prefect (this was 1956) I am writing down from a hundred yards away exactly what the males are doing as they spar, and the minute at which they are doing it. I had seen such matches before; indeed they were common enough that the hair covering the tops of the males' horns was completely worn away, leaving them bald.

The males lean over to snatch a few leaves from low thorn bushes, so I summarize the match and turn the page in my exercise-book, preparing to begin notes on their feeding behavior.

What the two males do next astonishes me. Star approaches the other male, whom I now recognize from the color between his spots as Cream, and begins not to hit him but to rub his neck gently along his trunk. Cream reciprocates by stroking Star's body with the top of his nose. What had seemed like a brawl is turning into a love-fest! For several minutes they rub their necks and bodies together in an apparently affectionate manner. Then Star, his pink penis now visible beyond its furry sheath, walks behind Cream and mounts him. Within a few seconds he slides off Cream's back and strolls behind a clump of bushes where I can no longer see him. Cream follows at a stately pace.

Wow! Homosexual behavior in giraffe? What would my aunt say? ("They shouldn't let young girls see that sort of thing," I later overhear her telling my uncle angrily after she has read my scientific paper describing this activity [Innis, 1958]. Who were "they" I wondered?)

Fifty years ago, homosexual behavior wasn't one of the things researchers, even those with a bent for what would come to be called sociobiology and then Darwinian psychology, expected to see in nonhuman animals. It would have made no sense. Why would this behavior have evolved in an animal such as a giraffe? It was of no use for reproduction. Were some giraffe gay and others straight? This species had not been studied in depth before, so this question had never been asked, let alone answered. Charles Darwin certainly hadn't considered homosexual behavior in *The Origin of Species*. Field biologists expected the activities of "their" animal to be adapted to its environment because of its evolution, so it could eat and digest available food, find safety from predators and mate to produce young at least as well adapted to their surroundings as their parents. Nothing about queer behavior.

During the late 1950s and 1960s, zoologists were no longer content to watch the activities of animals in laboratories or zoos as Solly Zuckerman, Robert Yerkes and Abraham Maslow had done. Scores of biologists, especially professors and graduate students, left their universities for periods of a few months or for years to study the behavior of animals in the wild, just as I did first to study giraffe. Homosexual behavior had been observed in zoos and laboratories, but was thought by many to be a consequence of captivity. Now biologists were seeing it in wild animals too.

A few researchers did report same-sex behavior as I did, but many did not (Bagemihl, 1999, 83ff). When some early field zoologists saw one animal mounting another in the wild, they assumed that it was a male mounting a female if they couldn't identify the sex of the participants. (Would researchers in the more open sexual climate of today be as ready to designate stereotyped male and female roles?) Others recorded homosexual behavior in their field notes but did not publish their data because they didn't want their colleagues to think they were gay or because they didn't know what it meant. In the mid-1970s Linda Wolfe, who was studying macaques in the wilds of Japan, found that if she mentioned the females' homosexual behavior people began to ask her if she had some kinky interest they didn't know about. When she wanted to have her results published, "referees accused her of doctoring the photographs and making up data" (Vines, 1999).

Homosexuality was often considered to be not only unnatural but pathological by many zoologists, especially those who studied animals in captivity (Bagemihl,

1999, 156ff). However, before long the same-sex behavior of captive animals was frequently also seen in the same species in the wild. Some researchers hypothesized that homosexual behavior was caused by a hormonal imbalance. This was tested in a breeding population of western gulls (*Larus occidentalis*) nesting on Santa Barbara Island in California in which there were many more females than males; apparently for lack of male mates some females had paired up with other females (Wingfield et al., 1982). These female couples established and defended breeding territories just as did male and female pairs, and laid clutches of as many as six eggs. However, none of the eggs was fertilized, so none hatched. The researchers tested the hormone levels in the blood of these female-paired birds which proved to be normal, so their behavior was not caused by one of the females being "masculinized" by androgens as had been postulated.

Other zoologists speculated without proof that homosexual activity could be caused by such things as toxins present in the environment. Toxins may indeed affect members of a population who have unusual levels of hormones, but these have not been correlated with homosexual behavior.

As more people began to report same-sex sexual activity, they often downplayed it or noted that it was "sexual perversion," "abnormal," "unnatural" or "aberrant," reflecting societal bias against gay men and lesbians.[1] Others described it but called it by other names such as, in bonobos, "greeting," "appeasement," "reassurance," "reconciliation," "tension-regulation," "social bonding," or "food-exchange" behavior—"almost anything, it seems, besides *pleasurable sexual* behavior" as Bruce Bagemihl (1999, 106) reported. Homophobia was being transferred, consciously or unconsciously, by scientists from the human to the animal world, just as sexism has been.

It is not surprising that sexual activity was particularly remarked upon in bonobos. They are the most inventive sexual beings known in both same-sex and opposite-sex couples. The sex they have each day is reported to relax them, to act as a bond between individuals and to replace the need for aggression (Waal, 1997, 101-5). Males sometimes hang from trees and "fence" with their erect penises, or rub their large scrota together; females rub their clitorises together while hugging each other face to face, a pastime called G-G rubbing (for genito-genital); and individuals share lengthy french kisses. While opposite-sex behavior is usually genital-genital, by contrast homosexual activity is far more creative, comprising genital-genital, oral-genital, anal-genital, anal-anal or manual-genital contacts (Pavelka, 1995, 23). One zookeeper was startled on being kissed by a male bonobo to find the animal's tongue in his mouth. Frans de Waal (1998) suggests that the bonobo is so little known just *because* of its extremely sexual behavior which upsets many zoologists and those who read their work.

Valerius Geist who, while studying the behavior of mountain sheep in the wild, saw males mounting each other, called this activity "aggressosexual" behavior in his early work on this species. In his book *Mountain Sheep and Man in the Northern Wilds* (1975, 97-98), Geist states that when he saw his old friend D-ram, who had defeated subordinate S-ram in battle, repeatedly mounting S-ram as if he were a female in estrus, he was aghast. He writes that he had used the word "aggressosexual" because "to state that the males had evolved a homosexual society was emotionally beyond me. To conceive of those magnificent beasts as 'queers'—Oh God!" He records that he claimed for two years that in mountain sheep, aggression and sexual behavior could not be considered separately because each was the reverse side of the same coin. Then, however, he faced reality and repudiated "that drivel!"; he called "a spade a spade and admitted that rams lived in essentially a homosexual society."

Zoologists nowadays are increasingly likely to report homosexual behavior if it occurs in "their" species. We now know it is common in the animal world; males have sex with males and females have sex with females in over 400 species of insects, spiders, fish, lizards, frogs, snakes, birds and mammals (Bagemihl, 1999). In the animals investigated so far most have members which practise same-sex sexual behavior, so the number 400 will be far higher once the behavior of additional species has been studied.

Sometimes more sexual behavior goes on between same-sex pairs than between males and females. Although human society may think of homosexuality as deviant, it is often an important expression of sex in a species. In giraffe, for example, ninety-four percent of mountings in one survey were homosexual (Bagemihl, 1999, 392). In gorillas, both females and males spend a great deal of time in same-sex sexual behavior. For male chimpanzees, up to a third or a half of sexual interactions, depending on the troop, is between same-sex individuals (p. 277). In bonobos homosexual activity, especially among females, is as common as sexuality between males and females. Each female participates in genital rubbing with another female, on average, every two hours or so (p. 273). For orangutans, either homosexual or heterosexual activity occurs depending on which two animals meet during their largely solitary lives (p. 286).

That animals often indulge in homosexual behavior is still largely a secret in the non-zoological world. When scientists write popular articles and books about animals, especially those directed at children, any mention of homosexuality remains taboo.[2] Recently a fascinating television program on homosexual behavior was completed by Saint Thomas Productions called "Animal Homosexuality" or "Out in Nature: Homosexuality in Animals." Because of its subject matter this documentary has only been aired a few times, sometimes along with a disclaimer at the beginning that some viewers may find the material offensive. Such a disclaimer is, needless to say, highly unusual for a nature film (pers. comm. Paul Vasey, Aug 1, 2001).

The difficulty many people have in dealing with the reality of homosexual behavior in animals reflects the large amount of homophobia in Western society. People who are adamantly against gay men and lesbians insist that this is because same-sex sexual behavior is always "unnatural." However, as we have seen, it is entirely natural among animals (including human beings). To claim otherwise is to demean the millions of gay people worldwide. In an effort to support several of my gay students in the early 1980s, I myself read hundreds of books and papers on animal behavior to enable me to write the first review article proving that homosexual behavior is common and widespread in vertebrate species (Dagg, 1984b).

Proponents of Darwinian psychology have a hard time with homosexuality. How can they interpret it? Heterosexual behavior results in offspring who carry the genes of their parents; homosexual behavior has no such outcome. If virtually all behavior occurs because of genetic evolution, how can homosexuality be explained? Their answer is with a number of far-fetched possibilities: kin selection, pseudo-heterosexuality, a substitute for heterosexuality, mistaken sex identity, rehearsal for heterosexuality, a recessive gay gene, to increase heterosexual behavior, reproductive competition and sperm-swapping. Darwinian psychologists have a remarkable capacity for inventing such evolutionary explanations for behavior, but most of these are fanciful, far-fetched, and/or tainted with heterosexual bias as we shall now see (Bagemihl, 1999, 124ff).

The most common suggestion to explain homosexuality is the kin selection theory (Wilson, 1975, 555). Homosexuals could be important in an evolutionary framework because, even though they don't have many or any offspring themselves, they help their more fecund relatives (with whom they have most genes in common including perhaps recessive "gay genes"?) to raise their young successfully. Maybe they are able to give extra food to their relatives or help protect the young in their group. Kin altruism occurs in some animals such as wolves, where the pack comprising mostly closely-related individuals helps raise the young of the alpha male and female. It is also common among lion females who nurse other cubs besides their own; pride females are all related, so anything a female does for a "nephew" or "niece" or grandcub benefits her own genes to some extent (Schaller, 1972a). If a recessive gene or genes were responsible for homosexual behavior, the relatives could have them and pass them along to their offspring, yet still be heterosexual themselves. However, there is no evidence for the existence of such a gene, nor is kin selection an evolutionary feature of human beings (Bobrow and Bailey, 2001).

Another proposal from Darwinian psychology is that homosexuality is a substitute for pseudoheterosexuality, an idea derived from Freud and other early psychoanalysts: in homosexual activity, one partner is seen in the male and one in the female role, the roles mirroring those often believed to be present in gay men and in lesbians. Thus female geckos from many Pacific Islands, *Lepidodactylus lugubris*, are said to play a male role if they mount other geckos, as they often do. For some reason males of this species are rare; on some islands there are none at all, so the females reproduce parthenogenetically, without the need for sperm. This doesn't stop the females from behaving sexually. In old films female geckos can be seen copulating by pressing their cloacas together (Werner, 1980). The mounting females were characterized as "masculinized," demonstrating this by their behavior, their social rank or their territorial superiority, an explanation that would be unacceptable today without concrete evidence.

Pseudoheterosexuality can't be applicable to many animals because for them, same-sex activity isn't the same as that present between opposite-sex couples. In the ostrich, for example, a male and female copulate away from the other birds (Sauer, 1972). First they walk about together, quietly and slowly, then bend down to feed in a ritually synchronized and nervous fashion. Up to twenty minutes later the cock drops to the ground, fluffs his tail and begins sweeping the ground with first one wing and then the other. At the same time he twists his neck about in a corkscrew fashion, swinging it left and right and back and forth while rocking his body and giving a booming call. When the hen soon squats nearby on the sandy ground herself, the cock leaps to his feet and mounts her.

In contrast to this mating ceremony, the homosexual dance of the ostrich begins often with one male in a group of up to forty males rushing toward his chosen partner at up to thirty miles an hour and stopping suddenly in front of him. Then he starts to dance in a frenzy a series of pirouettes, whirling around beside his friend in bursts, each lasting several minutes. Following this he drops to the ground beside his chosen and begins the same display of rocking and moving his neck in a corkscrew fashion that he would use with a female, although he carries it on much longer, for up to twenty minutes. As he is doing this he inflates and deflates his throat but makes no sound. His partner meanwhile pays little or no attention to this apparently demented exercise which does not end with copulation.

Homosexual activity may also be unlike heterosexual activity in frequency as we have seen for giraffe. Among gorillas, heterosexual activity only occurs when a female is in estrus, about every four years, and then only with one or two males. By contrast, homosexual activity is far more common as researcher Juichi Yamagiwa, an associate of the late Dian Fossey, found. Every day he climbed a tree in the jungle around the Virunga Volcanos to spy on a group of male gorillas comprising two large silverbacks, two younger blackbacks and two subadults, none closely related (Yamagiwa, 1992). Balanced among its branches he recorded what each of these animals was doing at ten minute intervals, which was often having sex. During his seven-month stay at the Karisoke Research Center he observed ninety-seven homosexual mountings solicited often by "social staring." An individual, usually a young one making a panting noise, approached another to within several feet to peer into his face. About half the time this triggered mounting by the male who was approached. He did so in either a front-back or a front-front position, thrusting to ejaculation and dismounting with a deep sigh, his semen sometimes visible on his partner's fur (Bagemihl, 1999, 281).

These couplings are not random because gorillas have preferred companions with whom they have sex; some males are satisfied with only one partner while others have up to five in succession, with individual pairings lasting from a few months to a year or more (p. 281). The silverback mounts other males but does not allow himself to be mounted. Otherwise, either male will mount his partner during copulations. Which then could be called the female-acting individual? Preferred partners are half-brothers or younger males; some gorillas "guard" such favorites, fighting to protect them from the attentions of other males (although aggression is less in all-male groups than can be the case in mixed-sex groups).

Another Darwinian psychological hypothesis to explain homosexual behavior in animals is that it is a substitute for heterosexuality (Bagemihl, 1999, 134ff); this reflects human behavior in prison where much homosexual behavior takes place because there is no possibility of opposite-sex partners. Again, this is not a useful model for other animals. For giraffe, Star and Cream had sex even though adult females were nearby. Sometimes, ignoring female giraffe in the area, three young males necked as a group, rubbing their bodies and necks together and touching each other gently with their heads.

Homosexual behavior may be rampant among female primates too, as in a captive troop of fifteen Japanese macaques whom two researchers observed during four mating seasons. As well as being involved in heterosexual activities, the eight to eleven females when in estrus formed pairs (called dyads) over time with almost all the other females present (with the exception of their mothers, daughters or sisters). Ignoring the males entirely, these pairs spent part of their time engaged in sexual activity (Chapais and Mignault, 1991). In each dyad, either female would mount the other or sit or lie on her back, giving pelvic thrusts or rubbing her clitoris against her partner. When one macaque wanted the other to mount her, she slapped the ground, gave high-pitched cries and presented her hindquarters. The rest of the time the twosome groomed each other or huddled together. Each pairing lasted for a few days or weeks; if a female were still in estrus after a partnership dissolved, she would often join forces with another female to form another dyad.

Another explanation for homosexual behavior is that of mistaken sex identity: a male mounts another male because he mistakenly thinks the male is a female (Bagemihl, 1999, 148ff). This seems highly unlikely if not ridiculous. Sometimes there is homosexual activity in a species such as the ostrich in which the black and white male looks quite unlike the brown female, and sometimes it is lacking in species in which the sexes closely resemble each other. As well, the mistake would only involve an initial error; it would not explain why homosexual activity would continue for some time, or might be initiated by the second animal. Of course, just because human beings think two sexes resemble each other doesn't mean they are identical. We know from sophisticated measuring devices that the sexes of some species look quite different under ultraviolet light (starlings), have calls human beings cannot hear that are of very high or very low frequency (brown rat, elephant) and emit unique smells or pheromones.[3]

A more unlikely suggestion is that same-sex sexual activity occurs because it acts as a rehearsal for heterosexual intercourse: young animals practise mounting each other so that the males will be able to perfect their heterosexual skills for when they mature, making them superior lovers (Bagemihl, 1999, 183). However, this leaves most questions unanswered. It doesn't take into account that females and males of all ages mount other animals and that some individuals engage in same-sex mounting both before and after heterosexual copulations. A few individuals take part only in same-sex activities, so what are they practising for? Others come to homosexuality when they are old: does this mean that their previous heterosexual behavior was practise for their senior years? Many individuals never engage in homosexual behavior, so why don't they also need to practise copulation?

One theoretical possibility with a genetic rationale is that females with one gay gene, carriers for the presumed recessive condition, could have more offspring than other heterosexual females: perhaps more milk for their offspring, or a physique or behavior pattern especially attractive to males. (For example in human beings a specific gene involved with hemoglobin protects a person from malaria when only one is present, even though it has another effect entirely, causing sickle-cell anemia, when a person inherits this gene from both parents.) However there is no evidence that such carriers for homosexual behavior exist.

Some theorists have suggested that homosexual behavior occurs because it increases heterosexual behavior (Bagemihl, 1999, 185ff). Because many females mount other females when they are in heat, the hypothesis goes, males who see this are stimulated and eager to have sex with the mounter. (Is this similar to heterosexual men being turned on by watching porn videos of lesbian love-making? But why aren't women aroused by gay male sexual activity?) Heterosexual activity may equally trigger homosexual activity as can be seen during the mating season in some monkey species when males mount females, females mount females, and males mount males (Dagg, 1984b). Others postulate that males (such as African elephants) may mount each other to stimulate their own libidos so that they can then move on to mate with females. However, this hypothesis fails because homosexual behavior often takes place outside the breeding season or when no member of the other sex is present.

A more implausible suggestion is that homosexual activity fosters reproductive competition: a female might form a pair-bond with another female to monopolize her time so that she won't mate with a male to produce young who will compete with her own young; similarly a male might distract another male rival to reduce or redirect his sex drive. However, homosexual pairings seem to comprise friendly rather than competitive relationships. As well, homosexual behavior often occurs outside the breeding season and there is no evidence that its presence reduces heterosexual behavior.

The most unlikely explanation for homosexual behavior is surely that of sperm-swapping in birds (Bagemihl, 1999, 191). A male tree swallow may deposit his sperm in the cloaca of a second male which, when the second male touches cloacas with a female, will theoretically be transferred to her reproductive tract. But why would the second male take part in such a scenario? Why wouldn't he defecate to remove his rival's sperm and then replace it with his own?

Innumerable studies prove that homosexual behavior is carried out almost entirely by individuals who also copulate heterosexually. If there were genes for homosexual behavior, they would theoretically be passed along to the next generation. This satisfies the tenets of Darwinian psychology, but there is no evidence that such behavior is genetic in animals. Whether homosexuality may have a genetic component in human beings is discussed in the next chapter.

At the present time only a few individual animals are known to be exclusively homosexual, a condition present more commonly in people. For the black swan of Australia and New Zealand, about thirteen percent of individuals in any one year are in same-sex pairings (Bagemihl, 1999, 55,179,489). Sometimes male pairs take over the nest and eggs of a mated pair, incubate the eggs and raise the cygnets themselves. In other pairs one bisexual male mates with a female and then the pair chases her away after she has laid her eggs. Male pairs dominate their flock because their combined strength, greater than that of heterosexual pairs, enables them to acquire the largest and best territories in the area. However, such achievement does not mean that they pass on their genetic inheritance more successfully than heterosexual couples; this is because some of their cygnets are unrelated to either male (when they have taken over the eggs and nest of a mated pair) and in the other clutches only one male shares genes with the young (p. 179).

An exclusively homosexual female has been observed among Japanese macaques of a colony in Texas; she formed consortships with a number of females during her lifetime but never with a male, so she never reproduced (Pavelka, 1995, 22). In domestic rams, up to sixteen per cent don't mate during a breeding season, and ten percent mate with males even if females are available (Adler, 1997). Few wild individuals in the animal world have been observed so closely over their lifetime that one can be sure they have never mated with a member of the opposite sex, so we do not know how common such exclusive homosexuality is.

From thousands of recent studies of animals we now know a great deal about homosexual behavior which:

- occurs in hundreds of species (and undoubtedly in many thousands more that have not yet been studied);
- does not occur in some species that have been much studied (howler monkeys);
- is generally rarer than heterosexual behavior in each species;
- is usually present in animals who also mate with the opposite sex, although it occurs exclusively in at least a few individuals;
- is immensely varied, especially in species with large brains (primates, dolphins);
- may occur in one sex of a species (male giraffe) but not in the other, and;

- may occur throughout the year, in contrast to reproductive behavior which usually takes place only when the female is in estrus.

Some of the less far-fetched suggestions above may indicate how homosexuality might increase reproduction in a few species, but none even begins to provide a rational evolutionary framework for it. The answer to why homosexual behavior is so widespread seems rather to be that animals are sensual and sexual, and as such find sexual pleasure with members of their own or the other sex. Animal life is not organized solely around procreation any more than is that of human beings. Animals like to move about, prefer to use one paw rather than the other, look for favored food, possibly admire a sunset, maybe masturbate. None of these activities depends on enhancing their reproductive capabilities—they are just something animals do, like having sex with a male or female friend.

Notes

1. However, nowadays some people have a bias against heterosexuality, regarding it as an inferior way of life designed by and for a patriarchal society.
2. As an example of homophobia, the Toronto *Globe and Mail* which calls itself Canada's National Newspaper printed, a few days before Valentine's Day in 1995, a photograph of two romantic giraffe with their necks entwined headed "The Telling Image." The legend underneath it read "The world's best neckers?" I wrote to the newspaper to point out that the two participants were not a heterosexual couple but both male, but the editor refused to publish my letter.
3. In connection with observers not knowing the sex of individual animals, long ago at the Edinburgh Zoo keepers called two king penguins Eric and Dora when they saw them engaged in sexual behavior (Vines, 1999). Later Eric's name was quietly changed to Erica when she was discovered to be female. Another penguin couple, Bertha and Caroline, were renamed Bertrand and Charles when keepers realized they also had been misjudged.

Chapter 13

Genetics Versus Culture? —Human Homosexuality

This chapter will discuss human homosexuality from two perspectives, first that of heredity (genetics/biology) and second that of history and culture.

Heredity: Genetics/Biology

> There was jubilation by millions of people when National Public Radio announced on July 15th, 1993, that apparently a Gay Gene had been discovered by Dean Hamer and his colleagues working at the National Cancer Institute in Washington. Many gay men celebrated this breakthrough by having tee-shirts made thanking their mom for their Xq28 gene (Ridley 1999, 107). Hamer proposed to patent the gene when it was finally identified so that it could not be used for prenatal diagnosis. He didn't want pregnant women asking for an abortion because they were homophobic.

A Gay Gene wasn't actually what the media said, but it was implied, and most listeners probably came away with the impression that there was such a gene (Satinover, 1996, 109ff). This impression was reinforced the next day with articles in the *Wall Street Journal* ("Research points toward a Gay Gene") and the *New York Times* ("Report suggests homosexuality is linked to genes"). Was this indeed the break-through that many Darwinian psychologists had sought?

Homosexuality has flummoxed Darwinian psychology because it doesn't fit neatly into the theory of evolution. We have seen that it is widespread throughout the animal kingdom and present in many or most members of some species, even though its practice is contradictory to reproduction, the standard against which sexual behavior is measured in an evolutionary perspective. Does a certain trait in an animal make it more likely that this animal will have more young than its peers? If so, the trait will be successful and passed on to future generations. If not, it will die out.

Because reproduction is the cornerstone of all evolution, Darwinian psychologists have been intent on linking it somehow with homosexuality, no matter how tenuous the possible connection as we saw in the last chapter; this would indicate that homosexuality has a genetic component. One can theoretically imagine a mutation occurring that turned an individual, because of his or her genetic inheritance, toward same-sex rather than opposite-sex partners, but two men or two women living together exclusively will not have children and the new gene(s) will not be passed into the next generation. (We ignore here test tube inseminations of the sperm of gay men because these were not part of the evolution of our ancestors, although progeny born of them will undoubtedly interest future Darwinian psychological researchers.) No matter how many mutations occur, and there would have to be a huge number to account for all the exclusive homosexuals in the world, they would not lead anywhere as far as evolution is concerned.

Fig 13.1 Theoretical Schemes for the Sexual Preference Axis. Black for heterosexual, white for homosexual and shades of gray for bisexual orientations.

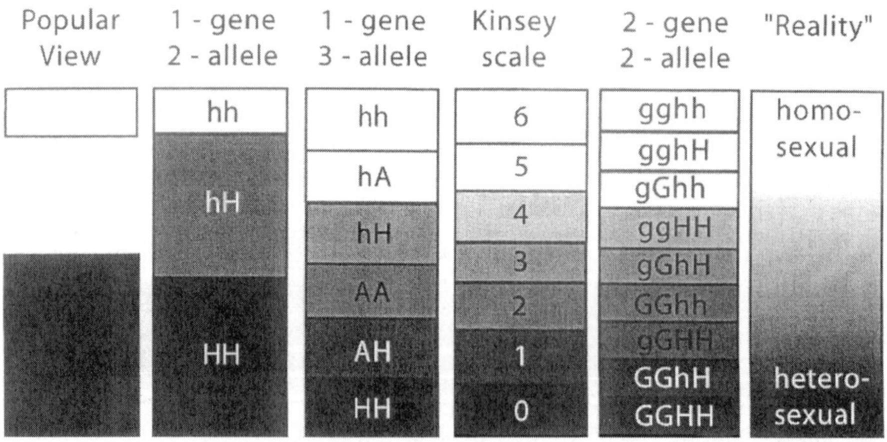

Source: MacIntyre and Estep, 1993

Homosexuality in human beings is not a clear-cut condition. If we consider columns of a chart with numbers of heterosexuals at the bottom and of homosexuals at the top (Figure 13.1, column 1), it is evident that the popular conception of all people being either straight or gay is invalid (MacIntyre and Estep, 1993). There is no clear-cut difference between the two, as column 6 indicates. Homosexuals may have occasional intercourse with someone of the other sex, making them bisexual. The Kinsey Scale (column 4) was devised to classify more precisely individuals' tendencies toward bisexuality and homosexuality. Genetic possibilities for homosexuality are indicated in columns 2, 3 and 5. If there is a single gene for sexuality with two possibilities of straightness and gayness as indicated in column 2, then a person with two straight alleles (an allele is one type of the gene) would be heterosexual, one with two gay alleles would be gay, and one with one of each would be bisexual. We shall see shortly that this simple model is highly unlikely.

If the gene for sexuality has three alleles, as in column 3, there is a much greater possibility for variation which better reflects the human condition. Even more possibilities occur if there are two genes with two alleles each (column 5), or any higher number of genes and/or alleles; Pillard and Bailey (1998) speculate that there could be "dozens or even hundreds of alleles relevant to sexual orientation." This polygenic condition is similar to the inheritance of skin color which involves a number of different genes and alleles so that it is impossible for an expecting black woman and her white mate to predict the exact color of their child.

If a gene S for sexual orientation should be found on the X or Y chromosome, this would affect its expression differently in men and women. A woman who by definition has two X chromosomes but no Y chromosome would be a carrier if she had this S gene. A man by contrast might reflect this S gene in his behavior, as it would not be masked by a second gene (in that a man has one X and one Y chromosome).

Do any type of genes connected with homosexuality actually exist, and if so, what kind of genes are they? What is the evidence of a genetic basis for homosexuality, a genetic base essential for the principles of Darwinian psychology to apply? Evidence of possible heritability comes from studies of family trees and especially twin studies, although the latter have produced extremely variable results. Franz Kallman, for example, reported that of eighty-five gay men he studied who had identical (monozygotic or MZ) co-twins, 100 per cent of their co-twins were also homosexual, although he later conjectured that his sample of mentally ill and institutionalized men was biased (Byne and Parsons, 1993). Other researchers report correlations for male MZ co-twins both being homosexual as ranging from forty-seven to sixty percent and for concordance in female MZ twins as forty-eight percent (Pillard and Bailey, 1998). This is far higher than one would expect by chance because in the United States today about three to four per cent of the male and one to two per cent of the female population are estimated to be exclusively homosexual or virtually so (Pillard and Bailey, 1998).

These data seem to correlate heredity with homosexuality to some extent because roughly half of homosexual monozygotic twins have co-twins who are also homosexual. But perhaps the similarity in sexual orientation between MZ twins is accounted for entirely by their experiences of developing at the same time in the same womb, looking virtually identical and growing up in the same family and culture?

The above data equally implicate non-genetic factors because about half of homosexual MZ twins do *not* have a homosexual co-twin. Family environment certainly has some effect because for fraternal or dizygotic (DZ) twins (who share as many genes on average as other non-twin siblings), the range in several studies for both co-twins being homosexual in males was zero to twenty-two percent and in females the average was sixteen percent (Pillard and Bailey, 1998). Theoretically the issue could be decided by having MZ twins raised in different environments, but this rarely occurs and the degree of separateness and similarity of households is often an issue (Segal, 1999). Researching the incidence of homosexuality in twins and in families has sparked no explanatory genetic model that can be tested.

For scores of years there has been an uneasy truce between those camps which thought sexual orientation was caused by an individual's personal experience in early life and those which opted for heredity. From the 1940s until the late 1970s, culture was in the ascendancy (Byne and Parsons, 1993). People postulated that a boy became gay because he was raised as a girl, or hadn't been exposed to girls when young, or had been seduced by boys or men, or had a possessive mother, or was shy with girls or been rejected by them (West, 1977, 84). No such causes necessarily led to homosexuality, but some psychologists thought that they could have had some influence on a boy's sexual orientation.

The most common (and misogynist) view was that boys grew up to be gay because they had possessive, dominating mothers who smothered them with love and kept them tied to their apron strings (West, 1977, 86); correlated with this were the boys having distant, weak, ineffectual fathers. An alternate explanation could be that the fathers became cold and distant because their sons liked to play with girls' toys; this then might have induced their wives to become overly attached to their sons to compensate. Whatever the truth, the development of a human being from infancy to adulthood is endlessly complex and for ethical reasons impossible to research in detail.

Researchers more recently turned to a biology-based question: Perhaps the concentration of testosterone in a man's blood affected his sexual orientation? (Testosterone is called the "male hormone" even though it also occurs, in small concentrations, in women.) Some reasoned that homosexuality reflected a lack of "normal" male sexual behavior which should translate into a deficiency of the male hormone testosterone in gay men. However, being given hormone treatments did nothing to change gay men into heterosexuals, and research found little or no difference in the hormone content of the blood of gay and heterosexual men. Not that researchers didn't try to prove this possibility one way or the other. By the 1980s, huge amounts of time and money had been poured into research on this issue, even though it must have been clear fairly early on that there was little to this different-levels-of-hormone hypothesis. Of twenty-five studies, twenty found no differences in hormone levels, three found lower testosterone levels in gay men while two found they had elevated levels (Meyer-Bahlburg, 1984, 377).

In the 1980s, when it seemed that testosterone was probably *not* correlated with sexual orientation, for lack of a better idea scientists leaned toward an integrationist model, with both nature and nurture involved in determining one's sexuality (Byne and Parsons, 1993). Presumably, because many MZ twins are both homosexual, there is some sort of genetic or prenatal influence that predisposes a person toward his or her sexual orientation. This tendency could be further influenced by a person's experience in his or her early life.

Even so, research on testosterone continues. A recent study found that a cause of homosexuality in some men is birth order; statistically, a man who has older brother(s) and a related low level of testosterone in his blood at birth is relatively more likely to be gay than other men (Blanchard and Bogaert, 1997). This could be because his mother, after bearing a son, built up an immune response to testosterone that affected her subsequent male offspring; this scenario could help explain the relatively high percentage of twins who are both homosexual as discussed above. A related study suggests that both lesbians and gay men may have been exposed to more male hormones than usual before birth as a result of their mother bearing former sons. This exposure is claimed to be responsible for the index finger of lesbians being shorter than the ring finger on the right hand (Williams et al., 2000) although this is a condition also present in many straight women.

New research also indicates that many gay men have *extra high* levels of male hormones in their blood; far from being effeminate, they can be said to be more like supermales with, compared to heterosexual men, larger genitalia and more sexual partners during their lifetime (Williams et al., 2000). Current research on the differences between straight and gay people now focuses on brain structure, handedness, cognitive ability, body size, hearing ability, startle and blink responses, and fingertip ridges (Johnson, 2004, 155ff). These characteristics point to prenatal influences which confirm that homosexuality is at least in part biological.

Another line of research introduced at the beginning of this chapter was led by Dean Hamer, a gay man who for years searched the human genome for a gay gene. In their book *The Science of Desire: The Search for the Gay Gene and the Biology of Behavior* (1994), he and Peter Copeland describe the hunt for a gene or genes connected to male homosexuality. Hamer and his colleagues collected and examined DNA samples from over one thousand extended family members of seventy-six gay men. They found a marker (not the gene itself, but close to it) on the X chromosome (from the mother), Xq28, which was apparently linked to homosexuality because the gay men in the group had it and the heterosexuals did not. The site of Xq28 at the end of the long arm of the X chromosome was too crowded with genes for a possible homosexual one to be identified.

The jubilation of the gay contingent at the discovery of what seemed to be a gay gene was matched by the gloom of those who wanted to believe that a gay man with enough desire could change his orientation. The latter, among others, found fault with Hamer's research (as Risch et al., 1993). They wanted especially to know exactly how a gay man was defined, because Alfred Kinsey in his research had divided homosexuals into six groups depending on their sexual behavior as we saw in Figure 13.1 (Kinsey et al., 1948, 638). Is a man gay if he has had many male partners but then married, apparently happily? If he married, had children, and then became openly gay as Oscar Wilde did? If he thought about men but remained celibate, never acting out his fantasies, because he wanted to keep his job? If he lived openly as a gay man but occasionally had sexual flings with women? Opponents of Hamer's research insisted that his sample size of gay men was too small and that his results would only apply at best to a restricted number of people which Hamer had never denied.

Some researchers tried to replicate Hamer's work. Eventually, in 1999, George Rice and his colleagues, who felt strongly enough about the issue to fund their research out of their own pockets, reported that Hamer's findings did *not* apply to a larger group of gay male sibling pairs from Canadian families. They claim their results repudiate the existence of an X-linked gene underlying male homosexuality.

Perhaps it is best for society that sexual orientation is not caused by a single gene as many gays had hoped. If this were so (although it is highly unlikely given the lack of success in finding one so far), it would set up a new political dichotomy. Gay men would presumably be less open to harassment initially, but not in the long-term. Chandler Burr (2000), a gay man who claims he would consider genetic surgery to "correct" his orientation if this were possible, argues that conservatives should in fact embrace a gay gene, say GAY-1. Then, with advanced technology, doctors could insert an allele for that gene, STRAIGHT-1, into a gay man to in effect "straighten" him out. With advanced technology pregnant women, given DNA tests that showed they were carrying embryos with the GAY-1 gene, could elect to have an abortion. Burr is delighted with this scenario, writing that "the possibility that abortion will be used as a form of sexual eugenics might make liberals, who have long fought for the right to abortion in every circumstance, think twice." Such abortions would destroy individuals who would have enriched our world, philosophically and artistically and every other way, from a gay perspective.

The euphoric announcement of the existence of a gene for a human behavior, followed by a later low key realization that the announcement was premature and probably incorrect, is a melodrama that has played out in research not only on homosexuality, but also on alcoholism, bipolar disorder and schizophrenia. A review of 135 scientific research papers dealing with the cause of sexual orientation concludes that "there is no evidence at present to substantiate a biologic theory, just as there is no compelling evidence to support any singular psychosocial explanation" (Byne and Parsons, 1993)."[1]

Currently it appears that a person's sexual orientation is not based on one or two genes but depends instead on the interaction of his or her genetic inheritance (including personality traits), the hormones he or she was exposed to as an embryo, his birth order and his or her familial and social milieu as sexuality emerged. Heterosexuality and homosexuality are not two distinct entities, but rather the endpoints of a range of sexual possibilities. Human beings are born with the potential of expressing themselves sexually in many different ways, a finding beyond the explanatory grasp of Darwinian psychology.

History and Culture

All social behaviors of an individual animal involve genetic makeup (G for genotype) acted upon by the environment (E) and culture (C) which influences him or her. The simplistic probability that an individual will have a certain behavior is:

$$G + E + C,$$

> keeping in mind that "+" doesn't mean these influences are added together; rather, they may or may not all be present, and all interact with each other.

In "primitive" animals such as insects and fish, G represented as instinct will be by far the major component of their behavior. As we go "up" the evolutionary scale, E becomes progressively more important, with C involved as well in "higher" animals in which information is passed from one generation to the next not genetically, but by observation and learning. In animals such as monkeys, apes and human beings, sexual behavior in an individual is *always* an interaction among genotype, environment and culture (Johnson, 2004, 201). Despite the apparent belief of many Darwinian psychologists, there is no need to prove that every animal behavior must be connected with evolution via reproduction, and this includes the propensity to engage in homosexual behavior.

Let's consider how homosexuality emerged in the evolution of primates and of human beings. As we saw in the last chapter, homosexual behavior seems endlessly variable and haphazard in animals, but it is not always random because at least in primates it shows an evolutionary progression (Vasey, 1995). Judging from the large array of thirty-three species of monkeys and apes in which homosexual behavior occurs, it has been present since the Oligocene thirty million years ago, yet it is not present in the earliest primates, the prosimians (such as lemurs and lorises). As more advanced primates evolved, their increasingly sophisticated brains enabled sexual behavior to be decoupled from reproduction; such behavior, including homosexuality, could be used instead for social purposes.

Homosexual behavior differs in the two main groups of monkeys which have evolved separately in the Old and New Worlds. In the New World monkeys (platyrrhines) it is less complex—less frequent with no extended homosexual socializing or consorts and with same-sex interactions apparently restricted to play and dominance displays. For Old World monkeys (catarrhines) homosexual behavior is more elaborate, involving frequent same-sex interactions, consort bonding, and alliances with political implications around issues of reconciliation and tension regulation. As well, there is explicit competition for same-sex sexual partners. For the most advanced apes, our closest relatives, homosexuality is common in bonobos, chimpanzees, orangutans and gorillas as we saw in the last chapter.

Over the past century homosexuality has been encountered in many different societies by anthropologists in their field work, although a number of them refrained from mentioning it in their publications, perhaps feeling that such goings-on must be an anomaly. Unlike current homosexual activity in many Western countries which often involves two men or two women living together in long-term relationships, that from early cultures fell mainly into two different realms: transgendered behavior and initiation into sex.

An example of a transgendered person was a berdache, an aboriginal American dressing and acting like a member of the opposite sex. This word was first applied to men who dressed as women, did women's work and took other men, usually chiefs, as sexual partners. Female berdaches who dressed as men participated in male activities such as hunting and warfare along with other men (Mondimore, 1996). Berdaches were an important part of their communities, commonly acting as shamans, healers and seers. Their presence has been documented in geographic areas world-wide—Siberia, Borneo, Indonesia, Vietnam, Thailand, Tahiti, the Philippines, India, Africa and Latin America (Dynes and Donaldson, 1992, xi-xii).

The second category, initiation into sex, was seen as a positive one in which a young boy had semen implanted in him by an older male to give him virtue and power (xi); this masculinized him. In this system a boy was involved in homosexual relationships with older men while he was young, but became heterosexual when he married. Such pederasty, valued in early Greek times and in many preliterate communities, is now regarded with abhorrence in the Western world.

By 1951, an analysis of hundreds of field research reports showed that at least two-thirds of societies studied by anthropologists had some homosexual component (Ford and Beach, 1952). Additional studies, more sensitive work and less reticence now indicate that homosexual behavior is present in virtually all but the tiniest human groups (Dynes and Donaldson, 1992, p. x,xv).

Is homosexual behavior similar in animals and people? If they aren't the same, can they both be a product of Darwinian psychology? Such a facile comparison is impossible, because there are so many animals with so many varied behaviors to compare with the behavior of one species, human beings. However, in several ways homosexual behavior is similar in both animals and human beings: it is usually less common than heterosexual behavior and it can take place at any time of the year just as can opposite-sex behavior in people. If human and animal homosexual behaviors are placed on the same line spectrum of possible behaviors, there is nothing to justify any strong claim of uniqueness for human homosexuality.

Animals don't care about the rights or wrongs of mating behavior. If they want to have sex with a pal, they go ahead and have it as we have seen, regardless of whether their partner is the same or opposite sex as themselves. Culture complicates this issue for human beings. Many societies adopt rules of acceptable social behavior which may be broken by some people, but which should not be *seen* to be broken, and if seen should be punished. Recent societies and religions which have wanted increased populations or adherents have made laws banning homosexuality (usually of men, because women were assumed to be incapable of it), fearing that if men were off having sex with each other there would be fewer husbands impregnating their wives to produce children. Christina Lamb (2002, 105) reports that sodomy is very common in Afghanistan because women are sequestered; she suggests that the anger of Taliban men may relate to their having been raped when younger.

The change from homosexuality being regarded by preliterate societies as a natural and positive force to one in which it was considered unnatural and evil occurred gradually. It was castigated in early Jewish writings and the Bible, whose influence spread widely from about 500 through to 1500 A.D. (Mondimore, 1996, 24). By the fourteenth century, the Catholic Church had made sodomy a criminal offence and pressured European monarchs and their countries to follow suit. Some nations made it punishable by death, as Saudi Arabia still does, using decapitation to terrorize the populace (Saunders, 2004). Homophobia has been reinforced by parental fears that one of their children might marry a homosexual who would be less likely to give them grandchildren (Wallace, 1979, 57).

(The focus on homosexuality had the amusing side-effect a hundred years ago of scholars assuming that it was caused by urbanization [Pillard and Bailey, 1998, 349]. Gay men were relatively common in cities but seemed not to be in rural areas, a situation that still holds true today. This dichotomy was rather a result of gay men and lesbians moving from farming regions to cities where they were more likely to meet other people like themselves and to carry on their lives without harassment.)

In the past thirty years there has been a huge change in Western attitude toward gay men and lesbians who now play positive roles in television and movies, are elected for public office and hold Gay Pride marches that attract millions of participants and watchers. Their contributions, especially to the arts, are widely acknowledged and appreciated, and gay marriages are becoming increasingly acceptable.[2] A Gay Index has even been established that ranks cities with a large number of gay residents; such tolerant, gay-friendly urban areas (San Francisco is number one) are found statistically to attract large numbers of creative people who work in the arts and high-tech industries (Florida, 2002, 258).

This new openness which has enabled homosexuals to come out of the closet and begin to live together openly has had its down side for homosexuality, though, should it be inherited to some extent. Up until recently, gay men usually felt forced by restrictive societies to marry and have children. Ironically, should there indeed be a gay gene, permissive societies where gay men are able to live as they wish may be the first to experience the extinction of male homosexuality, while the presumed-gay gene lives on in repressive societies where gay men are unhappily married (Hamer and Copeland, 1994, 183).

At present there is a chasm between those who enjoy or are tolerant of homosexuality and those who condemn it, a chasm that affects what research is done on the subject, who does the research and who believes the results. This abyss is reflected in a 2002 American survey in which sixty-six per cent of Democrats believed homosexuality was something a person was born with while sixty-one per cent of Republicans believed that it was due to such factors as upbringing and environment (Hacker, 2003, 15).

If one were against homosexuality for whatever reason, one's wish might be that the "condition" turn out to be non-genetic. If it were a "lifestyle choice" (although it is unclear why anyone would choose this "lifestyle" which is widely condemned by some and which leads many to self-hate and suicide [Health Canada, 1994]), then maybe gay men could be shown the error of their ways. Maybe they could be changed into normal heterosexuals? Although this is considered impossible for true exclusive homosexuals, it continues to be a hope offered by those wanting to "save" homosexuals from themselves.

By contrast, many gays and/or liberals believe that homophobia would subside if it could be proven that homosexuality is a genetic condition. How could people be blamed for being gay or lesbian if they were born that way? If the "condition" were "natural?" (Or are they being too optimistic? We know that skin color is inherited, yet that hasn't helped black people find tolerance.) And as we have discussed, were there a single gene for homosexuality, homophobic people might choose to try to eliminate it in both embryos and adults.

Whether sexual orientation is related more closely to genetics or to environment, to nature or nurture, remains unknown and unimportant. We do know that Darwinian psychology, despite its vast efforts and often bizarre hypotheses, has been able to shed little light on the issue of sexual orientation.

Notes

1. This opinion annoyed gay activists who suggested Byne had an antigay motive for his research and a "right-wing agenda" (Horgan, 1993, 131). He has been approached by conservative groups hoping he will support their stand against allowing gay men into the military, which he has refused to do. He believes that homosexuality is not a "choice" and that a genetic model of behavior is, as we have seen, just as likely to provoke bigotry as to quell it.
2. Gay marriages would have the added advantage of helping to fight overpopulation in the world, the greatest problem facing humanity today. Unless we cut down on the number of babies being born, more and more of them as they grow up will suffer from famines and die of starvation, and more and more of the earth's resources will be depleted. If homosexual marriages were endorsed for those who wish them, partners would be able to live satisfying lives without adding children to the world population; if partners chose to adopt children, these would be enriched by their parents' gay perspective. Rather than the accolade "Mother of the Nation" being applied to fecund women, childless same-sex couples might become role models. I imagine, however, that Darwinian psychologists would still dream up an evolutionary reason for this development.

Chapter 14

Bypassing Academic Standards—"Race"

In 1999, Philippe Rushton, a Canadian professor at the University of Western Ontario, sent over 40,000 free copies of a small 106-page abridgement of his book, *Race, Evolution and Behavior* (1995a), to social scientists around the world (Gatehouse, 2000; Morton, 2000). To obtain addresses for this mailing, Rushton used the members' list of the American Anthropological Association. This association, annoyed at having its mailing list used without permission and illegally for this purpose, complained to the producer, Transaction Publishers at Rutgers University, New Jersey, which subsequently destroyed 55,000 copies of the booklet and printed an apology in its *Society* magazine (Davis, 2000; Lamey, 2000).

Unruffled by this set-back, Rushton organized the printing of 100,000 more of the booklets under the auspices of his Charles Darwin Research Institute, again funded by right-wing organizations, in order to send even more copies to universities world-wide.

What goes on here? Rushton's ideas on the subject of "race" and behavior were contained in his 334-page original book, well-publicized (in part because so many academics disagreed publicly with its findings) and available to anyone who cared to buy it or borrow it from a library. Why go to the expense of sending out at enormous postal cost so many thousands of copies of an inferior abridged version?

When Rushton was asked about this, he replied that he was forced into such a measure because the academic world was trying to silence him for his sociobiological ideas (Morton, 2000). This is curious, because the booklet itself states that Rushton has published six books and nearly 200 academic articles (p. 5), many of which are cited in his 1995 book. If the aim was censorship, it hasn't worked very well. Because studies on "race" which are poorly researched, as Rushton's are, are regularly debunked by mainstream academics, Rushton apparently decided to evade their criticism by in effect self-publishing his booklet and sending it directly to every possible academic who might read and be swayed by it. The booklet won't appeal to most academics, but it can be used by others as an apparently scientific resource to back racist views.

"You just keep repeating the same lie over and over and over again and before you know it, people begin to believe it," Prof. Mehler says. Barry Mehler, founder of the Institute for the Study of Academic Racism at Michigan State's Ferris State University (Gatehouse, 2000), notes that the Pioneer Fund (along with other right-wing organizations) has invested a great deal of money in Rushton's career—at least a quarter of a million dollars between 1986 and 1990 (Lind, 1997)—and has been paying him \$80,000 a year for which he appears as the face of right-wing and racist political groups (Wong, 2000).

Rushton means his booklet to be taken seriously: it begins with a series of praises for the 1995 original work from various book reviewers including three professors whose university affiliations are given. One writer compares Rushton with Darwin while another thinks he should be given a Nobel Prize (the professors don't go *that* far). Most or all of the glowing testaments are from right-wing conservatives and/or Darwinian psychologists.

Rushton's work is useful in revealing the vast chasm between such admirers and his detractors who have routinely panned his publications as racist. One calls his 1995 book "intellectually insulting and morally repugnant: a case of strong politics driving weak science" (Ahmad, 1995); another claims that it does a major disservice to the serious study of behavior and gives him the shudders (Blinkhorn, 1994); while a third wittily portrays the research as the "I wouldn't have seen it if I hadn't believed it" approach (Armelagos, 1997, 282). However, even some Darwinian psychologists find Rushton's work abhorrent; one author has accused his 1995 book of "combining numerous little turds of variously tainted data" into what is "merely a larger than average pile of shit" (Mihm, 2001, 49).

Not only is Rushton serious about his 1999 booklet, but he wants it to be accepted not as fiction or a polemic but as science. "The goal of this book is to be scientific," he writes (p. 9). But does it adhere to scientific standards? Are his plethora of facts, chosen out of a far larger assortment from his original book, accurate? Are all possible explanations considered for each of the traits he analyzes?

Scientific discoveries in theory advance by feedback. When a scientist publishes new results, other scientists either confirm them with their own further research or point out where the research has gone wrong. Does Rushton not realize this, even though he claims to be doing science? Many academics have pointed out errors in his research, but he usually ignores their help. Over the years he continues to publish virtually the same conclusions based on almost the same often flawed data.

Rushton's thesis is that human beings are divided into three races: orientals (East Asians), caucasoids (Europeans, South Asians, whites), and negroids (Africans, blacks). He relates these races to what evolutionary biologists call the r-K scale of reproductive strategies. At one end of the scale (r-selection) are species which have a high reproduction rate at the expense of parental care; for example oysters spawn 500 million fertilized eggs a year, but do not (needless to say) protect their progeny. Of this large family only a few young oysters will survive to adulthood. At the other end of the scale (K-strategy) are animals such as the orangutan who produce few young but give each a high level of maternal care, so that again a few survive to adulthood. Either method is evolutionarily effective (since species that use them continue to exist), as are intermediate strategies between these two extremes.

The r-K scale was conceived of as a big-picture way to compare the reproductive strategies of different groups of animals such as oysters and large mammals, but Rushton, apparently looking around to find a system that would fit his thinking about racial differences, decided to apply it within one species, human beings, thus extending the hypothesis into an entirely new arena for which it was never intended. He argues that orientals are more K-selected than whites, who are in turn more K-selected than blacks. The doubtful strategy of fitting Darwinian psychological data into hypotheses or systems that have been set up for other purposes entirely is repeated for data on fluctuating asymmetry, as will be discussed in Chapter 16. The tactic appears to give the hypothesis entirely undeserved credibility.

Rushton summarized his research agenda colloquially in an interview with *Rolling Stone*: "Even if you take things like athletic ability or sexuality—not to reinforce stereotypes—but it's a trade-off: more brain or more penis. You can't have everything" (Rosen and Lane, 1995). Does this make sense? Do scholars have limited sex because of their academic interests? There is no evidence of this. Paul Johnson in his book *Intellectuals* (1988) profiles a number of the world's most famous academic men, showing that almost all of them led energetic (and often repugnant) sex lives.

During human prehistory, Rushton (1995a, 219) reports, some human beings like ourselves, *Homo sapiens sapiens*, migrated from Africa where they evolved to inhabit the cooler areas of Europe about 110,000 years ago. A new group split from the eastern caucasoids about 41,000 years ago to become orientals who moved north and east into even colder lands. Rushton hypothesizes that the blacks who remained in Africa are the most r-selected "race" and therefore the most sexually active (although why need this be, when a single act of intercourse can produce a child?); he thinks that since they have remained in tropical surroundings they are less intelligent than the other "races" in which larger brains have evolved to cope with their new harsher environments.

Rushton thus theorizes that Africans are dull, whites are smarter and orientals are smartest of all. These seem like sweeping generalizations when we consider the civilizations in Africa which produced the Great Zimbabwe monument and the Benin bronzes despite widespread tropical diseases such as malaria, bilharzia and leprosy. By contrast, not long ago in China many women had their feet purposely mutilated so that they became cripples and poor peasants often starved to death. It is also strange that during human evolution Rushton believes hominids began with K-like behavior common to the apes, switched to r-like behavior as they evolved in Africa, and then that those who moved out of Africa switched back to K-like behavior.

Fig 14.1 Racial Groupings of the World's Major Populations and Linguistic Families

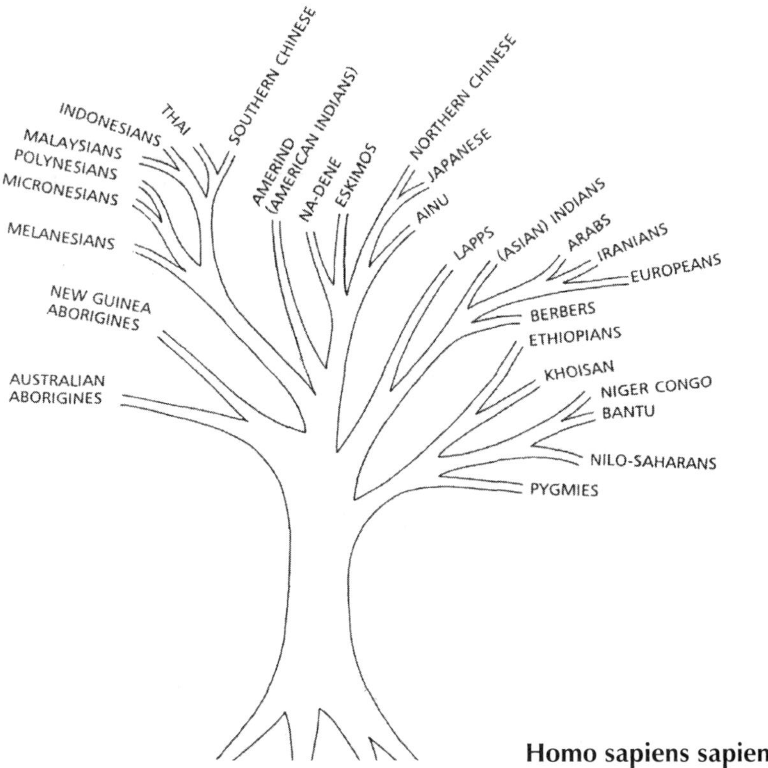

Source: Cavalli-Sforza and Cavalli-Sforza, 1995

For a scientific inquiry of Rushton's hypothesis, we must first decide whether human beings fit neatly into his three races. Mitochondrial DNA studies indicate that such a three-part division is far too simplistic (Cavalli-Sforza and Cavalli-Sforza, 1995, 66), as does common sense; for example east Indians and British whites are both "caucasoids," but their lifestyle, behaviors, number of children and social norms are very different. There is more DNA variation within African groups (such as between Tutsis at over six feet tall on average and pygmies at under five feet) than between whites and Chinese groups (Jones, 1999, 312; Venter, 2002). Japanese people and American aboriginals are both "mongoloids," but it is hard to imagine peoples with more different cultures. None of the physical traits that we usually associate with human races unambiguously corresponds to Rushton's races—neither skin color, hair type, body stature, blood group nor disease prevalence (Graves, 2001, 5).

Rushton spends much time comparing whites and blacks. He quotes a number of studies relating to Afro-Americans, but there was much miscegenation between blacks and whites in the days of slavery when black women were often raped by their white owners. Many blacks have as many genes from white forebears as black ones. Conversely, many whites have black genes from black forebears but lack those for dark skin pigmentation. In Brazil where the people have all shades of white to brown to black skin, a DNA study shows that a man's actual color is a poor indicator of his genomic African ancestry (Parra et al., 2002). Therefore to determine a person's heritage on the basis of skin color, which Rushton routinely does, is impossible.

Rushton may have it in for blacks, as we shall see, but he is positively smarmy to oriental people. Margaret Chon (1995, 239), a Korean woman, believes this is because he and other white men writing in a similar vein are anxious not to appear racist, which they would if whites were at the top of their superiority scale. She claims that the studies on which they base their IQ scale, for example, are few and poorly done. Related research shows that Chinese Americans owe their superior performance on IQ tests to a culture of hard work rather than heredity: in the 1920s they received average test scores of 65 to 70, in the 1950s after decades of education they were on a par with whites and in 1990 they scored above whites (Kutzik, 1995, 246).

Chon is angry that Asians are classified by Rushton and other white "experts" as a Superrace. This means that although Asian Americans are less wealthy than other American groups, they are ignored by social service agencies and by governments which could benefit their communities with voter assistance, better schools, better housing, health care and job training. By singling out their group rather than white groups made up of, say, Belgians, Portuguese or Italians, they become part of the racial fray in America, a buffer between blacks and whites. The false flattery means that Asians become targets of racism, with their intelligence seen as cunning, and rumors about their taking over the local economy or the world a reason for hatred and violence against them. In 1993 alone, at least thirty Asian Americans were murdered in homicide cases in which racial hatred was suspected or proven. Chon writes (p. 240) that "the accumulated rage of the black community cannot reach Beverley Hills or Bronxville, but it can make itself felt at Korean grocery stores in South Central Los Angeles and Flatbush."

To illustrate how Rushton has tried to prove his theory, we shall discuss his work under four headings: extensive use of anecdotal evidence, exploitation of numerical data with brain size as an example, the assumption that human evolution is happening today rather than in the distant past, and problems that occur when a book is abridged for mass consumption.

Anecdotal Evidence

Rushton's style differs from that of most scientists because he depends to a large extent on anecdotal evidence which is irrelevant to his r-K theory. In his 1995 book, for example, we find that mongoloid children learn to turn their heads later than white children (p. 149); that in Japan, the strong odor of a man was enough early in the 1900s to exempt him from military service (p. 162); that black women on average have lower voices than white women (p. 163); that black children are born earlier (which surely correlates with low birth weight and lack of prenatal care [p. 147]); that the muscles of East Africans produce little lactic acid so that they have great endurance (p. 163); and that in Thailand, female prostitutes report that size 52mm condoms bunch up during intercourse causing irritation (p. 167). Rushton even claims that Chinese babies are more highly evolved than black babies because they are slower to sit up! The real reason may be that many Chinese infants spend their early weeks or months tightly rolled in a blanket tied with a rope in what is called a "candle wrap." It amounts to a full-body straitjacket which prevents them from flexing their body and leg muscles (Wong, 1999).

Rushton also uses an anecdotal approach when he considers categories of behavior that are almost impossible to define. In one of Rushton's (1999, 19) charts, blacks are noted as being less cautious, more impulsive, more sociable, with a higher self-concept, and less likely to commit suicide than orientals. What do these categories mean? Is a cautious person one who hesitates to have children? Who does not put forward original ideas that might improve the lot of his group? Who looks for food only where she has found it before? What have these traits, if they are even valid, to do with reproductive strategy? Surely, following evolutionary theory, people who had a good self-concept were especially likely to choose a superior mate. People who were cautious might miss out in the mating game. Or they might not. Anyone who committed suicide was certainly out of the competition to produce young. Who is to say how people behaved many thousands of years ago? If these five characteristics were reversed for blacks and orientals, might they not be seen by Rushton as positive traits? Almost every page of Rushton's booklet contains such generalizations that are far too simplistic to be credible as science.

Exploiting Numerical Data—"Race" and Brain Size

Rushton devotes thirty-four pages in his 1995 book to the subject of brain size which he claims reflects a person's intelligence. Therefore, he assumes that the average size of the brains of members of a "race" reflects the average intelligence of that "race." (Racial groups and specific IQs will be considered in the next chapter.) To scientists, numbers are usually critical in proving a point, so let's consider his numerical data in detail to determine its accuracy.

Rushton (1995a, 131) states that orientals, whites and blacks have average sex-combined brain weights respectively of 1304 grams, 1309 gms and 1180 gms. He includes a table in his book with forty-three sets of measurements from various sources, but one-quarter of these sets are 100 years old, and three-quarters are from over fifty years ago; he omits a 1836 data-set on 320 brains published by Tiedemann which showed that brain size was similar in various "races" (Gould, 2002, 374). Inexplicably Rushton ignores current, more accurate information available from anthropologist and expert C. Loring Brace who has a vast database of head measurements; Brace reports that there is no significant difference among "races" (although he doesn't believe in the concept of race), and no connection between head or brain size and intelligence (Miller, 1995, 169). Even if some "races" should have bigger brains on average than others, there is no proof that brain size reflects intelligence.

What does the 124 gms difference in Rushton's racial data between the largest and smallest average brain weights mean? It is certainly conjectural when we know that the concept of race itself is untenable. It could reflect the difficulty and timing of extracting a dead person's brain and weighing it before it dried out. It could indicate the health of the person before he or she died. It could mean that biased scientists one hundred years ago made biased measurements as Gould has recounted (1981). It is questionable to represent a group of many millions of people with measurements from a few hundred or thousand individuals.

Even if we could accept the 124 gms weight difference for the brains of different races as valid, it means little when we consider individual variation in brain size (Rushton, 1995a, 106). For example, the brain weights of some brilliant men were low: poet Walt Whitman's brain weighed only 1,282 gms, author Anatole France's 1,017 gms and Franz Gall's 1,198 gms—Gall's brain weight was especially ironical because he was one of the founders of phrenology, the original "science" of judging mental abilities by the size and shape of localized skull areas (Gould, 1981, 92). At the other end of the scale the brains of zoologist Baron Cuvier and author Ivan Turgenev weighed respectively 1,830 gms and over 2,000 gms. So eminent European men can have a difference of nearly 1,000 grams in their brain weights, eight times the difference Rushton presents for his "races."

Rushton's theory is further undermined by data from women and from Neanderthal fossil skulls. Women have smaller brains than men, even when adjusted for their smaller body mass, yet by all measures they are equally as smart (Angier, 2000), a fact Rushton admits is "a nuisance" for his hypothesis and an "anomaly" (Wong, 2000). Because there are more women than men in the world, statistically it is men who should be Rushton's anomaly—men have larger heads but, according to Rushton's ideas, are comparatively dumber than women if brain size is held constant. In contrast with women, Neanderthals had larger skulls than human beings. If we followed Rushton's logic we would imagine that Neanderthals were smarter than members of *Homo sapiens sapiens*, but the fact that we are still here while Neanderthals have become extinct belies this.

Human Evolution Happened Prehistorically

Physically, races of human beings which developed long ago in different parts of the world look different. Presumably the skin of northern Europeans is pale because sunlight, needed to prevent rickets, is limited unlike in Africa; pygmies are small so they can move easily through jungles; and Kenyans often win marathons because they are well adapted to open areas and long-distance running (Krantz, 1980). Physiologically, blood groups and rare genetic disorders are often correlated with race too. With increasing intermarriage in the world, however, pure human races are now rare which is why using the term "race" is no longer tenable.

A major flaw in Rushton's work is his insistence that not only our distant past but our current behavior is shaped by evolution, although today Western societies protect the right of even evolutionary unfit people (such as those with genetic disorders) to reproduce. When the social behavior of various human groups differs today, it is largely because of their different cultures and religions. Here we shall consider examples of birth rate and of criminal behavior among Rushton's "races."

The basis of Rushton's r-K argument is that blacks have more children than the other two "races" and give each less care. Blacks may have more children today, but this was apparently not so during human evolution. Judging from present-day foraging societies such as the !Kung San of South West Africa, prehistoric African women averaged fewer than five children during their lifetime because each was breastfed for four years before the next infant was born (Howell, 1979, 128). If a woman delivered twins, one was killed because the mother was unable to cope with two babies during nomadic wanderings. I can find no evidence that Paleolithic women outside Africa had fewer young than this; indeed before 1875 European women had six children on average (Dagg, 1991), and often disposed of them to wetnurses or orphanages where they died from neglect.

Rushton (1999, 35) comments negatively on the large number of black American children now born out of wedlock, as if this ensures less parental care for them. Black marriages are now less common, but with the end of slavery in the United States marriage became a status symbol for blacks and by 1917, ninety per cent of all black children were born to married couples (Staples, 1981). Since then there have been progressively fewer weddings. This is obviously a case of cultural rather than biological behavior, as are many of his other examples. Rushton argues that such traits have been shaped by evolution, but he does not carry this theme to its logical conclusion. Why is having out-of-wedlock children an inferior characteristic? Indeed how can blacks be counted as inferior if they have a high rate of population growth, when for other species this is the main criterion of success?

Continuing his seeming obsession about black inferiority, Rushton states that blacks are more likely than whites or orientals to be in prison because of their genetic heritage. There are many blacks in jail, but how is this related to evolutionary theory? We don't know if paleolithic men had criminal behavior, or even what counted as a crime many thousands of years ago, so how can we postulate how it might have evolved? Can genetic inheritance account for the Nazi Germans who murdered millions of Jews and gay men? Or for the rulers who executed millions of Russians and Chinese under Communist rule? Since crime is anti-social, one would surmise that being a criminal would be a poor adaptation for community approval or for winning a spouse, and therefore a poor criterion for being an evolutionary success.

Although Rushton (1995b) states, in keeping with his thesis, that violent crime is greater in predominantly black nations than in predominantly white ones, and greater in these white nations than in predominantly Asian ones, a careful reanalysis of Rushton's Interpol data shows that there is no significant association between nations (considered as "races") and cross-national homicide rates (Neapolitan, 1998). Far from being genetically based, criminal behavior is correlated with poverty, alcohol, poor diets, lead-based paints, drugs and general desperation as we saw in Chapter 8.

Book to Booklet—Funneling and Popularizing

In writing his 1995 book *Race, Evolution, and Behavior*, Rushton must have read and sorted through tens of thousands of articles to collect those that supported his views about race. At the same time, he ignored articles and information that opposed them. For example, he makes much of the 85 average IQ score of blacks compared to the 100 score for whites, but he doesn't mention that about 15 points also separate Catholics from Protestants in Northern Ireland and Sephardic from Ashkenazic Jews, or that urban people score higher than rural people, and scores are higher for those with a high socioeconomic status than for a low one (Stevenson and Stigler, 1992). His mind thus acted as a funnel, including information that suited him and excluding information that did not support his views.

His funneling began again when Rushton abridged his 1995 book in order to produce his 1999 booklet: he cited in 1995 a few research results that do not fit into his theory, but omitted these from the booklet. For example, in it he cites a low average IQ score for black people while omitting data from studies that reported higher IQs for them. In one such study, a sample of about 4000 children of German mothers with black or white fathers (sired in Germany by American occupation troops following World War II) had similar IQs; black racism seems less virulent in Germany which has no history of mass slavery.

In his booklet Rushton has omitted a bibliography, making it impossible for readers to check his facts. However, he does allow himself enough room to address titillating subjects. He devotes half a page (p. 42) to speculate with long-dead authors about sex organs. He informs the reader that from the eighth to the sixteenth centuries, Arab Islamic literature revealed that black African men and women had high sexual potency and large organs. He tells us that nineteenth century European anthropologists reported on the position of female genitals (high in orientals, low in blacks, intermediate in whites), and the angle of erection in the penis (blacks with penises at right angles, orientals with penises parallel to the body, but no information on white penises—why not when the anthropologists all had them?). The statement about parallel penises is bemusing—parallel with the body because they didn't rise at all? In which case is intercourse possible? Or parallel because they rose so far their tip approached the belly button? In which case shouldn't this effort exceed that of the half-hearted perpendicular exertion of the black penis? And, tsk tsk, how did the male European anthropologists collect these data?

These same early "scientists" cited by Rushton claimed that orientals had the least prominent secondary sex traits in the form of visible muscles, buttocks and breasts, and blacks the most (but no information on whites is given). There are problems with these comparisons, the most obvious of which is whether the estimates of secondary sexual traits is reliable given their greater visibility in hot climates than in cold. Second, even if the differences as reported are correct, their cultural consequences for sexual behavior are a different issue. And finally, even if the differences of physical characteristics and sexual behavior are as Rushton argued (and condoms for Africans apparently are 53 mm wide compared to a width of 52 mm for whites and 49 mm for Asians [p. 42]), these "facts" do not lead to an obvious judgment of which race is inferior and which superior. After all, the advertisements for penis lengthening which invade our computer screens would appear to suggest that large size is devotedly sought, and those who possess it should be considered genetically blest.

Were all the strange observations of early researchers accurate? Rushton could have collected measurements on such things as penis angles, visible muscle and buttocks, to see if they were correct, but he did not do so. If he had searched the literature diligently he would even have found a study of penile length and body height published in 1899 which shows a positive correlation between the two measurements (Loeb, 1899); because orientals are on average shorter in height than whites, this may explain their shorter penises. (A recent report states that penis length varies not only with height, but also with foot size! [Siminoski and Bain, 1993]). From Rushton's booklet we are left with the presumption that as far as sexual organs are concerned, orientals and blacks fall into line with his theory of the r-K scale of reproductive strategies, even though there is no evidence that the angle of erection of a penis or the glimpse of a hearty buttock will mean that a person on average has more children than someone without similar attributes.

In conclusion, what do Rushton's ideas tell us about him as a scientist? His concept of race is so outdated as to be no longer valid; his data are often wrong, too vague to be useful, or irrelevant and anecdotal; he confuses the time in which human evolution occurred (which was not within human written history); he ignores data that do not support his thesis; and in condensing an academic book into a booklet that he hopes will be read by hundreds of thousands, he has produced a product that will spread often harmful misinformation. The well-known anthropologist Marvin Harris is said to have courted authority and prestige in his field by being "provocative, controversial and confrontational" (Casey, 1991, 11). It seems that Philippe Rushton must have the same compulsion for fame in order to behave in this same way.

Rushton, as an academic, should realize from the negative comments and critiques of large numbers of his peers to his research and publications that his analyses on race do not measure up to commonly-accepted academic standards. However, because he has tenure at his university he will not lose his position as a professor because of this. Probably he carries on his research on race for a number of personal reasons. He himself must be race-biased or he would be embarrassed to produce faulty research that feeds into racist beliefs. He has attracted the attention of the Pioneer Fund, connected with various racist and holocaust-denying pursuits (Miller, 1995; Shermer, 1997, 243), which has given him hundreds of thousands of dollars "for his research"—although Rushton's type of work is cheap, involving reading books and articles rather than laboratory experiments. And he likes the public attention he receives, even though much of it is negative—he is particularly eager to seek sympathy from audiences by complaining how misunderstood and reviled he has been by his detractors (Rushton, 1997).

Chapter 15

Politics Masquerading As Science —"Race" And IQ

If readers think an article or book is scientific—lots of big words, graphs, tables, appendixes—they think that what it says is true. Fiction appeals to the senses but science deals with facts one can trust. Or so people think.

In the 1990s, industry and business in the Western world adopted a leaner and meaner philosophy. Competition between rival companies became so fierce that many people lost their jobs. Yet taxes, which went in part to supply welfare payments, continued high. What better time to find a scapegoat for society's problems and sell a large number of books at the same time? Why not blame those at the bottom of the social scale, the welfare recipients, who were felt to sponge off the hard-working middle and lower classes?

Why not indeed? Along came the well-publicized book *The Bell Curve*: *Intelligence and Class Structure in American Life* (1994) by the late Richard Herrnstein and Charles Murray, both admirers of the work of Rushton (pp. 642-643). The bell curve describes the shape that frequencies of IQ scores depict when they are plotted against IQ scores for a large number of individuals. About ninety-six per cent of the population in the United States have IQ scores falling between 70 and 130, with the two per cent below 70 indicating mental retardation and the two percent above, exceptional brilliance (Lynn, 1995, 354). Most of those who live on welfare have IQs at the low end of the scale, and a disproportionate number of them are black. And the authors state that intelligence is largely inherited.

These raw facts set the scene. The book's thesis is that the world is controled, appropriately, by those with IQ scores on the right side (double meaning) of the curve including, of course, the two authors. Because of their intelligence, the smartest people are best adapted for power, wealth and opportunity (although the less fortunate must wonder why these advantages should accrue to evolutionary necessity rather than historical fortune and personal greed.)

Because American blacks and latinos have significantly lower IQ scores (averages of about 85) clustered on the left side of the curve than do the rest of Americans (averages of at least 100), the theory continues, these lower groups contribute to greater "illegitimacy" (a word I had hoped was no longer in use), crime, poverty, welfare dependency, unemployment and even workplace injury (Judis, 1995). According to the theory, because blacks and latinos have relatively large numbers of children who, like their parents, are of relatively low intelligence, their proliferation lowers the average intelligence of the American population and exacerbates the country's social problems. When affirmative action policies have been put in place, these people are given positions for which white people are better suited.

In the authors' view, this extreme predicament, the degeneration of a once great nation, demands desperate measures of which affirmative action is *not* one. Their suggestions include instead corraling a substantial minority of the dumber members of the population on a lavish version of an Indian reservation as permanent wards of the state (p. 526), preventing where possible poor women from having babies (p. 549), redirecting some funds to smart children from those who are dumb (who benefit little from funding because their low intelligence is genetic and not amenable to improvement) (p. 442), terminating current affirmative action programs (p. 475ff), abolishing welfare payments (so that poor women are not paid to have their inferior children [p. 548]), and restructuring immigration policy (so that skilled people are recruited at the expense of non-skilled relatives of recent immigrants [p. 549]). These measures are so draconian that were they put into effect, they would change the entire face of Western society; it is important, therefore, to address Herrnstein and Murray's concerns.

To ensure that their book be taken seriously, its 871 large pages are graced with a suitable academic paraphernalia of tables and graphs replete with a large number of notes, appendixes and references cited. To guarantee a good sale, advance copies of the book were kept from academic reviewers (most of whom would prove to be critical) so that their fault-finding couldn't dampen initial purchases (Jacoby and Glauberman, 1995, ix). The book was featured on the covers of *Newsweek*, *The New Republic* and *The New York Times Book Review* and by television stations CBS, NBC, CNN and ABC (Horowitz, 1995). As a good marketing ploy, the authors created controversy by extolling their own courage in daring to tell the truth about poverty/race and IQ despite Political Correctness, a truth they asserted others were too frightened to address: "They fearlessly pursue the Truth no matter where it leads, though interestingly enough it leads unerringly to answers that advance the ideological positions both men have long held," one reviewer notes sarcastically (Kennedy, 1995, 182). In the first two months of publication, 400,000 copies of the book were printed (Kamin, 1995).

Another successful ploy Herrnstein and Murray used was to flatter the reader as a member, like themselves, of the superior cognitive elite on the right side of the bell curve. They set up an "us/them" dichotomy which by the end of the book has become an "us *versus* them" antagonism (Gardner, 1995b, 70). "We" are the thoughtful, intelligent readers of their book who went to college and care about the future of the United States. "They" are the pitiful others who aren't very smart, who would never read books like theirs, and who are infinitely more likely to be their country's problem rather than its solution. As *The Bell Curve* puts it, "High cognitive ability is generally associated with socially desirable behaviors, low cognitive ability with socially undesirable ones" (p. 117). Periodically throughout their book, Herrnstein and Murray (1994) remind the reader of his or her superiority. The authors imply that the reason these elite haven't risen up already against their pathetic inferiors is that they know far too little about them, a gap the authors rectify with their book. When readers are so highly praised, they are likely to take the message of the book seriously despite its flaws. Some of them will have already lost jobs or university places given instead to blacks and latinos through affirmative action.

Of course, the thesis that Herrnstein and Murray present could be true. What evidence is there that it is not? Suspicion is aroused by the fact that their premise is not original, but rather a rehash of views that have been around for 100 years or more. Their basic concept is a hardline conservative one whereby one blames the individual for his or her misfortune rather than the hardships they have had to face such as racism, job discrimination or even bad luck. Herrnstein was a long-time advocate of the inheritance of intelligence; Murray (who as a youth helped burn a cross in his hometown of Iowa [Herbert, 1995, 249]) had focused on the drain of tax money into welfare payments to poor people with too many children, as outlined in his book *Losing Ground* (1984); he is said to be outrageous and to "throw stink bombs" to gain attention (Raspberry, 1995). Together, with their Harvard University connections to inspire reader confidence, they must have realized they could produce a book incorporating both their interests, a book they hoped would shift the political climate of the United States to the right and rationalize conservative indifference to the poor, a book that would be a best-seller because of intense interest on both sides of the political spectrum in the subject. (The publishers knew it would sell well because an article by Arthur Jensen written ten years earlier about the slim possibility of raising a person's IQ score was the sixth most cited article in the social sciences in 1978 [Jacoby and Glauberman, 1995, ix].)

The misgiving kindled by the men's right-wing backgrounds and the significance of their charges are enough to make any middle ground or left-wing reader carefully examine the data they use to prove their thesis, which we shall do here. We shall ask first what exactly IQ measures; discuss to what extent intelligence is inherited; consider whether it is possible to raise IQ scores significantly; and finally decide if an IQ score is relevant to a person being on welfare. (Flaws in *The Bell Curve* that will not be discussed here include the authors' suspect use of statistics [Gould, 1995, including the data of Ken Owen who specifically stated that his IQ results were not valid across cultures][1]; their cultural bias [Hacker, 1995]; their dismissal or ignorance of at least six studies showing that blacks can be as smart or smarter than whites [Nisbett, 1995, 38]); and their extolling the single intelligence factor 'g' even though its use is now considered outdated by most psychologists [Gould, 1995].)

What Does an IQ Score Mean?

How come IQ scores are important enough to be used to define everyone's place in society? Can they really be that predictable? Can they really be that infallible? Intelligence tests were invented in 1904 by Alfred Binet in France to identify children who were not doing well in school so that they could be helped with their studies.[2] The IQ score for an individual was derived from the totals of the four different parts of the test—for memory, reasoning, definitions and numerical ability.

How accurate are IQ scores? Among the homogenous population for which an IQ instrument is formulated, the tests work fairly well. An individual who takes several IQ tests at different times usually has similar scores, although they may vary somewhat depending on his or her mood, attitude and well-being at testing time, and whether she or he hates school too much to care about the test. But there are striking exceptions to general replicability: for example Gary Ross (1995, 256), a black student growing up in Buffalo, reports that he had an IQ score of 94 in grammar school, 114 in junior high school, 127 in high school, and 133 as an adult.

For a test to be fair, questions asked must cover information to which all those tested have been equally exposed. In reality, this is impossible. Children who have travelled a great deal or who live in a home where books and good conversation are routine tend to have higher scores than their less advantaged peers.

Nor are the lack of comparable backgrounds of respondents the only problem with IQ scores. Most psychologists today believe in a theory of multiple intelligences including and beyond what are measured by IQ tests (Gardner, 1999). A person who composes music or sight-reads musical scores with ease has musical intelligence; a crystallographer who studies crystalline chemicals has an exceptional ability to visualize structures in three-dimensions, or spatial intelligence; a gymnast has excellent kinesthetic sense; a person who gets along well with others has superior social intelligence; and an inventor full of new ideas has creative intelligence.[3] None of the people with these kinds of intelligences will necessarily score well on IQ tests.

The greatest problem with IQ scores, however, is that although they were devised to help children with their schooling, they are now commonly used to define whole populations and cultures in a manner for which they were never designed. To prepare an IQ instrument, researchers devise culture-appropriate questions for a homogenous population, then test anywhere from 200 to 10,000 individuals in that population (Chrisjohn et al., 1997, 208) to come up with an average value (100), with the same number of individuals having scores above and below. Then any other members of the population can be tested against this norm.

An IQ test is valid if it was normed for a population in question but invalid if it was not, which is often the case. For example, if a test were drawn up for black children, it would not be valid for aboriginal or white children who have different cultural experiences. This means that a comparison of IQ scores for blacks and whites in America such as Herrnstein and Murray routinely use is inappropriate because these people belong to different cultures. As an extreme example, members of the Zulu tribe in southern Africa who could hardly read the English sentences of IQ tests were asked to make decisions about such things as electrical appliances, microscopes, and "Western type of ladies' accessories" about which they knew virtually nothing (Kamin, 1995, 83). No wonder their average IQ score was low! The way to test for racial bias is to norm all the cultural questions in an instrument for all the whites in an area and to norm these same questions in another instrument for all the blacks in the same area. If each group has about as many respondents who know the answers as who do not, then racial bias has been addressed.

Using such silly data as those for the Zulus, Rushton claims (1995a, 137) that the average IQ of Africans on the whole continent of Africa south of the Sahara is 70, which equates with mild mental retardation. It is apparently important to Rushton that Africans be seen to have a low IQ so that the higher IQ scores of American blacks, who have significant white heritage, can be ascribed to this heritage. It is also important because black Africans, although they have a similar genetic background to black Americans, were not subject to slavery; therefore a low IQ cannot have been the product of American racism which led to slavery.

In their recent book *Race: The Reality of Human Differences* (2004), Vincent Sarich and Frank Miele repeat and elaborate on the anachronistic figure of 70 for the average IQ score of black Africans. They soothe their appalled readers by noting that this figure corresponds to someone of about twelve years of age who "can do all manner of things, including driving cars and even fixing them" (p. 230) and who therefore is *not* to be considered virtually mentally retarded. Like Herrnstein and Murray and like the Americans whose right-wing views are collected in *Contemporary Voices of White Nationalism in America* (2004, Swain and Nieli), Sarich and Miele opt for a concept of "Meritocracy in the Global Marketplace" (p. 260f); they are content, both ethically and economically, to be the beneficiaries of this vision. But what a culturally impoverished society it would be!

Is IQ Inherited?

The core of Herrnstein and Murray's work is that intelligence is inherited and cannot be changed to any extent during a person's lifetime. They believe America is in the predicament it is, in respect to intelligence and class, because of this. Arthur Jensen (1973, 89) states that a person's intelligence "is the result of a large number of genes each having a small additive effect," as if factors such as education, health, social interactions, and physical environment were not involved.

Although one's IQ score is based on both one's genes and one's life experiences which are inextricably entwined, twin studies do indicate that IQ scores are related to a person's genetic inheritance. When the IQ scores of specific pairs of people are compared, they vary on average (Segal, 1999, 58):

6 points between MZ twins who have the same genes,
10 points between DZ or fraternal twins,
14 points between full siblings, and
17 points between unrelated individuals picked at random.

Herrnstein and Murray (1994, 23) state that "Cognitive ability [as represented by IQ scores] is substantially heritable, apparently no less than forty percent and no more than eighty percent"—a huge range that makes one wonder how accurate these values are; by subtraction from 100 percent, they leave between sixty and twenty percent of one's IQ score based on environmental factors. Robert Plomin (Wright, 1999) and Howard Gardner (1995a, 27) both speculate that about half of one's IQ score is related to genetic and half to environmental factors, but Gardner also states that over ninety per cent of one's fortune does *not* lie in one's heredity. What does this mean?

For Gardner, a high IQ score does not guarantee success in life. We know, for example, that many once-great businesses have been destroyed after the founding genius was succeeded as head by his children and later his grandchildren, triggering the aphorism "You can hire better than you can sire" (Pitts, 2000). If the intelligence his descendants possessed was to a large extent genetic, why did the businesses fail?

Similarly, if equally bright children are born into a black ghetto and into a white middle-class professional home, their chances of success are vastly different. The black boy, if he is lucky, may escape the ghetto and move into the middle class but the white boy will almost certainly go to good schools, become involved in sports and club activities, have good resources and influence from his family and friends, and live in a positive physical and social environment (Raspberry, 1995). Unlike the black boy, he could reasonably aspire to be American president (although his wealth, politics, social skills, motivation and ambition would be far more important than his intelligence if he were to succeed.)

Since inheritance has some place in intelligence, some women decide to improve their chances of having a superior child by being inseminated with sperm from high achievers. Millionaire Robert Graham in 1980 set up a sperm bank in California with donated sperm from successful men including several Nobel Prize winners (one of them William Shockley who expounded the belief that blacks are genetically inferior to whites), top professionals, and some Olympic athletes (Goodwin, 2000). Today there are over 230 children with sperm bank fathers. Some of these children are brilliant, but given their birth circumstances, undoubtedly all of them have attentive if not domineering mothers who urge them to take full advantage of their potential, so it is impossible to know how much of their intelligence is due to their genes. Some of the children have done well at university but some have become rebels and one, at eight years of age, has never spoken a word, communicating by using a voice synthesizer and with symbols denoting key words; doctors can find no physical reason for his muteness. Another is brilliant in math, but had a difficult youth with an eccentric, dominating mother, being breast fed until he was four and wearing diapers until five (Laurence, 2001).

Theoretically, if individuals today want to produce bright children they should team up with a member of a "primitive" tribe (Diamond, 1997, 21). All Western babies are kept alive if at all possible and most live to reproduce no matter how intelligent they are. By contrast, a traditional New Guinean, for example, has managed to survive despite murder, tribal warfare, accidents and dearth of food, meaning that he or she is far more likely to have inborn intelligence. In addition, lacking television,

New Guinean children spend their youth actively interacting with people and the environment, the best possible stimulation for optimal mental development.

Recently, reflecting how little we actually know about the inheritance of intelligence, microbiologist Robert Plomin suggests that it is governed by hundreds if not thousands of genes with even major genes accounting for no more than about one per cent of heritability (Wright, 1999); geneticist Steve Jones (1999) speculates that cognitive ability may be explained by as few as fifty out of many thousands of genes; and Aryeh Routtenberg and his colleagues (2000) surmise that if people are like mice and other mammals, there may be a single gene/protein, GAP-43, which correlates with mice (and people?) being really smart.

Is the IQ of Groups Set in Stone?

The thesis behind *The Bell Curve* is that the IQ one is born with is hard to change. Herrnstein and Murray (1994, 19) point out that an individual's IQ score may not give much information about that person (for example, that of Gary Ross mentioned above), but that a population's average score does. The populations that most concern them are middle-class whites and lower-class people, especially blacks; the former have an average IQ score of over 100 and the latter one of about 85 (although as we have seen, these scores are not really germane because people from black and white cultures cannot be compared using a single instrument.) Their belief is that there is little possibility of educating dull children into being smart, so money should not be wasted on this enterprise.

Assuming that IQ scores are valid to some extent, why do blacks at present have lower averages than whites? American blacks are mostly descended from slaves who were kept in horrific conditions often for many generations, so that family ties were completely disrupted. Following the end of slavery, blacks were forced into segregated and inferior conditions for another ninety years. Black society still suffers from dysfunction, with nearly seventy per cent of black children living without their fathers, making life difficult for both mothers and children (Peretz, 1995). About one-third of blacks live in poverty related to this history of turmoil including women who smoke, drink and take drugs during and after their pregnancies (Patterson, 1995, 208).

Low IQ scores are correlated with many adverse biological and environmental conditions:

- Low birth weight in babies is associated with poor cognitive development during their growth (Richards et al., 2001), and black babies are more likely than white babies to have a very low birth weight (Trends..., 1997).
- In China, children kept safely tied in sandbags during their early years because both parents work all day in the fields score very low on IQ tests (Wong, 1999).
- Babies given formula instead of breast milk have lower IQ scores (Lucas et al., 1992).
- Infants living in poverty who suffer malnutrition, or children born with ailments such as fetal alcohol syndrome (caused by their mothers' drinking during pregnancy) have low scores because of underdeveloped brains (Genovés, 1970, 108)—an immense global problem that is scarcely being addressed.
- Children who have higher than normal levels of lead in their bodies have reduced intelligence (Schnaas et al., 2000).
- Children with iron deficiency are more likely to do poorly in math (Halterman, 2001) although their math improves if they have an older sibling in school (Smyth, 2001).
- A deficiency of iodine in the diet can lower the IQ of a population by as much as 13 per cent (Picard, 2002).
- Taking the drug Ecstasy along with pot lowers a young person's test scores for general intelligence (Gouzoulis-Mayfrank et al., 2000).
- So does becoming infected by the parasite *Toxoplasma gondii* from cat feces (Highfield, 2000).
- Individuals whose first language is not English do relatively poorly on American IQ tests (Ngana-Mundeke, 2000), as do those with dyslexia (who often have difficulty reading the instructions) and those who come from inferior schools and desperate home conditions (Kozol, 1996, 155).

The most striking universal disadvantage for any toddler is not being spoken to much in the home. Diligent researchers who taped and counted oral interactions with individual children found that by age three, an average child in a professional family would have accumulated experience with forty-five million words, one in a working-class family with twenty-six million words and one in a welfare family with only thirteen million words (Hart and Risley, 1995, 198). In addition, the disadvantaged children were exposed to a more limited vocabulary and to far more negative comments from their parents (Don't do that! Quit it! No!) (p. 199). Correlated with this is a far lower IQ which at age three indicates a developmental lag in a child rather than an estimate of his or her capacities (p. 143).

IQ performance may even fall with age if a person lives in horrific surroundings as a study of school children in rural Georgia showed. Arthur Jensen (1977) collected IQ scores from 1479 older and younger siblings of both black and white pupils; those of the white children stayed fairly constant, but those of the blacks decreased significantly between the ages of five and sixteen. The white children were from low and low-middle income homes, but these homes were splendid compared to those of the blacks who came from the worst environment possible, "as severely disadvantaged, educationally and economically, as can be found anywhere in the United States today." (Significantly, although Rushton cites many papers by Jensen which support his r-K theory discussed in the last chapter, he does not cite this study which helps refute it.)

Environment and culture have had a huge effect on black youth living in poor ghettoes. This underclass may actively discourage intellectual achievement, with good black students sometimes ostracized because they are "thinking white" (Besharov, 1995); for this reason many middle-class parents flee the ghetto if they can. In one experiment, black families were randomly assigned to live either in black middle-class city areas or in white suburbs of Chicago. Of the black children who grew up in the white suburbs, ninety-five per cent finished high school and fifty-four per cent went on to college; of those raised in the city, the numbers were lower—eighty per cent and twenty-one per cent respectively (Besharov, 1995). There is no doubt that poverty and social dysfunction account for the low IQ scores of poor blacks, and that as they leave poverty and the ghettoes behind, their IQ scores will climb to approach, equal or exceed those of whites.

Despite the pessimism of Herrnstein and Murray, there is ample evidence that the IQ of groups can improve. For example, IQ scores have risen dramatically world-wide, about twenty IQ points every thirty years, with people now able to answer far more IQ questions posed long ago than respondents could then (Flynn, 1998, 27). This phenomenon, called the Flynn Effect, is correlated with fewer children per family, better health, better nutrition for those living in poverty, better media circulation and increased travel; environment *can* therefore make an enormous difference to a community's average IQ scores (Neisser, 1998).

IQ performance may also rise with better education. One comparative study of children in Taiwan and the United States showed that although during kindergarten their scores were similar, by fifth grade the Chinese scores were far higher (Stevenson and Stigler, 1992). Another study of 1440 Japanese, Chinese and American children in Grades 1 and 5 found that although the Japanese and Chinese children scored better on intelligence tests, this was *not* because they had higher intellectual abilities, but because of their constant studying (Stevenson et al., 1985). Chinese and Japanese students excel on IQ tests because they attend classes for longer hours on more days a year than Americans (240 vs 180 days), work harder in school and at home doing school work and have dedicated teachers and parents who encourage and coach them constantly (Stevenson and Stigler, 1992). A depressing Japanese adage is: "Fail with five hours of sleep; pass with four."

Although Herrnstein and Murray are cynical, there are a variety of practical ways in which IQ scores of groups can be improved: good nutrition for pregnant women and their children will increase the IQ of blacks living in poverty (Gates, 1995; Herrnstein and Murray, 1994, 392); well funded preschool programs such as the Abecedarian project can raise the score of attending youngsters as much as 16 points, although this increase fades somewhat after the children begin school (Besharov, 1995, 361); and good schooling itself can raise the score of a child from two to four points (Herrnstein and Murray, 1994, 414).

Do IQ Scores Matter in Real Life?

The Bell Curve assumes that a person's success in a job depends on his or her IQ score, but no such link has been proven: former president of Harvard University, Derek Bok, states that "test scores have a modest correlation with first-year grades and no correlation at all with what you do in the rest of your life." People with low IQ scores can perform remarkably well with training and people with high IQ scores (for example members of Mensa) are no more likely to succeed in the top echelons of business or education than are those with ordinary brainpower (Raspberry, 1995).

Studies (and common sense) show that different jobs require different types of intelligences: managers are effective if they are able to sense a variety of tacit messages in the workplace—the ability to operate in complex human situations is vital, yet unrelated to the skills tapped in IQ tests; people who become experts do so because of their education and training far more than their inborn talent (Gardner, 1995b, 66). No one speaks of an "intelligent poet," or an "intelligent chef," or an "intelligent businesswoman," even if that person pulled herself up by her bootstraps

(Hacker, 1995)—their success depends almost entirely on hard work and motivation.[4] A measured "Intelligence" concerns academics infinitely more than business people, who indeed are often suspicious of those with more than one degree. Their opinion of a worker depends on the worker's level of production, as it should.

Nor are highly successful people necessarily highly intelligent. For his book *The Millionaire Mind* (2000), Thomas Stanley found that the average millionaire of the 1300 he surveyed made Bs and Cs in college. These prosperous individuals may not have been very good scholars, but they were creative and practical, chose careers that matched their abilities and were willing to take calculated risks to get ahead. They depicted their success not as a result of their genetic inheritance but as due to their honesty, self-discipline, getting along well with others, having a supportive partner and working hard.

Just as there is little correlation between IQ and job performance, there is little correlation between IQ and class. Couples with high IQ scores usually have children whose IQs revert to a more average level (Hacker, 1995). Harvard University, in admitting the children of its alumni/ae to its campus, often has to set its standards below those for other applicants. (This affirmative action [which parents *don't* complain about], however, may be partly necessary because the children, brought up in a comfortable life style, have seen little need to overexert themselves with study.) Intelligence testing has even helped to undermine a class system. In England and Wales, "eleven-plus exams" for children aged ten or eleven were instituted after the second World War to select the brightest boys and girls to attend the grammar schools which led to university (Blinkhorn, 1994). These exams, which enabled many poor children to gain a good education which they otherwise could not have afforded, helped break down class barriers.

Herrnstein and Murray focus on the critical need in the United States to reduce numbers of groups that have low IQ score averages such as poor black people. What about other groups? Whites in Tennessee and rural Georgia also have significantly lower scores than whites in the Northeast; shouldn't equal efforts address their intellectual drag on the nation? Should these people too be sent to an isolated reservation along with poor blacks? But no one calls national and negative attention to this population's low IQ scores because they are white; if IQ differences are noted, this is done in a sensitive and sympathetic way because, unlike blacks, these poor whites are considered core members of the American nation who have fallen on hard times, not people who are inherently dull (Patterson, 1995).

What about the upward mobility of pretty lower-class women who sleep their way to a good career? (Patterson, 1995). One way out of the poverty ghettos for a woman is with sex appeal. If Herrnstein and Murray really believe that people are poor because they have low IQ scores, why aren't they worried about poor women who obtain good jobs because of sex, or who sleep their way into the intelligent elite and sometimes have children by elite men? Aren't these women in the most direct way possible undermining the nation's intelligence by producing inferior offspring?

To some contributors quoted in *The National Review, The Bell Curve* "confirms ordinary citizens' reasonable intuition that trying to engineer racial equality in the distribution of occupations" goes against nature (Fraser, 1995, 1). To hundreds of scientists, however, the book is fatally flawed by the errors it contains and the false suppositions it makes. If the United States really believes that all Americans should have an equal opportunity to succeed in life, then it must continue to combat the racism and dysfunction that mar the future of so many of its citizens.

Notes

1. Herrnstein and Murray cite data from Owen (1991, 720) but omit his reference from the bibliography; Gould (1995, 11) believes that many of their data are relegated to complicated Appendixes so that their weakness will not be too evident.
2. Ironically, a federal judge in California has recently ruled, as a matter of law, that IQ tests be banned from use in schools to place dull children in classes designed to help them (Glazer, 1995); this was the very reason the tests were created.
3. The multiple intelligences documented by Gardner (1999, 41ff) are linguistic and logical-mathematical both typically valued in school; musical, bodily-kinesthetic and spatial especially notable in the arts; interpersonal and intrapersonal important in social interactions; and naturalist, spiritual and existential which he added to his list recently.
4. I have in my files an article noting that John Ertl who applied for graduate school in psychology at Queen's University in Kingston, Canada, scored "a near-moronic 77" on a standard IQ test; this result did not jibe with his high undergraduate marks so he was admitted anyway (hmmm—do we detect a bias even in psychology against IQ tests?) and he went on to earn a PhD.

Chapter 16

Hijacking A Valid Theory —Fluctuating Asymmetry

Do you want to have lots of healthy children? Then hope that your left ear isn't bigger or smaller than your right; hope that your ankles are the same size and the fingers on either hand the same length. According to Darwinian psychology, people who have appendages with the right and left ones of different sizes are less likely than those with more symmetrical ears or wrists or ankles to have a rosy reproductive potential. Darwinian psychologists equate such measurements with the reproductive success of human beings and with human evolution.

Fluctuating asymmetry (FA) is a new hot topic among Darwinian psychologists, but does it make sense in the many articles that focus on it? FA was explored originally in animals, but has been hijacked by Darwinian psychology to further its cause, no matter how unlikely it is to apply to people as will be discussed in this chapter. A theory gains credibility if it can ride on the coat tails of another that has already been widely accepted. We have seen in Chapter 14 that Philippe Rushton pirated the r-K theory postulated for animals in general and applied it to a single species, human beings, to support his biased ideas about human races. Similarly the theory of sperm competition, which has been studied especially in birds where females often mate with more than one male, has been hijacked by Darwinian psychologists as an inherited behavior pattern also present in human beings. This new application for sperm competition is also untrue, as we have seen in Chapter 11.

Fluctuating asymmetry (FA) is the least known of Darwinian psychology's pirated theories, all of which were hijacked in the past decade or two. To calculate the FA of an animal or a person, right and left measurements are taken for a variety of paired appendages such as ear heights and widths, wrist widths, ankles widths and finger lengths. If the respective right and left measurements are almost the same in an individual, then this superior being is considered to be symmetrical, or to have a low FA value; (the FA value is the value of the difference, ignoring whether the left or the right is the larger). If many of the measurements are different and/or if the differences themselves are large, then the individual is said to have a high FA value which is seen by Darwinian psychologists as a bad thing. FA values are obtained from individuals but often studied in populations for which the FA values are averaged.

What is the rationale for judging that a low FA value is good and a high FA value bad? The genes are the same on the right and left sides of the body, so morphological differences between the two sides are thought to be caused by unequal developmental forces within the body. These are usually caused not by a person's genetic inheritance but by environmental factors, as we shall see.

FA has been investigated in animals at least since 1932. Vertebrates and many invertebrates are built around the principle of bilateral symmetry, meaning that in general the right and left sides of an individual are similar; (this does not hold true for many internal organs, of course, since the heart is on the left side and the appendix on the right, both examples of directional asymmetry which does not interest us here.) Meticulous experts have found that right and left measurements of molar teeth in mice (*Peromyscus*), canine teeth in fossil horses (*Griphippus*) and microchaetae (tiny bristles) in fruit flies (*Drosophila*) differ in size (Van Valen, 1962). What do such differences mean?

In the various non-human animals studied, FA is correlated with some sort of developmental instability in individuals as Anders Møller and John Swaddle describe, giving hundreds of examples in their book *Asymmetry, Developmental Stability, and Evolution* (1997). Rarely asymmetry may be a consequence of genetic abnormality or of inbreeding (p. 116, 118), but usually it is a result of environmental stress caused, during an individual's development, by such factors as malnutrition, extreme temperatures, environmental pollution, loud noise, high population density or parasitic infection (p. 135). A review of FA in humans found that individual traits probably do not have a significant genetic component either (Livshits and Kobyliansky, 1991).

Why is FA of interest to Darwinian psychologists when it is rarely caused by a genetic condition? An individual may have a left appendage different in size than a right one, caused perhaps by being subject to pollution while growing up, but why does this matter when the condition is not genetic and therefore is not passed on to his or her progeny? Darwinian psychologists make a big thing out of "good genes" being associated with a low FA value, but as we shall see, this is speculation.

Inbreeding is the main human example of a high FA caused by heredity. In 1961 residents of Tristan da Cunha, an isolated island in the south Atlantic Ocean, were evacuated to Britain when a volcano eruption threatened their homeland. They were healthy but the subject of great biological interest because of inbreeding—they were descended from a founding population of only thirteen people. Researchers found that their right and left upper canine teeth were often of different sizes, indicating fluctuating asymmetry, and concluded that this was a negative measure of population fitness (Bailit et al., 1970). As another example, members of an equally healthy community of Mennonites living in Mexico also had a high FA because they were highly inbred (Livshits and Kobyliansky, 1991, 458).

We can compare these groups with another that was not inbred but suffered great environmental stress. This was the Kwaio people from the island of Malaita in the Solomon Islands where conditions are so adverse that there has been no thought of trying to woo Western tourists. The island has rugged terrain, few roads, 185 inches of rain a year, settlements from 300 to 900 metres above sea level and night temperatures as low as seven degrees C. Researcher H.L. Bailit was horrified at the islanders' ill health when he visited the island in 1966 (Bailit et al., 1970). Because their diet consisted largely of sweet potatoes which lack protein, most of the Kwaio people suffered from such ailments as upper respiratory infections, malaria, yaws and parasites. Bailit made molds of the teeth of 400 individuals which also showed differences in the size of right and left comparable teeth, indicating a high degree of fluctuating asymmetry. The researchers concluded that the high FA value was related to the poor level of health and nutrition in the population; there was little correlation between the state of health of people related to each other, indicating that the heritability of FA was low.

Most people in the Western world are neither inbred nor have they been subject to great environmental stress. An exception are children with fetal alcohol effect (FAE) or the more serious fetal alcohol syndrome (FAS) born to some women who drank alcohol during their pregnancies. They exhibit FA in the form of asymmetrical teeth or other asymmetries (sometimes called phenodeviants) (Møller and Swaddle, 1997, 142). For these people FA is certainly correlated with lack of fitness, given the difficult life they face because of their disability.

Research indicates that FA values in Western people in general are somewhat variable. They change to some extent in healthy growing boys and girls: when the FA values of large numbers of youngsters of different ages were calculated, they decreased both absolutely and relatively until age ten, increased during puberty, and decreased again after age fifteen at least to age eighteen, the oldest age group measured (Wilson and Manning, 1996). Individual men can have short-term (within twenty-four hours) changes in the asymmetry of their soft tissues, correlated apparently with their hormones (Manning et al., 2002). And for 965 twenty-six-year-old men and women, there was no association between FA values and an array of health measures including blood pressure, blood cholesterol, cardiorespiratory fitness and periodontal disease (Milne et al., 2003).

A Case Study

What about the notion that symmetrical people (with low FA values) have on average a better reproductive future than other people? Steven Gangestad and Randy Thornhill (1997) decided to study "cheating" on their partners (called by the more scientific-sounding name of EPCs by the authors, for extra-pair copulations) in college men and women to elucidate this possible evolutionary strategy during human evolution. We have already seen in Chapter 10 that males and females "cheating" on their spouse was proposed to explain why and how the two sexes maximize their chances of producing superior progeny. (This theory supersedes the widespread earlier theory originating with Darwin that females, interested in the quality of a partner, are choosy about whom they mate with compared to males who opt for quantity and copulate with as many females as possible.)

In their article "The evolutionary psychology of extrapair sex: The role of fluctuating asymmetry," Gangestad and Thornhill (1997) hypothesize that although short-term mating ("cheating") outside a long-term relationship has costs (e.g., it may destroy or weaken the long-term relationship, it may trigger jealous violence, or it may increase the spread of sexually-transmitted diseases), it also has benefits. The Darwinian basis of cheating on one's partner seems to be as follows: Partnerships have developed during the evolution of our ancestors because they are the most effective method of raising healthy children. Sex within the partnership helps to keep the relationship bond strong. Yet men and women are often not satisfied with remaining faithful to their partner. According to the authors' Darwinian reproductive theory, men mate with as many women as possible while women, too, may mate with a number of men; the women, however, tend to choose superior men in the hope of securing sperm with "better" genes than those of her partner to fertilize her eggs. These will develop into children she will raise with her partner even though, unknown to him, he is not the father. The many people nowadays who have extramarital affairs may think they do so because it is exciting and fun, but this does not invalidate the hypothesis.

To determine whether there was a correlation between "cheating" on their partner and the FA values of young people, Gangestad and Thornhill studied 203 heterosexual romantic couples who had been together for at least one month and at least one of whom was taking a university psychology course (for which he or she received credit for taking part in this research). The average age of the men was twenty-one years (range seventeen to forty years) and of the women twenty years (range seventeen to thirty-nine years). Some of the subjects had children with the current or previous partner(s), but these children were not part of the study (although in reality they were the only tangible results of reproductive success since most of the respondents were young adults). Each person was asked to fill out a questionnaire giving information about themselves and their sex lives, and their photographs were taken so that judges could tabulate their physical attractiveness. (The inference in the study is that symmetrical people are attractive people, but surely ugly people can be symmetrical, too!)

Each person's asymmetry (and probably no person is completely symmetrical for all these measurements) was calculated by measuring seven parts of their anatomy on each side: foot width, ankle width, hand width, wrist width, elbow width, ear length and ear width. (In a second session, the index and fifth finger lengths were also included). The difference between each pair of measurements was divided by the average measurement and then these values were summed across all characters to obtain the person's total FA value.

The authors predicted, and found to be true from their research results, that the most symmetrical men (with a low FA) were most likely to have cheated on their partners and have affairs, that the women who cheated were more likely to cheat with these symmetrical men than with men with a higher FA, and that symmetrical men had the greatest number of affairs outside their partnership. They found that the physical attractiveness of men (but not of women) was also correlated with these EPCs.

The authors' results from the measurements, the attractiveness ratings, and the questionnaires are set out in seven complex tables which include 250 numbers and 80 statistical tests of significance. These extensive data seem to give the research solid authenticity, but in fact the theory and methodology of the research have many problems which fatally undermine the results. What are these problems? Let's consider two main aspects of this research: the evolutionary connection between the students and their nomadic forebears many thousands of years ago, and the concept of "good genes."

Harvard Jo as Pleistocene Pat?

This case study considers the question of cheating on their partners and body asymmetry in modern young men and women, and the light these factors shed on the evolution of human beings. What sort of a question is this posed by Gangestad and Thornhill? If characteristics are claimed to be important in a species' evolution, they must be shown to have benefited the reproductive success of individuals of that species. How can we know which individuals will be successful by this measure when the people being studied are mostly college students? None of them has finished his or her child-bearing years and most haven't even begun them. At any university a great number of copulations take place, but the number of children produced from these is minimal, given that most couples use birth control or opt for abortion if birth control fails. Gangestad and Thornhill have asked a question that cannot be answered.

Actually, perhaps the question could be answered, but only if the subjects in the experiment were over fifty years of age (usually beyond child-bearing), an age group difficult to target compared to students under a professor's control. These older individuals might not have an accurate memory of their youth and their choice of young lovers, but at least the researchers would know how many children each person had produced, the essential criterion for evolutionary success.

Behind Darwinian psychology is the premise that human social behavior evolved in prehistoric times over many thousands of years, and that what may seem like random actions nowadays arise from past adaptations. Gangestad and Thornhill chose to study extra-pair sex because (p. 70) "EPCs in college relationships can bring about many of the same disruptive consequences that extrapair sex in marriages brings about. Hence, EPCs in student relationships may shed light on evolutionary hypotheses." However, college romances do not emulate marriage as the authors concede (p. 70); they used students because they were convenient and because cheating outside of their romantic partnerships was not uncommon. We are asked to compare marriage, which usually has dependent children, with a relationship of as little as one month by mostly young students exploring new relationships which are usually short-term, serial, almost never produce children, and are seldom concerned with the daily necessity of earning a living/procuring food and shelter.

Does this make any sense at all? Why do they assume our ancestors even lived in marriages? We have seen that polygamy is present in most human cultures, and that female chimpanzees and bonobos, the species which human beings most resemble, would think a marriage relationship ridiculous. When they are in heat, they mate raucously with as many males as possible.

What are other problems with the authors' hypothesis?

a) Modern young women often have a number of lovers before they settle down to raise a family, if indeed they ever do, so there isn't any reason for them to assess their boyfriends as father material. Surely their choices of bedfellows are more likely to be a school mate or a media star look-alike, a professional athlete or a professor? Why not choose a comedian or a big-man-on-campus who is touted as a great catch? Or why not avoid handsome men who often seem too smooth to be trusted? Barb may bed Bob because he has a great sense of humor, then Bert because they belong to the same bird-watching group, then Ben because he helps her with her art history course. She doesn't care what they look like. She would howl with laughter if she were told that one of her choices (how does one decide which man counts in the theory when they are so different?) was subconsciously chosen as a potentially good father. Our ancestors didn't have birth control, so they might have had children by any of their lovers. And there weren't that many men to choose from, given the small populations of foraging human groups.

b) Many studies report that men tend to choose women who are physically attractive while women are inclined to select partners who have resources (e.g., money or class in Western history, hunting skills in various societies studied by anthropologists) (Wiederman and Allgeier 1992). Gangestad himself (1993, 206) states that "women probably evolved to prefer mates who, all else being equal, possess what we might refer to as investment potential." Yet in this case study the women did not behave according to Darwinian expectations: they did not seek out men from rich families or with good earning potential with whom to have EPC sex. Therefore behavior "ingrained" in our species from prehistoric times is *not* necessarily reflected in current behavior as the authors' hypothesis implies. Nor need the cheating behavior of the students be related to behavior among our prehistoric ancestors.

c) A person's high FA is said to be related either to inbreeding or to a stressful environmental upbringing. But surely few university students, usually middle-class, are either inbred or have been stressed environmentally while growing up in anything like the way the Kwaio were on their desperate little island. FA seems like a factor that would vary little among the students. Even if a student did have a high FA for some reason, what this really matter to a mate? One might only admire them for overcoming a disadvantaged childhood.

d) The number of students who were seventeen and eighteen in the study of cheating lovers did not have as stable an FA as they would have had if older, nor perhaps did those older than eighteen, given that no such individuals were analyzed in the study mentioned above (Wilson and Manning, 1996). Because of this, Gangestad and Thornhill's 1997 data are tainted to some unknown extent.

e) The experimental data say nothing about whether the man a woman cheats with has a lower FA than her stable partner although the authors note, without evidence, that "Men most willing to invest in a mateship…may be those less able to achieve short-term matings" (p. 73). They may be or they may not be. In the absence of any evidence, their data have no relevance for their thesis that women cheat on their partners in order to improve the genetic inheritance of their children.

f) The authors hypothesize that cheating on one's mate has been an important part of human evolution. However, they give no evidence that modern men who cheat on their partners have more offspring than other men, which is the test of an evolutionary successful reproductive strategy. It is assumed in the article (since there are presumed evolutionary benefits) that men who cheat on relationships and have sex with more women than other men will also have more offspring. However, this is impossible to assess since the reproductive future of most of these young adults is ahead of them. It may be that philanderers are more inclined to use contraception than are other men so that their behavior has less chance of detection. If they do have more children as a result of a "roving eye," they are perhaps poor fathers, as this behavioral trait may disadvantage their offspring.

g) People often lie when questioned about their sex lives, as we have seen earlier.

"Good Genes"

Most parents would like to produce children with "good genes." What does this mean? Gangestad and Thornhill tell us that people with symmetrical body parts have good genes, or at least genes that are better than those who have more asymmetrical appendages. But as we have seen above, high levels of FA are correlated with extremely stressful environmental conditions but only rarely with genetics. Why do Darwinian psychologists claim that "good genes" are connected to FA? Laura Betzig, editor of *Human Nature: A Critical Reader* (1997), states that "good genes" reside in those who look healthy—"colorful, energetic, symmetrical" (p. 4). She writes that "men with 'good genes' better resist environmental stress. They grow more regular; and they grow larger" (p. 5). The "good genes" are presumed to make a person resistant to pathogens because pathogen resistance and lack of mildly harmful new genes are said to be marked by an individual's FA. However, this has never been shown to be true and would be almost impossible to prove experimentally.

Could good genes be proven to be related to FA? Why not? One need only pinpoint people who have these genes and then measure the symmetry of their appendages. The rub, of course, is that no one knows what these "good genes" are. They are defined by Helena Cronin (1991, 193-5) as those occurring in individuals with a robust constitution, since this may be the only external evidence of genotype that a prospective mate can monitor. More broadly, she states that "good genes" may also include other genetic attributes that attract a mating partner.

Even though genetic factors are an unimportant feature of FA, and even though no one can define the actual genes that make up the genotype "good genes," readers are expected to assume on faith in this research project (and in many others) that "good genes" are correlated with FA. Needless to say, there are a number of problems with this:

a) Measurement differences between right and left appendages are typically so small that people are unaware of them; Betzig (1997, 5) notes that they can be as little as 0.1 or .01 mm. If people don't realize they exist, how can FA affect social behavior? One research team believes it is because FA and facial attractiveness (rated by photographs) are correlated, at least in men (Gangestad et al., 1994). Why not then use facial attractiveness as the criterion for comparison? Is it because this is seen as too subjective, while FA produces a number which seems more scientific?

b) Judging from the earlier studies of FA mentioned above, the teeth are the best measure of asymmetry. If FA was useful in evolution because it alerted possible mates about an individual's disabilities, why would the teeth be targeted instead of some other more visible body part? Anyone planning to marry was and is unlikely to examine the teeth of his or her prospective spouse to check for inbreeding.

c) Birth order, unrelated to inheritance, which also affects FA has not been taken into account in FA Darwinian psychological research. Men with older brothers are more likely than other men to have a high FA value (Lalumière et al., 1999).

d) People who look healthy and therefore presumably possess the enigmatic "good genes" may, in fact, be carriers of genes involved with ailments such as juvenile diabetes, Huntington's disease, hemophilia, Tay-Sachs disease, sickle-cell anemia or cystic fibrosis. Some of their genes may be very bad indeed.

e) People who have a noticeably asymmetric appendage may look healthy and robust and to most eyes a good catch as a mate: one scientist I know has one ear noticeably larger than the other, but also an excellent job and a rosy future. Is it possible his ears will seal his fate? Is this why some men grow long hair?

f) People may have asymmetry for reasons unconnected to "good genes." Lesbians, for example, are said to have right index fingers (often used for FA measurements) shorter than their right ring finger (Williams et al., 2000). Hard-hitting players of racquet sports such as tennis, badminton and squash and manual workers such as carpenters have a dominant arm larger than the one they use less (Dagg and Griffin, 1998). Such people have a higher FA value than comparable nonathletic/ nonmanual workers, so they would be categorized as not having especially "good genes" because of their asymmetrical muscular development. By any other measure, such a person would be considered particularly fit and healthy.[1]

g) Betzig (1997, 5) states that those with "good genes" and a low FA tend to be larger than those without. This is perplexing. In the past, poor nutrition prevented people from reaching their potential full height. How would Pleistocene women know if a small man, a potential mate, had been malnourished as a child or if he was small because he lacked "good genes?" Neanderthal people were larger than ourselves, but can we assume they couldn't have had "good genes" because they became extinct? However, they did exist for one hundred thousand years. The stature of pygmy peoples would surely also confound the "increased size" attribute since their small size is adaptive to their environment.

h) "Good genes" have been cited as responsible for resistance to pathogens and environmental stress, for body symmetry, and for increased size. Could one genotype (="good genes") simultaneously govern these three characteristics? We have no idea. It certainly has not been proven to be so.

i) Researchers may bias their results to keep them in line with their expectations. For example, one study found that in Dominica children growing up with stepparents had lower body weights than those living with biological parents (Flinn et al., 1999). This was their major conclusion which backed the hypothesis that biological parents are more willing than stepparents to care for their children as discussed in Chapter 2. However, the article also reported that the stepchildren had a lower FA than other children, which was completely unanticipated. The authors did not admit that this undercut their results, but only stated: "Why stepchildren had significantly lower FA than others warrants further investigation."

j) Different studies measure the FA of individuals using different appendages (some or most of ears, wrists, ankles, hands, arms, elbows, fingers, calves, finger ridges etc), so that it is often impossible to compare results across studies.

k) People from different regions around the world have different values for FA; these are not taken into consideration in American studies which include people of these cultures (Dittmar, 1998; Gangestad and Thornhill, 1997).

l) Facial attractiveness is *not* related to physical health and "good genes," at least in the long term (Kalick et al., 1998). Researchers collected photos of 164 young men and of 169 young women, all born between 1920 and 1929, which thirty-two male and female raters judged for attractiveness. The researchers then delved into the health history of each subject and found that there was no correlation of their attractiveness with their health either at the time the photos were taken or subsequently. The raters tended to think that the people with the most attractive faces *were* the healthiest, but this was not the case; one might even conclude that a person's face could be a *false* representation of his or her health and suitability as a mate. The researchers also found that attractiveness was not related to the number of children born by the subjects.

The "best" individual plants and animals (judging by such things as strength, reproductive potential, longevity etc) are produced by parents who have dissimilar genotypes. Such outbreeding or heterosis has produced famous farm crops (hybrid corn) and superior domestic animals. The people who are likely to have not only "good genes" but "best genes" are those with mixed race parents. It is strange that Darwinian psychologists do not champion this well-known scientific truth or the brown-skinned people who sometimes personify it.

Human social behavior is virtually impossible to research. People can't be manipulated like mice and observed as if what they do is entirely mediated by their genes. Although babies are pure biology when they are born, as they grow up they are influenced to their very core by their culture and their experiences. Research such as that of Gangestad and Thornhill is bound to fail even if it were not riddled with false assumptions and faulty data, as theirs is. Fluctuating asymmetry is an interesting phenomenon to a few zoologists, but it has little to say to social scientists.

Note

1. Matthew Griffin and I (1998) proved this by measuring the right and left wrist widths of sixty-nine people, thirty of whom were serious, long-term tennis players or manual workers. The wrist measurements on their dominant side were statistically "highly significantly" larger than their other wrist. It is of political interest that although our results show that past research could have been inaccurate because of this unconsidered "exercise asymmetry," two Darwinian psychological journals refused to publish our short paper even though it would have allowed future researchers to collect more accurate data by taking our findings into consideration.

Chapter 17

Evolution By Crafty, Curvy Women And Their Body Parts?

Does she lie about her baby? Does she have a wasp waist? Is one breast larger than the other? Are her two ankles symmetrical? Darwinian psychologists are obsessed with women as objects. All of these questions fascinate scores of university researchers who spend years trying to answer them. Yet there is no evidence—how could there be?—that our foraging ancestors and evolutionary forces cared about such things.

Many Darwinian psychologists aren't much interested in how people actually behave in real life situations. Instead, they dream up an evolutionary hypothesis, then dredge up evidence using models or university students to show that it is true and rush into print. Some use incorrect assumptions and inaccurate data to prove their points, taking advantage of the reality that although a behavior cannot be *proved* to be genetic, the possibility cannot be *disproved* either. In any case it doesn't much matter if their hypothesis is disproved, because other researchers will gain papers and credit by demonstrating this, citing the original researchers as they do so. This busywork keeps hundreds of professors and graduate students cheerfully engaged with research published by sympathetic journals and presses. We have from their perspective a win/win/win situation: with each published paper or book professors add to their curriculum vitae and their likelihood of career advancement, graduate students obtain higher degrees that provide an entrée to the comfortable professoriate, and presses make money producing large numbers of publications that appeal to the lay public.

This chapter will consider three recent hot topics of research: Do children usually look like their fathers? Do all men prefer sexy women with wasp waists? Does women's reproduction depend on their sexy body parts? It will end by mentioning briefly some other may/might weasel studies that are published but reach no conclusion.

Do Most Children Resemble their Fathers?

In 1995, Nicholas Christenfeld and Emily Hill announced that year-old infants had evolved to resemble their fathers more than their mothers, following up several earlier papers on the subject (Daly and Wilson 1982; Finegan and Mackenzie, 1990; Regalski and Gaulin, 1993; Pagel, 1997). This finding aroused renewed interest in both the scientific and the popular press, and undoubtedly controversy in the homes of many young children. Scientists remained puzzled because a baby's assortment of genes should determine who he or she looks like, and these genes are equally from either parent. The hypothesis behind this announcement was that if babies resemble their fathers, the fathers will be more likely to believe that the mother has not cheated on them with another man and therefore will be more willing to help raise the child.

Soon two Belgian psychologists organized an experiment to try to replicate the research (Brédart and French, 1999). They asked 180 undergraduate students (what would research professors do without their captive undergraduates?) to match photographs belonging to twenty-eight Caucasian families. Each family had produced five photos for the researchers—of the mother, the father, and three of the same child when one, three and five years of age. In a number of randomized tests, the students were asked to match a child's photo to its mother who was one of three women, or to its father who was one of three men. The students did not match the children to the father more frequently than to the mother (and indeed more than half the time had the children with the wrong parent), so their conclusion did not support that of the earlier report. Children *don't* especially resemble their fathers.

These researchers developed a new hypothesis to explain their results which repudiated the former one. They argue that if children resemble their father closely enough that he knows they are his, he will also know if they are *not* his. In that case he might refuse to help raise them which would be counterproductive for the mother and the child. This, however, is odd because children may resemble their mother whether or not she has cheated, or they may resemble neither parent. What we have here is an attempt to rescue a hypothesis by yet another explanation which is even more unlikely.

The following year, other researchers reported that it didn't necessarily matter if a baby didn't look like his or her father. The mother could overcome this problem by oohing and aahing over the newborn while assuring the father (and his relatives) that the baby looked just like him (McLain et al., 2000). This is what interviewers found new mothers did when they questioned them in the hospital, even though non-related judges matched photographs of the baby more often to the mother than to the father. The authors state that the mothers' comments "may be an evolved or conditioned response to assure domestic fathers of their paternity." Or they may not. Probably many mothers comment that their baby resembles the father realizing that he will be feeling left out by the female-focused process of childbirth. This common-sense notion is perhaps unacceptable to Darwinian psychologists because it emphasizes a woman's intelligence and empathy rather than her evolved genetic inheritance. In any case, not to worry. The six papers focusing on the important subject of whether children usually resemble their fathers produced citations for the resumes of thirteen researchers which will improve their chances of getting grants and advancing in the academic world.

And there is hope in the future. If this latest Darwinian psychological hypothesis is disconfirmed, the ingenuity of researchers will once again be called into play. Perhaps there is a gene responsible for rationalization which attracts its possessors to the field of Darwinian psychology?

Do All Men Prefer Women with Wasp Waists?

Let's consider the evolution in Darwinian psychology of a hypothesis about the sexy shape of women. Devendra Singh (1993a,b) from Texas had the bright idea of researching men's special interest in women with hourglass figures such as Marilyn Munroe. He popularized the Waist-to-Hip Ratio (WHR) which is the circumference measurement of a woman's waist divided by the circumference measurement of her hips, so that a woman with hips larger than her waist has a lower ratio than one whose waist and hips are the same size (ratio value of 1). Marilyn Monroe had a WHR of 0.7. The great apes have neither discernible waists nor buttocks, so this is a new silhouette of primate anatomy. Singh noted that healthy girls at puberty deposit more fat on their buttocks and hips than around the waist, giving women a curvy, sexy body and a low WHR value. By contrast, women with tubular bodies suffer disproportionately from infertility because of hormone disorders and from the risk of various diseases such as adult-onset diabetes. "The WHR is therefore an accurate indicator of health status and fertility, and male preference for low-WHR females is considered to be one of the best-supported examples of a sexually selected adaptation for assessing mate quality" (Yu and Shepard, 1998).

Fig 17.1 Schematic Figures of Women with Varying Waist-to-Hip Ratios (WHR)

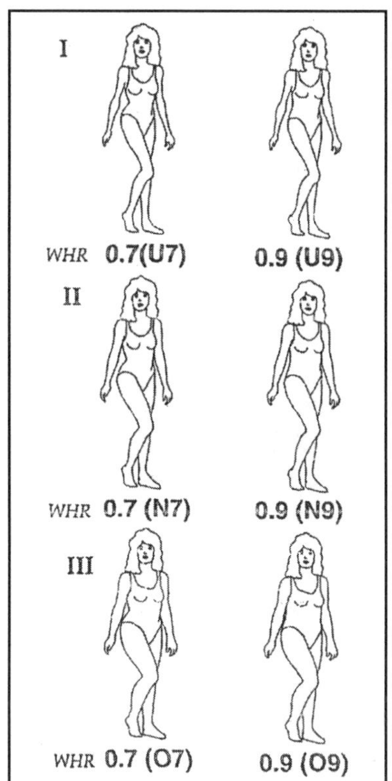

Used in many WHR studies

U = underweight

N = normal weight

O = overweight

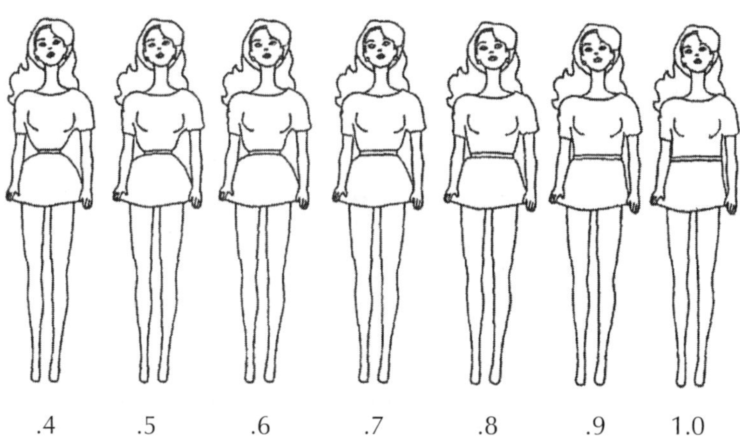

Source: Personality and Individual Differences 30, Marlowe and Wetsman, Preferred waist-to-hip ratio and ecology, pp. 481-489, 2004

Singh's 1995 research involved giving male college students a course assignment of studying line drawings of female figures with two types of body shapes in which the waist was much smaller (WHR of 0.7) and nearly as big as the hips (WHR of 0.9). He also asked them to rate three types of breasts—each equal in size, one slightly larger than the other, and one larger yet than the other. The men, after deliberation, decided that women most willing to engage in short- and long-term relationships were those with a low WHR and symmetrical breasts. The weak conclusion of the research was that "WHR and breast asymmetry may signal different aspects of overall female mate quality." Or they may not. The statement simply rephrases the original question. The men perceived all the figures of women as being equal in reproductive capability, but this fact is glossed over and not included in the abstract.

Researchers jumped on this new sexy shape index with glee, incorporating WHR into many studies in their effort to show that it was "culturally invariant," meaning that men around the world agree that low WHR women were/are, based on reproduction and evolution, the best. Thornhill and Grammer (1999) reported proudly that its value held true for thirty Austrians and thirty Americans. Because the Americans comprised five hispanic, three oriental and three Amerindian young men who shared the views of the nineteen caucasians, they felt that it held true across cultures as well (although three men isn't very many from which to generalize for a whole society), ignoring the fact that all the Americans were subject to American culture.

However, there was a problem. Why were Darwinian psychologists testing men who live in a Western culture, who watch endless movies and television portraying stylized women? Why not ask men who live in preliterate societies similar to the ones in which human beings evolved? A survey of anthropological literature showed that Hottentot women actually did fit their hypothesis—in times of famine they had greatly enlarged stores of fat in their hips (steatopygia) which lowered their WHR—but their unusual shape wasn't what Darwinian psychologists had in mind. Instead, they surveyed a few "primitive" men from other groups.

Seventy men of the Hadza tribe of Tanzania who looked at depictions of a variety of women's figures in two studies chose the shape of their preferred mates not as women with a curvy shape, but those who were big and tubular and presumably could work hard (Wetsman and Marlowe, 1999; Marlowe and Wetsman, 2001). Isolated men of the Matsigenka population in Peru who practise slash and burn agriculture agreed with them (Yu and Shepard, 1998). One respondent from an isolated Peruvian village reported that the figure of an overweight women with a tubular shape was healthy, while an overweight woman with a smaller waist "was skinny in the waist" and perhaps suffering from diarrhea. To him, all the thinner women were unhealthy if not "almost dead"—to be fat is valued in preliterate societies where food is often limited. When men from this group who had moved away from their villages and lived a more Western lifestyle were tested, their preference for women more closely approached that of Western men. (All of these "primitive" men must have been bemused by the research of which they were a part.)

That men in nomadic and semi-nomadic groups prefer tubular-shaped large women invalidates the WHR hypothesis that because women with sexy bodies are healthy and fertile, men's behavior evolved to choose them as mates. So now a new premise has evolved: women's shapes in small traditional communities are perhaps not a priority: kin rules govern mate choice to a large extent and every one knows everyone else anyway, including "direct information about mate quality, such as age and history of illness" (Yu and Shepard, 1998).

Physical features may be important not necessarily in preliterate societies but in modern Western society where strangers meet frequently and sexy bodies are the best way for men to judge a woman as a possible mate. One researcher believes that this is what WHR is for: to judge a woman's potential for sex and to see if she is pregnant from a distance (Hassebrauck, 1998) because when a man comes closer he will be far more interested in her face. But then, of course, he will be bemused because WHR is not correlated with facial attractiveness (Thornhill and Grammer, 1999) and, as we saw in the last chapter, facial attractiveness is not correlated with physical health (Kalick et al., 1998). So now we have an evolutionary hypothesis that doesn't apply to societies most like our ancestors', but may apply in modern industrial nations.

A final blow to the original WHR hypothesis is that even Western men don't necessarily prefer women with hourglass figures. For one project, waist and hip measurements were calculated for 577 centerfold "bunnies" from *Playboy*, a hugely successful magazine that reflects in its pages the type of women contemporary men like to look at (Voracek and Fisher, 2002). The gradual trend from 1953 to 2001 showed that early on men preferred the body type of Marilyn Monroe but that currently they favor women with smaller breasts, thicker waists and thinner hips.

In summary, over the ten years since a hypothesis (about women's WHR and male preference) was postulated, it has been tested in various studies and found wanting, and now will be discarded. Had the original hypothesis been tested in the same various ways *before* publication, it would have never seen print. But never mind: the public has been titillated by widespread media reports and many researchers have had articles published on the subject which will be cited and for which they will be rewarded in academia. It is a win-win situation, except for science.

But wait. It seems that the hypothesis, even though disproven, has *not* been discarded by Darwinian psychologists. In their recent books both Geoffrey Miller in *The Mating Mind* (2000, 248) and Eric Gander (2003, 178) in *On Our Minds* refer to the waist-to-hip hypothesis as if it is still valid. Gander also ignores the present-day reality that many fertile young women and mothers are tubular and obese, whereas many older women retain their shapely figures.

Sexy Body Parts

Unfortunately, women's waists and hips aren't the only body parts that intrigue scientists such as the seven men involved in WHR studies whose work is reported above. The accepted Darwinian psychological hypothesis is that attractive women with symmetrical body parts will attract most men and produce more children on average than other women. Scores of research experiments have been based on women's body parts to prove this thesis, but to what effect?

As an example of men dedicated to women's body parts, Randy Thornhill (author of the misbegotten book on rape discussed in Chapter 9) and Karl Grammer (1999) solicited, at a cost of $50 each, ninety-two caucasian women to pose nude for photographs of their faces, of their fronts with their faces covered, and of their backs. These photographs, reminiscent of pornography, were then scrutinized by the thirty American and thirty Austrian men mentioned above who judged which images were the most attractive. The authors arrive at the mundane conclusion that women's bodies are shaped by estrogen at puberty and also "probably by developmental adaptations for symmetry" (although there is no evidence given to support this suggestion). They conclude that if a woman looks good she's probably healthy, although they state this fact more pedantically: "Thus women's physical attractiveness in face and body honestly signals hormonal and perhaps developmental health."[1]

In another experiment, researchers videotaped twenty-five women dressed in grey leotards standing with their feet far apart (Tovée et al., 2000). They measured seven of the women's appendages (feet, ankles, wrists, hands, elbows, ear lengths, ear widths) for asymmetry, then changed the appearance of each body with a software computer program to make it completely symmetrical so that this could be compared with the original image (since all people are asymmetrical to some extent). After the women's faces on each image had been masked out, sixty male and female students compared each body's symmetrical and asymmetrical images to see which they preferred. They couldn't tell them apart. A second experiment using only male observers found that they liked the symmetrical bodies slightly better (choosing them eleven out of twenty times which is hardly a striking preference). The researchers conclude, in any case, that the size of a woman's body and its shape takes precedence over its symmetry when a man evaluates it.

Such experiments are a waste of time and money for a number of reasons. First and most importantly, it is silly to assume that a picture of a woman or a number calculated from measurements of her appendages (FA value) is the same as the woman herself. (Mail order brides do exist, but usually because men are too shy or inept to find a woman in their own social circle.) Research studies make no mention of personality. Does it not occur to these earnest "scientists" that some contemporary women are fun to be with, some are competitive, some are witty, some are excellent cooks? (or, in prehistoric times during which human beings evolved, that some females were fun, some competitive, some witty, some superior skinners of antelope?)

In his book *The Mating Mind*, Geoffrey Miller (2000, 355) notes that on average couples (no matter how symmetrically perfect) exchange a million words before they conceive a child together; during this oral phase of their relationship much can go wrong: "Personalities clash. Arguments go unresolved. Incompatibilities arise. Jokes fall flat. Boredom ensues." Yet neither what people talk about nor how they act is considered important in the abundant research on mate choice, although these attributes are usually what inspire a man to marry. One article does caution that research subjects make judgments about "pen-and-paper people" that may not be representative of potential mates in the "real world" (surely an understatement) (Weiderman and Dubois, 1998) and another does worry that nonphysical factors are important but ignored in mate-choice research, but few Darwinian psychologists pay attention (Kniffin et al., 2004).

Second, "best" mates are said to be symmetrical individuals (Gangestad and Thornhill, 1997). However, there is no body of research proving that symmetrical women (or men) have more children, and no evidence that this was so in prehistoric times. The research subjects who make up the vast majority of participants in these studies are college students who haven't even begun having children, so how could there be? Indeed in one experiment respondents reported that they preferred images of human faces that were somewhat *asymmetrical* (Perrett et al., 1999). Many people find plain faces interesting and not the visage showcase "where harmful mutations show themselves most readily as unusual proportions and asymmetries" (Miller, 2000, 249). Any number of women who seem to observers to be asymmetrical, unattractive and even unhealthy are still happily married and producing children, the criterion of evolutionary success. By contrast, attractive women sometimes choose to become "trophy wives" by marrying upwardly mobile men. Such middle and upper class families usually have few children, so these "best" women may pass on *fewer* genes than other women.

Third, the assumption has been that symmetrical people are healthier than other people which is why they should make a superior spouse. However, there has been no association found between people's symmetry (FA value) and their health, either past, present or future (Rhodes et al., 2001).

Fourth, the assumption is that ogling somehow equates with child production. One researcher found that seventy college students were especially interested in studying the appearance of attractive women and men (e.g., they looked sooner and longer at computerized pictures of their faces and body parts). These attractive images were of youthful, healthy and sexually mature women, or of men displaying status and dominance (Hassebrauck, 1998). Is this information useful for human evolution? Does it show that the male and female voyeurs in the study will mate with such target people and have a more than usual number of children with them? Of course not. We know what some people like to look at but not whom, if any, they will have children with.

To carry this assumption further, scores of women may sleep with a man, but this does not mean they expect to or will have children with him. Certainly not nowadays. In the case study of the last chapter 406 students and lovers of students were having sex, but probably no children were born because of this. In prehistoric times, too, when women produced a child only every four years, they must have copulated hundreds of times between each mating that produced a child.

As I was reading these strange research papers I began to wonder who could have funded them. Would granting agencies be happy with the end products? I found, perhaps not surprisingly, that about two-thirds of the papers acknowledged no funding at all for carrying out the research. The others thanked sources such as Unilever Research; Belgian, American and Australian granting agencies; several universities; and a NATO fellowship provided by the Royal Society, London.

May/Might Weasel Studies

The recent Darwinian psychological literature is full of suggestions for adaptations based on evolution—may/might weasel studies. The authors don't know if their results mean anything and neither do we. As the following goofy examples indicate, they certainly seem unlikely and either defy, or are, common sense:

- Female vervet monkeys prefer to play with a doll and a pot while their male counterparts opt for a ball and a toy car (Alexander and Hines, 2002). A picture book and a stuffed dog attract both sexes equally. Although the evolutionary link between people and these monkeys was broken perhaps fifty million years ago, the authors note that these "preferences may contribute to present day sexually dimorphic toy preferences in children." (What can one say?)
- Postpartum depression may be an adaptation evolved so that afflicted mothers will know to reduce care of their children and it "may help them negotiate greater levels of investment from others" (Hagen, 1999). (It also sometimes results in death for women and their babies! The author Edward Hagen may not have read Voltaire's *Candide*, but he shares his Panglossian optimism to identify good in the suffering of others.)
- Women don't tell others their age "as putative deception in mate search tactics" (Pawlowski and Dunbar, 1999). (In fact, of course, as we all know, sometimes they do and sometimes they don't. When and how they do or don't varies historically and in different cultures depending, among other things, on whether there is a cultural bias toward youth and fertility or toward age and wisdom.)
- When women look at slides of attractive women their face muscles contract in a threat or defensive display "as they have encountered a high-status competitor that possibly threatens their reproductive success and social status" (Hazlett and Hoehn-Saric, 2000). (Yeah, right. In our ancestors' small nomadic societies, women saw mostly the same few women, sometimes their relatives, every day. Would they really have evolved special muscle contractions because of this?)
- Many women around the time of ovulation prefer men with more masculine faces (Penton-Voak and Perrett, 2000), although British and Japanese women in general apparently prefer men with more "feminized" faces (Johnston et al., 2001). (This is science? Can any rational person take such evolutionary nonsense seriously?)

Virtually all our female ancestors in prehistoric times had children, whereas reproduction for males was more chancy—some could have had many children (spreading their genotype widely) but others none. Why, then, don't Darwinian psychologists focus on men rather than on women? Why not research what characteristics make one man a more successful sire than another? Is it a sexual bias because most of the researchers are male?

In summary, virtually all of the current Darwinian psychological research based on whom one chooses as a mate and which mates will have the most children is nonsense. Undergraduate students can be badgered by any number of professors to take part in research projects, but since they haven't yet reproduced and their future number of children is unknown, both professors and students are wasting their time.

Note

1. The question of hormones is discomfiting for the authors because the female hormone estrogen, which is presumed to make women feminine and attractive, is also strongly implicated in some female cancers, "suggesting that it interferes with homeostasis [FA] of the body." As well, some metabolites of estrogen may be toxic. The authors counter these negative suggestions with the curious logic that the genes correlated with the hormones may be correlated with illness and death, but they are still somehow "good genes"; because of the "good genes" attractive women have, their very beauty advertizes the fact that they are healthy enough to overcome any toxic effect of estrogen.

Chapter 18

Conclusions

Darwinian psychologists are gung ho for dreaming up human adaptations. No matter on what social behavior they focus, they can think up an evolutionary reason for why it evolved. Not only that, but they urge researchers from a variety of disciplines to help them in their exciting quest to unravel the mysteries of human nature: "Tube snaking in the wave of scientific revolution is fun. It is my profound hope that a few clever readers will come in and swim" (Betzig, 1997, xiv). Anthropologists, sociologists, philosophers, political scientists, animal biologists and physicists have all joined the happy band churning out books and articles on sociobiological themes. Unfortunately, scientists who focus on a topic of behavior and present counter arguments *against* Darwinian psychology are not welcome (as I was unwelcome because of my research showing that infanticide by male lions is not an evolutionary strategy [Chapter 1]).

Geneticists are notably lacking among Darwinian psychologists even though genetics is the basis for all matters of inheritance. This is because Darwinian psychologists use genetic inheritance not as a framework but as a mantra; their analyses of specific behaviors, although theoretically based on genetics, virtually never indicate how the genetics might work. Would a certain behavior be correlated with a recessive gene? a dominant gene? many genes? a gene on either of the sex chromosomes? They offer not even a guess.

Darwinian psychologists seem to have a right wing bias, either conscious or subconscious; their findings too often provide a framework for policy makers who want to blame the victims in society by claiming that much of human social behavior is genetic rather than learned and cultural. They favor the status quo. It is far easier politically nowadays to cut off funding for social work than to provide more money to address difficult problems of the poor.

This bias most notably affects people who aren't white, unlike virtually all Darwinian psychologists. Any non-white group that doesn't fit easily into white North

American or European culture may find itself vilified as the chapters on crime, "race" and IQ describe. One study generalizes that the women most evolved to catch a man have "a small nose and small feet and pale [sic], hairless skin" (Barber, 1995).

The conservative bias also affects women, because the topics that captivate Darwinian psychologists are ones that downplay feminine importance—infanticide, aggression, dominance, rape, sperm competition and war. There is little research on such things as cooperation, childcare and social community which are of interest to most women.

The Darwinian psychological approach also demeans gays and lesbians. It implies that their sexual orientation is abnormal, but nevertheless tends to insist that their "condition" *must* have an evolutionary rational as discussed in Chapters 12 and 13. Darwinian psychologists seem unable to accept that homosexuality is a manifestation of one type of many possible sexualities.

In this book we have made a number of generalizations related to Darwinian psychology. These are:

1) In non-human animals social behaviors are usually inherited as evolutionary adaptations.

2) Human beings have evolved from their primate ancestors to have a large brain; because of their intelligence, people's social behavior is largely based not on their genetic inheritance but on sex, personality, experience and culture.

3) Darwinian psychology contends that most or much of human behavior is genetically inherited from ancestral primates. This is true for basic behaviors which we share with chimpanzees and bonobos—sociality, aggression, maternal care of young, distinctive male and female behaviors caused by hormones, copulation usually between opposite sexes, a preference for the familiar and the incest taboo.

4) Specific human universal social behaviors, not present in chimpanzee and bonobos, have evolved in the past six millions years including a tendency for social monogamy, cooperation within communities, interest by fathers in their children and communication by speech.

5) Other human behaviors seem to have no evolutionary component and are based therefore on culture and individual personalities. These include territoriality, rape, infanticide, dominance hierarchy, and male dominance. They also include most of the hundreds of "universal" human behaviors beloved of some anthropologists such as war and having false beliefs.

6) Proponents of Darwinian psychology tend to think up evolutionary explanations to account for observed human characteristics, then marshal data to prove they are true.

7) Zeal in marshalling the data leads too often to fatal errors and to shoddy science:

- assuming that current behavior is a genetic inheritance from our nomadic ancestors—e.g., currently Western men may prefer a woman with a curvy body but men of traditional nomadic or semi-nomadic communities do not;
- ignoring the behavior of real people—e.g., real people marry not because their partner is good looking or symmetrical, but because he or she is kind/sympathetic/a good sport/smart/industrious/educated/funny/a good cook/has a great job/take your pick;
- fabricating data—such as the mythical kamikaze sperm that are supposed to attack alien sperm in a woman's body;
- ignoring data that contradict the hypothesis—e.g., claiming increased infanticide by stepparents without considering societies such as Sweden in which easily-obtained abortions mean that all babies are wanted;
- using data that are outdated—e.g., using head or brain measurements that are sometimes over 100 years old instead of those from accurate modern databases;
- citing data incorrectly—e.g., arguing that there is rape in animals such as fish, frogs and monkeys when this is not true.

Darwinian psychology has been summarized as "The point of life is the proliferation of life" (Betzig, 1997, 1). This is true in hundreds of thousands of studies on thousands of species of plants and animals, but it is controversial for human beings who are intelligent enough to have major individual and cultural as well as biological agendas. If the point of life is reproduction, why is so much of human activity devoted to circumventing it? (Dagg, 1991). Why do many couples decide to have no children? Why do women use birth control and have abortions? Why do natural parents sometimes abuse, kill or desert their children? Human reproductive behavior reflects a couple's wishes, not the inherited behavior of their biological progenitors. Men and women in the West take control of their own reproduction.

Darwinian psychologists act as if every facet of human behavior has a genetic component. This is a gross exaggeration. Human beings act as they do primarily because of their sex and their personality which, admittedly, *is* based to some degree on heredity; however, a person's personality is shaped to a huge extent by culture and by his or her education and experience. Proponents wonder if science will unravel human behavior to such an extent that "we will lose the capacity to believe in individual moral responsibility? This dilemma confronts *all* scientific approaches to behavior" (Daly and Wilson, 1987, 306). Given the major flaws that exist in Darwinian psychology, however, there is no need to worry about this for a very long time.

Because Darwinian psychology is popular among laypeople, new "discoveries" about human nature are widely reported in the mass media. However, these findings tend to foster a social climate that alienates rather than encourages disadvantaged people. Far from promoting improvement in people's lives, the discipline indicates that any change in human social behavior is difficult and unlikely. Yet its research is often based on untrue premises, specious arguments and inaccurate data. The "findings" of Darwinian psychology should always be considered with deep suspicion.

Appendix A

The following suggestions by Darwinian psychologists (and sometimes for them, free of charge, by Jones and Dagg), have been formulated to explain why various human characteristics may have evolved. Readers, please feel free to fill in the unused letters as the spirit moves you. The problem with these suggestions, of course, is not necessarily that most of them are ridiculous, but that they cannot be tested, which means that they are not scientific.

A: Acne. This may prevent young people from having sex until they are old enough to reproduce (Jones in Levin, 2001).

B: Beards. Beards evolved to display a man's confidence; should it be grabbed in battle, the owner still shows he feels able to win. Women do not grow beards because they are uninterested in fighting (Zahavi and Zahavi, 1997, 213).

C: Chewing Gum. This activity has "developed exclusively as a displacement feeding device. It provides the necessary tension-relieving 'occupational' element, without contributing damagingly to the overall food intake" (Morris, 1967, 196).

D: Dancing. Chimpanzees make many swaying and jigging movements which "also accompany the mood-provoking musical performances of our own species" (Morris, 1967, 137). Human beings have elaborated and expanded the movements of their primate ancestors, giving them a talent to impress a prospective mate.

E: Eyebrows. Dominant people (such as men) have thicker and heavier eyebrows than women and children so that when a man registers a threat with puckered eyebrows, his intention is clearly known to his subordinates who will then obey him (Zahavi and Zahavi, 1997, 212)

F: Flashes, Hot. Women's faces turn red because of hot flashes experienced during menopause; this tells men that the woman is no longer fertile so they should not waste time with her (Dagg).

G: Gambling. For lower class people gambling substitutes for the drive to hunt; whereas work is a substitute for hunting for middle class people, for the lower class their work is so repetitive and predictable that workers resort to gambling to add risk and spice to their lives (Morris, 1967, 190).

H: Hair. Hair grows continuously (unlike in other species) so that it can be neatly fashioned to show off the owner's dexterous hands. A coiffeur proclaims to possible future mates that the owner has the time to care for his or her hair as well as patience, skill and imagination in doing so (Zahavi and Zahavi, 1997, 211).

I:

J:

K: Kiss. A kiss evolved to test bonds of romantic friendship to ensure that one has a reliable partner (Zahavi and Zahavi, 1997, 218).

L:

M: Menstruation coincides with the phases of the moon so that primitive women, who cycled together, did so when the moon was a mere sliver and the earth was therefore darkest and least helpful for predators who smelled the blood (Shlain, 2003).

N: Nose and facial wrinkles. Noses and wrinkles grow longer and deeper respectively with age "to enable more dominant individuals to display their intent [of friendship or enmity] more clearly" (Zahavi and Zahavi, 1997, 213).

O:

P: Phobias. Claustrophobia and agoraphobia are useful in that they reveal a person's weakness which may repulse (or attract) a stable mate (Dagg).

Q:

R: Red cheeks. Red cheeks evolved as an indication of good health to attract a superior mate (Zahavi and Zahavi, 1997, 214). Yet see F for hot flashes.

S: Spectacles. Spectacles or glasses reveal information about a prospective mate because "mild-mannered individuals tend to select thin-rimmed or rimless spectacles"; this enables them to minimize "stare exaggeration" and the counter-aggression it arouses (Morris, 1967, 165).

T:

U:

V:

W: Whipping. Rhythmic whipping of bent-over schoolboys by a school master is related to the rhythmic pelvic thrusts of a dominant male. The reddening of the boys' buttocks may recall to the schoolmaster "the flushing of the primate female hindquarters when in full sexual condition" (Morris, 1967, 168).

X:

Y:

Z: Zoophilia. This is a sexual attraction for animals—"Figure that one out for yourselves" (Jones in Levin, 2001).

Bibliography

Abraham, Carolyn. 2002, Dec 14. *Globe and Mail* (Toronto), A1,6.

Adler, Tina. 1997, Jan 4. *Science News* 151: 8-9.

Ahmad, Waqar. 1995, Jul 22. *New Scientist* 44-45.

Alexander, Gerianne M. and Melissa Hines. 2002. *Evolution and Human Behavior* 23,6: 467-479.

Allen, Caitilyn. 1997. In Patricia Gowaty, ed. *Feminism and Evolutionary Biology: Boundaries, Intersections, and Frontiers, 515-521. New York: Chapman and Hall.*

Allen, Garland E. 1996. In Robert W. Sussman, ed. 1997. *The Biological Basis of Human Behavior* 374-387. New York: Simon and Schuster.

Altmann, Stuart. 1979. *Animal Behavior* 27: 46-80.

Anderson, Craig A. and Brad J. Bushman. 2002. *Science* 295: 2377-2379.

Anderson, Karen. 1991. *Chain her by One Foot: The Subjugation of Women in Seventeenth-century New France*. London: Routledge.

Angier, Natalie. 1995, Apr 22. *Globe and Mail* (Toronto), D8.

Angier, Natalie. 2000, Aug 23. *National Post* (Toronto), A15.

APA, 1996. American Psychological Association Presidential Task Force on Violence and the Family: http://womenissues.about.com/library/bldomesticviolencestats.htm

Archer, John. 1991. *British Journal of Psychology* 82: 1-28.

Ardrey, Robert. 1961. *African Genesis: A Personal Investigation into the Animal Origins and Nature of Man*. New York: Atheneum

Ardrey, Robert. 1966. *The Territorial Imperative: A Personal Inquiry into the Animal Origins of Property and Nations*. New York: Atheneum.

Armelagos, George J. 1997 [1995]. In Robert W. Sussman, ed. *The Biological Basis of Human Behavior* 279-287. Needham Heights, MA: Simon and Schuster.

Aromäki, Anu S., Ralf E. Lindman and C.J. Peter Eriksson. 1999. *Aggressive Behavior* 25: 113-123.

Athens, Lonnie H. 1989. *The Creation of Dangerous Violent Criminals*. London: Routledge.

Bagemihl, Bruce. 1999. *Biological Exuberance: Animal Homosexuality and Natural Diversity*. New York: St Martin's Press.

Bailit, H.L., P.L Workman, J.D. Niswander and C.J. MacLean. 1970. *Human Biology* 42: 626-638.

Baker, Robin. 1996. *Sperm Wars: The Science of Sex*. Toronto: HarperCollins.

Baker, Robin and Mark A. Bellis. 1995. *Human Sperm Competition*: *Copulation, Masturbation and Infidelity*. London: Chapman and Hall.

Balikci, Asen. 1970. *The Netsilik Eskimo*. Garden City, NY: Natural History Press.

Barber, Nigel. 1995. *Ethology and Sociobiology* 16: 395-424.

Barker, Kate. 2002, Winter. Bishop Strachan School Alumnae Magazine, 8.

Barley, Nigel. 1983. *The Innocent Anthropologist: Notes from a Mud Hut*. London: British Museum Publications.

Baron, Robert A., Joel H. Neuman and Deanna Geddes. 1999. *Aggressive Behavior* 25: 281-296.

Baron, Robert A. and Deborah R. Richardson. 1994. *Human Aggression* 2nd ed. New York: Plenum Press.

Bartlett, Thad Q., Robert W. Sussman and James M. Cheverud. 1993. *American Anthropologist* 95: 958-990.

Battin, Sara R., Karl G. Hill, Robert D. Abbott, Richard F. Catalano and J. David Hawkins. 1998. *Criminology* 36: 93-115.

Baumeister, Roy F., Laura Smart and Joseph M. Boden. 1996. *Psychological Review* 103,1: 5-33.

Beatty, John. 1968. In M.F. Ashley Montagu, ed. *Man and Aggression* 111-115. New York: Oxford University Press.

Beckerman, Stephen, Roberto Lizarralde, Carol Ballew, Sissel Schroeder, Christina Fingelton, Angela Garrison and Helen Smith. 1998. *Current Anthropology* 39,1: 164-167.

Beckwith, Jon and Larry Miller. 1976. *Harvard Magazine* 79: 30-33.

Beecher, Michael D. and Inger Mornestam Beecher. 1979. *Science* 205: 1282-1285.

Beer, Francis A. 1974. *How Much War in History: Definitions, Estimates, Extrapolations and Trends*. Beverley Hills, CA: Sage Publications.

Bercovitch, Fred B. 1991. *Ethology and Sociobiology* 12: 315-333.

Berger, Lee R. 2000. *In the Footsteps of Eve: The Mystery of Human Origins*. Washington, DC: Adventure Press/ National Geographic.

Berk, Richard, Paul R. Abramson and Paul Okami. 1995. In Paul R. Abramson and Steven D. Pinkerton, eds. *Sexual Nature Sexual Culture* 371-386. Chicago: University of Chicago Press.

Berkowitz, Leonard. 1990. In Betty Glad, ed. *Psychological Dimensions of War* 24-40. Newbury Park, CA: Sage Publications.

Bertram, Brian C.R. 1975. *Journal of Zoology* London 177: 463-482.

Bertram, Brian C.R. 1978. *Pride of Lions*. New York: Scribners.

Besharov, Douglas J. 1995. In Russell Jacoby and Naomi Glauberman, eds. *The Bell Curve Debate* 358-363. New York: Random House.

Betzig, Laura, ed. 1997. Introduction. *Human Nature: A Critical Reader*. New York: Oxford University Press.

Birkhead, Tim R. 1979. *Animal Behavior* 27: 866-874.

Birkhead, Tim R. 2000. *Promiscuity: An Evolutionary History of Sperm Competition and Sexual Conflict*. London: Faber and Faber.

Birkhead, Tim R. and A.P. Møller. 1992. *Sperm Competition in Birds: Evolutionary Causes and Consequences*. London: Academic Press.

Blanchard, Ray and Anthony F. Bogaert. 1997. *Behavior Genetics* 27: 45-54.

Blinkhorn, Steve. 1994. *Nature* 372: 417-419.

Bobrow, David and J. Michael Bailey. 2001. *Evolution and Human Behavior* 22: 361-368.

Boehm, Christopher. 1999. *Hierarchy in the Forest: The Evolution of Egalitarian Behavior*. Cambridge, MA: Harvard University Press.

Boyanowsky, Ehor. 1999. *International Journal of Law and Psychiatry* 22,3-4: 257-271.

Boyd, Neil. 2000. *The Beast Within: Why Men are Violent*. Vancouver: GreyStone Books.

Brédart, Serge and Robert M. French. 1999. *Evolution and Human Behavior* 20: 129-135.

Brennan, Patricia A., Emily R. Grekin and Sarnoff A. Mednick. 1999. *Archives of General Psychiatry* 56,3: 215-219.

Broude, Gwen J. and Sarah J. Greene. 1976. *Ethnology* 15: 409-429.

Brown, Donald E. 1991. *Human Universals*. Philadelphia: Temple University Press.

Browne, Janet. 1995. *Charles Darwin: A Biography* vol 1. New York: Knopf.

Browning, Christopher R. 1992. *Ordinary Men: Reserve Police Battalion 101 and the Final Solution in Poland*. New York: HarperCollins.

Brunner, H.G., M.R. Nelen, P. van Zandvoort, N.G.G.M. Abelling, A.H. van Gennip, E.C. Wolters, M.A. Kuiper, H.H. Ropers, and B.A. Van Oost. 1993. *American Journal of Human Genetics* 52: 1032-1039.

Buck, Naomi. 2002, Jul 12. *Globe and Mail* (Toronto), A16.

Burr, Chandler. 2000. Website: (http://members.aol.com/gaygene/pages/standard.htm).

Buss, David M. 2000. *The Dangerous Passion: Why Jealousy is as Necessary as Love and Sex*. New York: Free Press.

Byne, William and Bruce Parsons. 1993. *Archives of General Psychiatry* 50: 228-240.

Cadoret, Remi J., Leslie D. Levee and Eric Devor. 1997. In Maurizio Fava, ed. *Anger, Aggression, and Violence: The Psychiatric Clinics of North America* 301-322. Philadelphia: Saunders.

Carneiro, Robert L. 1994. In S.P. Reyna and R.E. Downs, eds. *Studying War: Anthropological Perspectives* 3-27. Langhorne, PA: Gordon and Breach.

Carrithers, Michael. 1989. In Signe Howell and Roy Willis, eds. *Societies at Peace: Anthropological Perspectives* 187-209. London: Routledge.

Casey, Geraldine J. 1991. In Anne E. Hunter, ed. *On Peace, War, and Gender* 1-33. New York: Feminist Press.

Cavalli-Sforza, Luigi Luca and Francesco Cavalli-Sforza. 1995 (1993). *The Great Human Diasporas: The History of Diversity and Evolution*. Reading, MA: Addison-Wesley.

Chagnon, Napoleon A. 1968. *Yanomamö, The Fierce People*. New York: Holt, Rinehart and Winston.

Chagnon, Napoleon A. 1988. *Science* 239: 985-992.

Chance, Michael. 1956. *British Journal of Animal Behaviour* 4: 1-13.

Chapais, Bernard and Christiane Mignault. 1991. *American Journal of Primatology* 23: 171-183.

Charbonneau, Léo. 2001, Jan. *University Affairs* (Ottawa), 19,29.

Chon, Margaret. 1995. In Russell Jacoby and Naomi Glauberman, eds. *The Bell Curve Debate* 238-240. New York: Random House.

Chrisjohn, Roland, Deborah Pace, Sherri Young and Marcia Mrochuk. 1997. In Roland Chrisjohn and Sherri L. Young, eds. *The Circle Game: Shadows and Substance in the Indian Residential School Experience in Canada* 199-219. Penticton, BC: Theytus Books.

Christenfeld, Nicholas J.S. and Emily A. Hill. 1995. *Nature* 378: 669.

Chwialkowska, Luiza. 1999, Nov 16. *National Post* (Toronto), A9.

Clutton-Brock, T.H., M.J. O'Riain, P.N.M. Brotherton, D. Gaynor, R. Kansky, A.S. Griffin and M. Manser. 1999. *Science* 284: 1640-1644.

Coyne, Jerry A. and Andrew Berry. 2000. *Nature* 404: 121-122.

Cronin, Helena. 1991. *The Ant and the Peacock: Altruism and Sexual Selection from Darwin to Today*. Cambridge, UK: Cambridge University Press.

Culliton, Barbara J. 1975. *Science* 188: 1284-1285.

Cunningham, Emma J.A. and Andrew F. Russell. 2000. *Nature* 404: 74-76.

Curtin, Richard and Phyllis Dolhinow. 1978. *American Scientist* 66,4: 468-475.

Dagg, Anne Innis. 1983. *Harems and Other Horrors: Sexual Bias in_Behavioral Biology*. Waterloo, ON: Otter Press.

Dagg, Anne Innis. 1984a. *International Journal of Women's Studies* 7,2: 118-135.

Dagg, Anne Innis. 1984b. *Mammal Review* 14,4: 155-185.

Dagg, Anne Innis, 1991. In Anne Innis Dagg, Sheelagh Conway and Margaret Simpson, eds. *Women's Experience, Women's Education: An Anthology* 29-32. Waterloo, ON: Otter Press.

Dagg, Anne Innis. 1998. *American Anthropologist* 100,4: 1-11.

Dagg, Anne Innis. 1999, Dec. *Anthropology News* 20.

Dagg, Anne Innis. 2001. *American Anthropologist* 102: 831-834.

Dagg, Anne Innis and Matthew B. Griffin. 1998. A source of error in human fluctuating asymmetry measurements. Manuscript.

Dahl, Jeremy F., Kenneth G. Gould and Ronald D. Nadler. 1993. *American Journal of Physical Anthropology* 90: 229-236.

Daly, Martin and Margo Wilson. 1982. *Ethology and Sociobiology* 3: 69-78.

Daly, Martin and Margo Wilson. 1987. In Charles Crawford, Martin Smith and Dennis Krebs, eds. *Sociobiology and Psychology: Ideas, Issues and Applications* 293-309. Hillsdale, NJ: Lawrence Erlbaum Assoc.

Daly, Martin and Margo Wilson. 1988. *Homicide*. New York: Aldine de Gruyter.

Daly, Martin and Margo Wilson. 1998. *The Truth about Cinderella: A Darwinian View of Parental Love*. London: Weidenfeld and Nicolson.

Davies, N.B. 1983. *Nature* 302: 334-336.

Davis, Bernard D. 1976. *Harvard Magazine* 79: 26-30.

Davis, William. 2000, Apr. *Anthropology News* 15.

Dawkins, Richard. 1976. *The Selfish Gene*. Oxford: Oxford University Press.

Derocher, A.E. and O. Wiig. 1999. *Arctic* 52: 307-310.

Desmond, Adrian and James Moore. 1991. *Darwin*. London: Michael Joseph.

DeVore, Irven and Sherwood L. Washburn. 1963. In F.C. Howell and F. Bourlière, eds. *African Ecology and Human Evolution* 335-367. Chicago: Aldine.

Diamond, Jared. 1992. *Third Chimpanzee: The Evolution and Future of the Human Animal*. New York: HarperCollins.

Diamond, Jared. 1997. *Guns, Germs, and Steel: The Fate of Human Societies*. New York: Norton.

Dittmar, Manuela. 1998. *American Journal of Physical Anthropology* 105: 377-393.

Divale, William Tulio and Marvin Harris. 1976. *American Anthropologist* 78: 521-538.

Dixson, A.F. 1987. *Journal of Zoology* London 213: 423-443.

Dolhinow, Phyllis. 1999. In Shirley C. Strum, Donald G. Lindburg and David Hamburg, eds. *The New Physical Anthropology: Science, Humanism, and Critical Reflection* 119-132. Upper Saddle River, NJ: Prentice Hall.

Donohue, John J III and Steven D. Levitt. 2001. *Quarterly Journal of Economics* 116: 379-420.

Dunham, Will. 2001, Aug 12. *Toronto Sunday Star*, F8.

Dynes, Wayne R. and Stephen Donaldson. 1992. In Wayne R. Dynes and Stephen Donaldson, eds. *Ethnographic Studies of Homosexuality* Vol 2, vii-xvi. New York: Garland Publishing.

Eberhard, William G. 1990. *American Scientist* 78: 134-141.

Eibl-Eibesfeldt, Irenäus. 1979. *The Biology of Peace and War: Men, Animals, and Aggression*. New York: Viking Press.

Elwood, Robert W. 1991. *Animal Behavior* 42: 841-849.

Emlen, Stephen T., Natalie J. Demong and Douglas J. Emlen. 1989. *Auk* 106: 1-7.

Faludi, Susan. 1991. *Backlash: The Undeclared War Against American Women*. New York: Crown Publishers.

Faludi, Susan. 1999. *Stiffed: The Betrayal of the American Man*. New York: Morrow.

Farr, James A., Joseph Travis and Joel C. Trexler. 1986. *Animal Behavior* 34: 497-509.

Fedigan, Linda Marie. 1982. *Primate Paradigms: Sex Roles and Social Bonds*. Montreal: Eden Press.

Fedorowycz, Orest. 2002. Homicide in Canada - 2000. Ottawa: Statistics Canada - Catalogue no. 85-002-XPE Vol 21, no.9, p12.

Ferguson, R. Brian. 1989. *American Ethnologist* 16,3: 564-565.

Ferguson, R. Brian. 2001. *Anthropological Theory* 1: 99-116.

Finegan, Joan E. and Anita Mackenzie. 1990. *Canadian Psychology* 31: 300.

Flinn, Mark V., David V. Leone and Robert J. Quinlan. 1999. *Evolution and Human Behavior* 20: 465-479.

Florida, Richard. 2002. *The Rise of the Creative Class and How it's Transforming Work, Leisure, Community and Everyday Life*. New York: Basic Books.

Flynn, James R. 1998. In Ulric Neisser, ed. *The Rising Curve: Long-Term Gains in IQ and Related Measures* 25-66. Washington, DC: American Psychological Association.

Ford, Clellan S. and Frank A. Beach. 1952. *Patterns of Sexual Behaviour*. London: Eyre and Spottiswoode.

Fortune, R.F. 1932. *Sorcerers of Dobu: The Social Anthropology of the Dobu Islanders of the Western Pacific*. London: Routledge.

Frank, Laurence. 1994, Mar 5. *New Scientist* 38-41.

Fraser, Steven. 1995. In Steven Fraser, ed. *The Bell Curve Wars,* 1-10. New York: Basic Books.

Freeman, Derek. 1983. *Margaret Mead and Samoa: The Making and Unmaking of an Anthropological Myth*. Cambridge, MA: Harvard University Press.

Fukuyama, Francis. 1998, Sept/Oct. *Foreign Affairs* 24-40.

Gagnon, Lysiane. 2001, Dec 24. *Globe and Mail* (Toronto), A11.

Gander, Eric M. 2003. *On Our Minds: How Evolutionary Psychology is Reshaping the Nature-versus-Nurture Debate*. Baltimore: Johns Hopkins University Press.

Gangestad, Steven W. 1993. *Human Nature* 4: 205-235.

Gangestad, Steven W. and Randy Thornhill. 1997. *Evolution and Human Behavior* 18: 69-88.

Gangestad, Steven W., Randy Thornhill and Ronald A. Yeo. 1994. *Ethology and Sociobiology* 15: 73-85.

Gardner, Howard. 1995a. In Steven Fraser, ed. *The Bell Curve Wars* 23-35. New York: Basic Books.

Gardner, Howard. 1995b. In Russell Jacoby and Naomi Glauberman, eds. *The Bell Curve Debate* 61-72. New York: Random House.

Gardner, Howard. 1999. *Intelligence Reframed: Multiple Intelligences for the 21st Century*. New York: Basic Books.

Gatehouse, Jonathon. 2000, Jul 11. *National Post* (Toronto), A2.

Gates, Henry Louis Jr. 1995. In Steven Fraser, ed. *The Bell Curve Wars* 94-96. New York: Basic Books.

Geist, Valerius. 1975. *Mountain Sheep and Man in the Northern Wilds*. Ithaca, NY: Cornell University Press.

Genovés, Santiago. 1970. *Is Peace Inevitable? Aggression, Evolution, and Human Destiny*. London: Allen and Unwin.

Ghiglieri, Michael P. 1988. *East of the Mountains of the Moon: Chimpanzee Society in the African Rain Forest*. New York: Free Press.

Ghiglieri, Michael P. 2000. *The Dark Side of Man: Tracing the Origins of Male Violence*. Cambridge, MA: Helix/ Perseus Books.

Glad, Betty, ed. 1990. *Psychological Dimensions of War*. Newbury Park, CA: Sage Publications.

Gladstone, Douglas E. 1979. *American Naturalist* 114,4: 545-557.

Glazer, Nathan. 1995. In Steven Fraser, ed. *The Bell Curve Wars* 139-147. New York: Basic Books.

Glueck, S. 1960. *Journal of Criminal Law, Criminology and Police Science* 51: 283-308.

Glueck, S. and E.T. Glueck. 1950. *Unraveling Juvenile Delinquency*. Cambridge, MA: Harvard University Press.

Glueck, S. and E.T. Glueck. 1968. *Delinquents and Nondelinquents in Perspective*. Cambridge, MA: Harvard University Press.

Goldberg, Steven. 1973. *The Inevitability of Patriarchy*. New York: Morrow.

Gomendio, Montserrat, Alexander H. Harcourt and Eduardo R.S. Roldan. 1998. In T.R. Birkhead and A.P. Møller, *eds. Sperm Competition and Sexual Selection* 667-755. San Diego: Academic Press.

Goodall, Jane. 1968. *Animal Behaviour Monographs* 1: 161-311.

Goodall, Jane. 1986. *The Chimpanzees of Gombe: Patterns of Behavior*. Cambridge, MA: Belknap Press.

Goodall, Jane. 1999. *Reason for Hope*. New York: Warner.

Goodall, Jane. 2001. *Beyond Innocence: An Autobiography in Letters–The Later Years*. Boston: Houghton Mifflin. Edited by Dale Peterson.

Goodwin, Christopher. 2000, Jan 16. *Toronto Star,* F1,3.

Gordon, Deborah. 1999. *Ants at Work: How an Insect Society is Organized.* New York: Free Press.

Gould, Stephen Jay. 1981. *The Mismeasure of Man.* New York: Norton.

Gould, Stephen Jay. 1995. In Russell Jacoby and Naomi Glauberman, eds. *The Bell Curve Debate* 3-13. New York: Random House.

Gould, Stephen Jay. 2002. *I Have Landed: The End of a Beginning in Natural History*. New York: Harmony Books.

Gouzoulis-Mayfrank, Euphrosyne, Jörg Daumann, Frank Tuchtenhagen, Susanne Pelz, Steffanie Becker, Hans-Jürgen Kunert, Bruno Fimm and Henning Sass. 2000. *Journal of Neurology, Neurosurgery and Psychiatry* 68: 719-725.

Gowaty, Patricia Adair and Jonathan H. Plissner. 1998. *The Birds of North America* No. 381, 31 pp.

Graber, Robert Bates et al, 2000. *Meeting Anthropology Phase to Phase*. Durham, NC: Carolina Academic Press.

Graves, Joseph L., Jr. 2001. *The Emperor's New Clothes: Biological Theories of Race at the Millennium.* New Brunswick, NJ: Rutgers University Press.

Greenberg, James B. 1989. *Blood Ties: Life and Violence in Rural Mexico.* Tucson, AZ: University of Arizona Press.

Guze, Samuel. 1999. In Botkin, Jeffrey R., William M. McMahon and Leslie Pickering Francis, eds. *Genetics and Criminality: The Potential Misuse of Scientific Information in Court* 99-105. Washington, DC: American Psychological Association.

Hacker, Andrew. 1995. In Steven Fraser, ed. *The Bell Curve Wars,* 97-108. New York: Basic Books.

Hacker, Andrew. 2003, Mar 27. *The New York Review,* 14-16.

Haddow, A.J. 1952. *Proceedings of the Zoological Society of London* 122: 297-392.

Hagen, Edward H. 1999. *Evolution and Human Behavior* 20: 325-359.

Halterman, J.S., J.M. Kaczorowski, C.A. Aligne, P. Auinger and P.G. Szilagyi. 2001. *Pediatrics* 107,6: 1381-6.

Hamer, Dean H. and Peter Copeland. 1994. *The Science of Desire: The Search for the Gay Gene and the Biology of Behavior*. New York: Simon and Schuster.

Haraway, Donna. 1989. *Primate Visions: Gender, Race, and Nature in the World of Modern Science*. New York: Routledge.

Haraway, Donna. 2000. In Strum, Shirley C. and Linda M. Fedigan, eds. *Primate Encounters: Models of Science, Gender, and Society* 398-420. Chicago: University of Chicago Press.

Harcourt, Alexander and Frans B.M. de Waal. 1992. *Coalitions and Alliances in Humans and Other Animals.* Oxford, UK: Oxford University Press.

Harding, C.F. 1985. In Sunday, Suzanne R. and Ethel Tobach, eds. *Violence Against Women: A Critique of the Sociobiology of Rape* 59-84. New York: Gordian Press.

Harding, Robert S.O. 1977. *American Journal of Physical Anthropology* 47: 349-354.

Hare, James F. 1991. *Canadian Journal of Zoology* 69: 797-800.

Harris, Marvin and Eric B. Ross. 1987. *Death, Sex, and Fertility: Population Regulation in Preindustrial and Developing Societies.* New York: Columbia University Press.

Hart, Betty and Todd R. Risley. 1995. *Meaningful Differences in the Everyday Experience of Young American Children*. Baltimore: P.H. Brookes.

Hassebrauck, Manfred. 1998. *Evolution and Human Behavior* 19: 111-123.

Hausfater, Glenn. 1975. *Dominance and Reproduction in Baboons (*Papio cynocephalus*): A Quantitative Analysis*. Basel: S. Karger.

Hazlett, Richard L. and Rudolph Hoehn-Saric. 2000. *Evolution and Human Behavior* 21: 49-57.

Health Canada. 1994. *Suicide in Canada: Update of the Report of the Task Force on Suicide in Canada.* [Cat H39-107/1995E]. Ottawa: Minister of National Health and Welfare.

Herbert, Bob. 1995. In Russell Jacoby and Naomi Glauberman, eds. *The Bell Curve Debate* 249-251. New York: Random House.

Herrnstein, Richard J. and Charles Murray. 1994. *The Bell Curve: Intelligence and Class Structure in American Life*. New York: Free Press.

Highfield, Roger. 2000, Aug 8. *National Post* (Toronto), A2.

Hill, Kim and A. Magdelena Hurtado. 1996. *Ache Life History: The Ecology and Demography of a Foraging People*. New York: Aldine de Gruyter.

Hinde, R.A. 1974. *Biological Bases of Human Social Behaviour*. New York: McGraw-Hill.

Hodgins, Sheilagh, Lynn Kratzer and Thomas F. McNeil. 2001. *Archives of General Psychiatry* 58: 746-752.

Hoge, Warren. 2003, Jan 2. *New York Times International* A1,6.

Homer-Dixon, Thomas F. 1999. *Environment, Scarcity, and Violence*. Princeton: Princeton University Press.

Hoogland, John L. 1985. *Science* 230: 1037-1039.

Horgan, John. 1993, June. *Scientific American* 123-131.

Horowitz, Irving Louis. 1995. In Russell Jacoby and Naomi Glauberman, eds. *The Bell Curve Debate* 179-200. New York: Random House.

Hotta, Masanobu. 1994. *Animal Behavior* 47: 491-493.

Houpt, Simon. 2002, June 17. *Globe and Mail* (Toronto), R1,6.

Howard, Richard D. 1978. *Evolution* 32,4: 850-871.

Howell, Nancy. 1979. *Demography of the Dobe !Kung*. New York: Academic Press.

Howell, Signe and Roy Willis. 1989. In Signe Howell and Roy Willis, eds. *Societies at Peace: Anthropological Perspectives* 1-28. London: Routledge.

Hrdy, Sarah Blaffer. 1974. *Folia Primatologica* 22: 19-58.

Hrdy, Sarah Blaffer. 1999. *Mother Nature: A History of Mothers, Infants, and Natural Selection*. New York: Pantheon Books.

Humphrey, Nicholas. 2002. *The Mind Made Flesh*. Oxford: Oxford University Press.

Innis, Anne Christine. 1958. *Proceedings of the Zoological Society of London* 131,2: 245-278.

Itani, J. and A. Nishimura. 1973. In E.W. Menzel, ed. *Precultural Primate Behavior* 26-50. Basel: Karger.

Jacobs, Patricia A., Muriel Brunton, Marie M. Melville, R.P. Brittain and W.F. McClemont. 1965. *Nature* 208: 1351-1352.

Jacoby, Russell and Naomi Glauberman. 1995. *The Bell Curve Debate* ix-xiv. New York: Random House.

Jarvie, Jenny. 2000, Jul 24. *National Post* (Toronto), A2.

Jason, Janine, Jeanne C. Gilliland and Carl W. Tyler. 1983. *Pediatrics* 72,2: 191-197.

Jensen, Arthur R. 1973. *Educability and Group Differences*. London: Methuen.

Jensen, Arthur R. 1977. *Developmental Psychology 13*: 184-191.

Johnson, Olive Skene. 2004. *The Sexual Spectrum: Exploring Human Diversity*. Vancouver: Raincoast Books.

Johnson, Paul. 1988. *Intellectuals*. London: Weidenfeld and Nicolson.

Johnston, Victor S., Rebecca Hagel, Melissa Franklin, Bernhard Fink and Karl Grammer. 2001. *Evolution and Human Behavior* 22: 251-267.

Jones, Clara B. 1985. *Primates* 26,2: 130-142.

Jones, Steve. 1999. *Darwin's Ghost: A Radical Scientific Updating of* The Origin of Species *for the 21st Century*. New York: Random House.

Judis, John B. 1995. In Steven Fraser, ed. *The Bell Curve Wars* 124-129. New York: Basic Books.

Kaessmann, Henrik, Victor Wiebe and Svante Pääbo. 1999. *Science* 286: 1159-1162.

Kalick, S.M., L.A. Zebrowitz, J.H. Langlois and R.M. Johnson. 1998. *Psychological Science* 9,1: 8-13.

Kamin, Leon J. 1986. *Scientific American* 254: 22-27.

Kamin, Leon J. 1995. In Russell Jacoby and Naomi Glauberman, eds. *The Bell Curve Debate* 81-105. New York: Random House.

Keeley, Lawrence H. 1996. *War before Civilization*. New York: Oxford University Press.

Keenleyside, Miles H.A. 1972. *Copeia* 1972: 272-278.

Kennedy, Randall. 1995. In Steven Fraser, ed. *The Bell Curve Wars* 179-186. New York: Basic Books.

Kimball, Meredith M. 1989. *Psychological Bulletin* 105: 198-214.

Kinsey, Alfred C., Wardell B. Pomeroy and Clyde E. Martin. 1948. *Sexual Behavior in the Human Male*. Philadelphia: Saunders.

Klama, John. 1987. *Aggression: Conflict in Animals and Humans Reconsidered*. London: Longman Scientific and Technical.

Klopfer, Peter H. and Barrie K. Gilbert. 1966. *Zeitschrift für Tierpsychologie* 23: 757-760.

Kniffin, Kevin M. and David Sloan Wilson. 2004. *Evolution and Human Behavior* 25,2: 88-101.

Kovandzic, Tomislav V., Lynne M. Vieraitis and Mark R. Yeisley. 1998. *Criminology* 36: 569-599.

Kozol, Jonathan. 1996. *Amazing Grace: The Lives of Children and the Conscience of a Nation*. New York: Harper/Perennial.

Krantz, Grove S. 1980. *Climatic Races and Descent Groups*. North Quincy, MA: Christopher Publishing House.

Kummer, Hans. 1967. In Stuart Altmann, ed. *Social Communication among Primates* 63-71. Chicago: University of Chicago Press.

Kummer, Hans. 1968. *Social Organization of Hamadryas Baboons*. Basel: Karger.

Kutzik, David M. 1995. In Russell Jacoby and Naomi Glauberman, eds. *The Bell Curve Debate* 246-248. New York: Random House.

Lalumière, Martin L., Grant T. Harris and Marnie E. Rice. 1999. *Proceedings of the Royal Society of London, B* 266: 2351-2354.

Lamb, Christina. 2002. *The Sewing Circles of Herat*. New York: HarperCollins.

Lamey, Andy. 2000, Jan 31. *National Post* (Toronto), A1,10.

Laurence, Charles. 2001, Feb 7. *National Post* (Toronto), A1,12.

Leacock, Eleanor. 1980. In Mona Etienne and Eleanor Leacock, eds. *Women and Colonization: Anthropological Perspectives* 25-42. New York: Praeger Publishers.

Leacock, Eleanor. 1981. *Myths of Male Dominance*. New York: Monthly Review Press.

Leakey, Louis and Robert Ardrey. 1971. Munger Africana Library Notes #9, 25pp.

Leakey, Richard. 2001. *Wildlife Wars: My Fight to Save Africa's Natural Treasures*. New York: St Martin's Press.

Leibowitz, Lila. 1968. *Journal of Theoretical Biology* 21: 153-169.

Lerner, Gerda. 1987. *The Creation of Patriachy*. New York: Oxford University Press.

Levin, Martin. 2001, Apr 14. *Globe and Mail* (Toronto), D16.

Lind, Michael. 1997 [1994]. In Robert W. Sussman, *ed. The Biological Basis of Human Behavior* 306-309. Needham Heights, MA: Simon and Schuster.

Livshits, G. and E. Kobyliansky. 1991. *Human Biology* 63: 441-466.

Loeb, H. 1899. *Munchen Medizinische Wochenschrift* 46: 1016-1019.

Lombroso, Cesare. 1887. *L'Homme criminel*. Paris: Félix Alcan.

Lombroso, Cesare. 1911. *Criminal Man*. New York: Putnam's.

Lombroso, Cesare and William Ferrero. 1915. *The Female Offender*. New York: D. Appleton and Co.

Lorenz, Konrad. 1972 [1967]. *On Aggression*. London: Methuen.

Lucas, A., R. Morley, T.J. Cole, G. Lister and C. Leeson-Payne. 1992. *Lancet* 339: 261-264.

Lynn, Richard. 1995. In Russell Jacoby and Naomi Glauberman, eds. *The Bell Curve Debate* 354-357. New York: Random House.

MacIntyre, Ferren and Kenneth W. Estep. 1993. *BioSystems* 31: 223-233.

Malinosky-Rummell, Robin and David J. Hansen. 1994. *Psychological Bulletin* 114,1: 68-79.

Malinowski, Bronislaw. 1929. *The Sexual Life of Savages in North-western Melanesia*. London: Routledge and Kegan Paul.

Manning, John T., Alex R. Gage, Michael J. Diver, Diane Scutt and William D. Fraser. 2002. *Evolution and Human Behavior* 23: 95-102.

Markowitz, Fred E. and Richard B. Felson. 1998. *Criminology 36*: 117-138.

Marlowe, Frank and Adam Wetsman. 2001. *Personality and Individual Differences* 30: 481-489.

Martan, Jan and Benjamin A. Shepherd. 1976. *Journal of Experimental Zoology* 196: 79-84.

Maslow, Abraham H. 1936. *Journal of Genetic Psychology* 48: 261-277.

McLain, D. Kelly, Deanna Setters, Michael P. Moulton and Ann E. Pratt. 2000. *Evolution and Human Behavior 21*: 11-23.

McLeod, Peter J. 1990. *Canadian Journal of Zoology* 68: 402-404.

Mesnick, Sarah L. and Burney J. Le Boeuf. 1991. *Behaviour* 117: 262-280.

Mesquida, Christian G. and Neil I. Wiener. 1996. *Ethology and Sociobiology 17*: 247-262.

Meyer-Bahlburg, Heino F.L. 1984. *Progress in Brain Research* 61: 375-398.

Mihm, Stephen. 2001, May/Jun. *Lingua Franca* 43-49.

Miller, Adam. 1995. In Russell Jacoby and Naomi Glauberman, eds. *The Bell Curve Debate* 162-178. New York: Random House.

Miller, Geoffrey. 2000. *The Mating Mind: How Sexual Choice Shaped the Evolution of Human Nature*. New York: Doubleday.

Milne, Barry J., Jay Belsky, Richie Poulton, W. Murray Thomson, Avshalom Caspi and Jules Kieser. 2003. *Evolution and Human Behavior* 24,1: 53-63.

Milner, Larry S. 2000. *Hardness of Heart/ Hardness of Life.* Lanham, MD: University Press of America.

Mock, Douglas W. 1984. In Glenn Hausfater and Sarah Blaffer Hrdy, eds. *Infanticide: Comparative and Evolutionary Perspectives* 3-30. New York: Aldine.

Møller, Anders Pape and John P. Swaddle 1997. *Asymmetry, Developmental Stability, and Evolution*. Oxford: Oxford University Press.

Mondimore, Francis Mark. 1996. *A Natural History of Homosexuality.* Baltimore: Johns Hopkins University Press.

Moore, H.D.M., M. Martin and T.R. Birkhead. 1999. *Proceedings of the Royal Society of London* 266: 2343-2350.

Morris, Desmond. 1967. *The Naked Ape: A Zoologist's Study of the Human Animal.* London: Cape.

Morris, Desmond. 1994. *Bodytalk: A World Guide to Gestures.* London: Cape.

Morris, Robert T. 1918. *The Way Out of War: Notes on the Biology of the Subject.* Garden City, NY: Doubleday, Page.

Morton, Peter. 2000, Jul 12. *National Post* (Toronto), A10.

Murray, Charles. 1984. *Losing Ground: American Social Policy 1950-1980.* New York: Basic Books.

Nadler, R.D. and L.C. Miller. 1982. *Folia Primatologica* 38: 233-239.

Nagin, Daniel S. and Richard E. Tremblay. 2001. *Archives of General Psychiatry* 58: 389-394.

Neapolitan, Jerome L. 1998. *Criminology* 36: 139-151.

Neisser, Ulric. 1998. *The Rising Curve: Long-Term Gains in IQ and Related Measures.* Washington, DC: American Psychological Association.

Newell, Walter R. 2003. *The Code of Man: Love Courage Pride Family Country.* New York: HarperCollins.

Ngana-Mundeke, Annie. 2000, Apr. *Anthropology News* 25.

Nisbett, Richard. 1995. In Steven Fraser, ed. *The Bell Curve Wars* 36-57. New York: Basic Books.

Österman, Karin, Kaj Björkqvist, Kirsti M.J. Lagerspetz and T.K. Oommen. 1999. *Aggressive Behavior* 25,1: 58.

Owen, Ken. 1991. *Personality and Individual Differences* 13: 149-159.

Packer, Craig. 1994. *Into Africa.* Chicago: University of Chicago Press.

Packer, Craig. 2001. *American Anthropologist* 102: 829-831.

Packer, Craig and Anne E. Pusey. 1984. In Glenn Hausfater and Sarah Blaffer Hrdy, eds. *Infanticide: Comparative and Evolutionary Perspective* 31-42. New York: Aldine.

Pagel, Mark. 1997. *Animal Behavior* 53: 973-981.

Parekh, Bhikhu. 2000. *Rethinking Multiculturalism: Cultural Diversity and Political Theory.* Cambridge MA: Harvard University Press.

Parker, G.A. 1970. *Biological Review* 45: 525-567.

Parker, G.A. 1984. In Robert L. Smith, ed. *Sperm Competition and the Evolution of Animal Mating Systems* 1-60. Orlando, FL: Academic Press.

Parra, Flavia C., Roberto C. Amado, José R. Lambertucci, Jorge Rocha, Carlos M. Antunes and Sérgio D.J. Pena. 2002. *Proceedings of the National Academy of Sciences* 100: 177-182.

Patterson, Orlando. 1995. In Steven Fraser, ed. *The Bell Curve Wars* 187-213. New York: Basic Books.

Pavelka, Mary S. McDonald. 1995. In Paul R. Abramson and Steven D. Pinkerton, eds. *Sexual Nature, Sexual Culture* 17-36. Chicago: University of Chicago Press.

Pawlowski, B. and R.I.M. Dunbar. 1999. *Evolution and Human Behavior* 20: 53-69.

Pearson, Patricia. 1997. *When She was Bad: Violent Women and the Myth of Innocence.* Toronto: Random House.

Penton-Voak, I.S. and D.I. Perrett. 2000. *Evolution and Human Behavior* 21: 39-48.

Peretz, Martin. 1995. In Steven Fraser, ed. *The Bell Curve Wars* 148-155. New York: Basic Books.

Perrett, David I., D. Michael Burt, Ian S. Penton-Voak, Kieran J. Lee, Duncan A. Rowland and Rachel Edwards. 1999. *Evolution and Human Behavior* 20: 295-307.

Picard, André. 2002, May 21. *Globe and Mail* (Toronto), A5.

Pierotti, Raymond. 1991. *American Naturalist* 138: 1140-1158.

Pillard, Richard C. and J. Michael Bailey. 1998. *Human Biology* 70,2: 347-365.

Pitts, Gordon. 2000. *In the Blood: Battles to Succeed in Canada's Family Businesses.* Toronto: Doubleday.

Pollard, Irina. 1994. *A Guide to Reproduction: Social Issues and Human Concerns.* Cambridge, UK: Cambridge University Press.

Pollock, J.I. 1979. *Folia Primatologica* 31: 143-164.

Pontier, Dominique and Eugenia Natoli. 1999. *Aggressive Behavior* 25: 445-449.

Power, Margaret. 1991. *The Egalitarians—Human and Chimpanzee. An Anthropological View of Social Organization.* New York: Cambridge University Press.

Preston, Brian T., Ian R. Stevenson, Josephine M. Pemberton and Kenneth Wilson. 2001. *Nature* 409: 681-682.

Quinn, James S., Linda A. Whittingham and Ralph D. Morris. 1994. *Animal Behavior* 47: 363-367.

Raine, Adrian, Todd Lencz, Susan Bihrle, Lori LaCasse and Patrick Colletti. 2000. *Archives of General Psychiatry* 57: 119-127.

Raspberry, William, 1995. In Russell Jacoby and Naomi Glauberman, eds. *The Bell Curve Debate* 290-292. New York: Random House.

Regalski, J.M. and S.J.C. Gaulin. 1993. *Ethology and Sociobiology* 14: 97-113.

Reichard, Ulrich and Volker Sommer. 1997. *Behaviour* 134: 1135-1174.

Reynolds, Vernon. 1968. *Man* New Ser 3: 209-223.

Reynolds, Vernon. 1975. *Man* New Ser 10: 123-125.

Rhine, Ramon J. and Bruce J. Westlund. 1981. *Folia Primatologica* 35: 77-116.

Rhodes, Gillian, Leslie A. Zebrowitz, Alison Clark, S. Michael Kalick, Amy Hightower and Ryan McKay. 2001. *Evolution and Human Behavior* 22: 31-46.

Rice, George, Carol Anderson, Neil Risch and George Ebers. 1999. *Science* 284: 665-667.

Richards, Marcus, Rebecca Hardy, Diana Kuh and Michael E.J. Wadsworth. 2001. *British Medical Journal* 322: 199-203.

Ridley, Matt. 1999. *Genome: The Autobiography of a Species in 23 Chapters.* New York: HarperCollins.

Risch, Neil, Elizabeth Squires-Wheeler and Bronya J.B. Keats. 1993. *Science* 262: 2063-2065.

Roberts, Julian V. and Thomas Gabor. 1990. *Canadian Journal of Criminology* 32: 291-313.

Rose, Hilary. 2001. In Hilary Rose and Steven Rose, eds. *Alas, Poor Darwin* 106-128. London: Vintage.

Rose, Hilary and Steven Rose. 2001. In Hilary Rose and Steven Rose, eds. *Alas, Poor Darwin* 1-13. New York: Vintage.

Rosen, Jeffrey and Charles Lane. 1995. In Steven Fraser, ed. *The Bell Curve Wars* 58-61. New York: Basic Books.

Ross, Gary Earl. 1995. In Russell Jacoby and Naomi Glauberman, eds. *The Bell Curve Debate* 255-257. New York: Random House.

Ross, Patrick Jr and David Crews. 1977. *Nature* 267: 344-345.

Routtenberg, A., I. Cantallops, S. Zaffuto, P. Serrano and U. Namgung. 2000. *Proceedings of the National Academy of Science* 97,13: 7657-7662.

Rowell, Thelma. 1967. *Animal Behavior* 15: 499-509

Rowell, Thelma. 1969. *Folia Primatologica* 11: 241-254.

Rowell, Thelma. 1972. *The Social Behaviour of Monkeys.* London: Penguin.

Rowell, Thelma. 1974. *Behavioral Biology* 11: 131-154.

Rushton, J. Philippe. 1990. *Canadian Journal of Criminology* 32: 315-334.

Rushton, J. Philippe. 1995a. *Race, Evolution, and Behavior: A Life History Perspective.* New Brunswick, NJ: Transaction Publishers.

Rushton, J. Philippe. 1995b. *Psychological Reports* 76: 307-312.

Rushton, J. Philippe. 1997 [1990]. In Robert W. Sussman, ed. *The Biological Basis of Human Behavior* 222-225. New York: Simon and Schuster.

Rushton, J. Philippe. 1999. *Race Evolution and Behavior: Special Abridged Edition.* New Brunswick, NJ: Transaction Publishers.

Sampson, Robert J. and John H. Laub. 1993. *Crime in the Making: Pathways and Turning Points through Life.* Cambridge, MA: Harvard University Press.

Sapolsky, Robert M. 2001. *A Primate's Memoir.* New York: Scribner.

Sarich, Vincent and Frank Miele. 2004. *Race: The Reality of Human Differences.* Boulder, CO: Westview Press.

Satinover, Jeffrey. 1996. *Homosexuality and the Politics of Truth.* Grand Rapids, MI: Baker Books.

Sauer, E.G. Franz. 1972. *Auk* 89: 717-737.

Saunders, Doug. 2004, Jun 22. *Globe and Mail* (Toronto), A15.

Sauther, Michelle L. 1991. *American Journal of Physical Anthropology* 84: 463-477.

Sayers, J. 1980. Brighton Women and Science Group, ed. *Alice through the Microscope* 42-61. London: Virago.

Schaller, George B. 1972a. *The Serengeti Lion.* Chicago: University of Chicago Press.

Schaller, George B. 1972b. *A Kingdom of Predators.* New York: Knopf.

Schnaas, L., S.J. Rothenberg. E. Perroni, S. Martinez, C. Hernandez and R.M. Hernandez. 2000. *Neurotoxicology and Teratology* 22: 805-810.

Scott, J.P. 1945. *Comparative Psychology Monographs* 18,4: 1-29.

Segal, Nancy L. 1999. *Entwined Lives: Twins and What They Tell Us about Human Behavior*. New York: Dutton.

Segerstråle, Ullica. 2000. *Defenders of the Truth: The Battle for Science in the Sociobiology Debate and Beyond.* Oxford: Oxford University Press.

Severinghaus, C.W. 1955. *New York Fish and Game Journal* 2,2: 239-241.

Seymour, Norman R. and Rodger D. Titman. 1979. *Canadian Journal of Zoology* 57: 2421-2428.

Shaw, John. 2001, Aug 5. *Toronto Star* F7.

Shea, Christopher. 1999, Sep. *Lingua Franca* 23-25.

Shepher, Joseph. 1983. *Incest: A Biosocial View.* New York: Academic Press.

Shermer, Michael. 1997. *Why People Believe Weird Things: Pseudoscience, Superstition, and other Confusions of our Time.* New York: W.H. Freeman.

Shlain, Leonard. 2003. *Sex, Time and Power: How Women's Sexuality Shaped Human Evolution*. New York: Penguin.

Short, R.V. 1979. *Advances in the Study of Behavior* 9: 131-158.

Shostak, Marjorie. 1981. *Nisa, the Life and Words of a !Kung Woman.* Cambridge, MA: Harvard University Press.

Silk, Joan and Craig B. Stanford. 1999, Sep. *Anthropology News* 27-29.

Siminoski, Kerry and Jerald Bain. 1993. *Annals of Sex Research* 6: 232-235.

Simmons, N.M. 1980. In G. Monson and L. Summer, eds. *The Desert Bighorn* 124-144. Tucson: University of Arizona.

Singh, Devandra. 1993a. *Journal of Personality and Social Psychology* 65,2: 293-307.

Singh, Devandra. 1993b. *Human Nature* 4,3: 297-321.

Singh, Devandra. 1995. *Evolution and Sociobiology* 16: 465-481.

Smith, Robert L. 1984. In Robert L. Smith, ed. *Sperm Competition and the Evolution of Animal Mating Systems* 601-659. Orlando, FL: Academic Press.

Smuts, Barbara. 1992. *Human Nature* 3: 1-44.

Smyth, Julie. 2001, Jun 14. *National Post* (Toronto), A1,8.

Soltis, Joseph, Fusako Mitsunaga, Keiko Shimizu, Yoshimi Yanagihara and Masumi Nozaki. 1997. *Animal Behavior* 54: 725-736.

Stanford, Craig. B. 1999. *The Hunting Apes: Meat Eating and the Origins of Human Behavior.* Princeton: Princeton University Press.

Stanford, Craig B. 2000. *American Scientist* 88: 360-361.

Stanley, Thomas J. 2000. *The Millionaire Mind.* Kansas City: Andrews and McMeel Publisher.

Staples, Robert. 1981. In Charles H. Mindel and Robert W. Habenstein, eds. *Ethnic Families in America: Patterns and Variations* 2nd ed, 217-244. New York: Elsevier.

Stehn, R.A. and F.J. Jannett, Jr. 1981. *Journal of Mammalogy* 62: 369-372.

Stevenson, Harold W. and James W. Stigler. 1992. *The Learning Gap: Why Our Schools Are Failing and What We Can Learn from Japanese and Chinese Education.* New York: Summit Books.

Stevenson, Harold W., James W. Stigler, Shin-ying Lee, G. William Lucker, Seiro Kitamura and Chen-chin Hsu. 1985. *Child Development* 56: 718-734.

Stewart, Omer C. 1968. In M.F. Ashley Montagu, ed. *Man and Aggression* 103-110. New York: Oxford University Press.

Stokstad, Erik. 2002. *Science* 297: 752.

Storr, Anthony. 1968. *Human Aggression*. London: Allen Lane.

Strauch, Barbara. 2003. *The Primal Teen: What the New Discoveries about the Teenage Brain Tell Us about our Kids*. New York: Knopf.

Strum, Shirley C. 1987. *Almost Human: A Journey into the World of Baboons*. New York: Norton.

Sulloway, Frank J. 1996. *Born to Rebel: Birth Order, Family Dynamics, and Creative Lives*. New York: Pantheon Books.

Sussman, Robert W. 1995. *Reviews in Anthropology* 24: 1-11.

Sussman, Robert W. 2000. In Strum, Shirley C. and Linda M. Fedigan, eds. *Primate Encounters: Models of Science, Gender, and Society* 85-103. Chicago: University of Chicago Press.

Swain, Carol M. and Russ Nieli, eds. 2004. *Contemporary Voices of White Nationalism in America*. New York: Cambridge University Press.

Tang-Martinez, Zuleyma. 2000. In Strum, Shirley C. and Linda M. Fedigan, eds. *Primate Encounters: Models of Science, Gender, and* Society 261-274. Chicago: University of Chicago Press.

Tanner, Nancy Makepeace. 1981. *On Becoming Human*. Cambridge, UK: Cambridge University Press.

Temrin, Hans, Susanne Buchmayer and Magnus Enquist. 2000. *Proceedings of the Royal Society of London B* 267: 943-945.

Thomas, Caitlin. 1997. *Double Drink Story: My Life with Dylan Thomas*. Toronto: Penguin.

Thornhill, Randy. 1980. *Animal Behavior* 28: 52-59.

Thornhill, Randy and Karl Grammer. 1999. *Evolution and Human Behavior* 20: 105-120.

Thornhill, Randy and Craig T. Palmer. 2000a. *A Natural History of Rape: Biological Bases of Sexual Coercion*. Cambridge, MA: MIT Press.

Thornhill, Randy and Craig T. Palmer. 2000b, Jan/Feb. *The Sciences* 30-36.

Tiger, Lionel and Robin Fox. 1971. *The Imperial Animal*. New York: Holt, Rinehart and Winston.

Tovée, M.J., K. Tasker and P.J. Benson. 2000. *Evolution and Human Behavior* 21: 191-200.

Trends in the well-being of America's children and youth. 1997. U.S. Dept of Health and Human Services.

Triandis, Harry C. 1994. *Culture and Social Behavior*. New York: McGraw-Hill.

Urrutia, Lena P. and Hugh Drummond. 1990. *Auk* 107: 772-794.

U.S. Government Statistics. 2000. Washington, DC.

Van Lawick-Goodall, Jane. 1971. *In the Shadow of Man*. Glasgow: William Collins.

Van Valen, Leigh. 1962. *Evolution* 16,2: 125-142.

Vasey, Paul L. 1995. *International Journal of Primatology* 16,2: 173-204.

Venter, J. Craig. 2002, Apr 27. *Globe and Mail* (Toronto), F6.

Vines, Gail. 1999, Aug 7. *New Scientist* 33-35.

Voracek, Martin and Maryanne L. Fisher. 2002. *British Medical Journal* 325: 1447-1448.

Waal, Frans de. 1982. *Chimpanzee Politics: Power and Sex among Apes*. London: Cape.

Waal, Frans de. 1989. *Peacemaking among Primates*. Cambridge, MA: Harvard University Press.

Waal, Frans de. 1997. *Bonobo: The Forgotten Ape*. Berkeley, CA: University of California Press.

Waal, Frans de. 1998. *Current Anthropology* 39: 407-408.

Wachter, Bettina, Oliver P. Höner, Marion L. East, Waltraud Golla and Heribert Hofer. 2002. *Behavioral Ecology and Sociobiology* 52: 348-356.

Wallace, Robert Ardell. 1979. *The Genesis Factor*. New York: Morrow.

Wallen, Kim. 1995. In Paul R. Abramson and Steven D. Pinkerton, eds. *Sexual Nature Sexual Culture* 57-79. Chicago: University of Chicago Press.

Warr, Mark. 1998. *Criminology* 36:183-216.

Warren, P.S. 2002. *Auk* 119,2: 349-361.

Washburn, S.L. and Virginia Avis. 1958. In Anne Roe and George Gaylord Simpson, eds. *Behavior and Evolution* 421-436. New Haven, CT: Yale University Press,

Washburn, S.L. and Irven DeVore. 1961. *Scientific American* 204,6: 62-71.

Watson, Lyall. 1995. *Dark Nature: A Natural History of Evil.* New York: Harper Collins.

Weiping, Wu and Cai Longquan. 1999. *Aggressive Behavior* 25,1: 58.

Welty, Joel Carl. 1982. *The Life of Birds.* Philadelphia: Saunders.

Werner, Y.L. 1980. *Zeitschrift für Tierpsychologie* 54: 144-150.

West, D.J. 1977. *Homosexuality Re-examined.* Minneapolis: University of Minnesota Press.

Wetsman, Adam and Frank Marlowe. 1999. *Evolution and Human Behavior* 20: 219-228.

Whiten, A., J. Goodall, W.C. McGrew, T. Nishida, V. Reynolds, Y. Sugiyama, C.E.G. Tutin, R.W. Wrangham and C. Boesch. 1999. *Nature*, 399: 682-685.

Whitman, Karyl, Anthony M. Starfield, Henley S. Quadling and Craig Packer. 2004. *Nature* 428: 175-178.

Whitten, W.K. 1966. In Anne McLaren, ed. *Advances in Reproductive Physiology, Vol 1* 155-177. London: Academic Press.

Wiederman, Michael W. and Elizabeth Rice Allgeier. 1992. *Ethology and Sociobiology* 13: 115-124.

Wiederman, Michael W. and Stephanie L. Dubois. 1998. *Evolution and Human Behavior* 19: 153-170.

Williams, Terrance J., Michelle E. Pepitone, Scott E. Christensen, Bradley M. Cooke, Andrew D. Huberman, Nicholas J. Breedlove, Tessa J. Breedlove and Cynthia L. Jordan. 2000. *Nature* 404: 455-456.

Wilson, Edward O. 1975. *Sociobiology: The New Synthesis.* Cambridge, MA: Belknap Press.

Wilson, Edward O. 1998. *Consilience.* New York: Knopf.

Wilson, J.M. and J.T. Manning. 1996. *Journal of Human Evolution* 30: 529-537.

Wilson, James Q. and Richard J. Herrnstein. 1985. *Crime and Human Nature.* New York: Simon and Schuster.

Wingfield, J.C., A.L. Newman, G.L. Hunt, Jr and D.S. Farner. 1982. *Animal Behavior* 30: 9-22.

Witkin, Herman A., Sarnoff A. Mednick, Fini Schulsinger, Eskild Bakkestrom, Karl O. Christiansen, Donald R. Goodenough, Kurt Hirschhorn, Claes Lundsteen, David R. Owen, John Philip, Donald B. Rubin and Martha Stocking. 1976. *Science* 193: 547-555.

Wong, Jan. 1999. *Jan Wong's China.* Toronto: Doubleday.

Wong, Jan. 2000, Sep 23. *National Post* (Toronto), R6.

Woodbury, A.M. 1941. *Ecology* 22: 410-411.

Wrangham, Richard W. 1974. *Animal Behavior* 22: 83-93.

Wrangham, Richard W. 1997. *Science* 277: 774-775.

Wrangham, Richard and Dale Peterson. 1996. *Demonic Males: Apes and the Origins of Human Violence.* Boston: Houghton Mifflin.

Wright, Karen. 1999, Nov 23. *National Post* (Toronto), A17.

Yamagiwa, Juichi. 1992. *Primates* 33,4: 523-544.

Yerkes, Robert M. 1939. *Quarterly Review of Biology* 14: 115-136.

Yoon, Carol Kaesuk. 2002, Jan 3. *New York Times, National* A16.

Yu, Douglas W. and Glenn H. Shepard. 1998. *Nature* 396: 321-322.

Yu, Hing-Sing. 1994. *Human Reproductive Biology.* Boca Raton: CRC Press.

Yurk, H., L. Barrett-Lennard, J.K. Ford and C.O. Matkin, 2002. *Animal Behavior* 63,6: 1103-1109.

Zahavi, Amotz and Avishag Zahavi. 1997. *The Handicap Principle: A Missing Piece of Darwin's Puzzle.* New York: Oxford University Press.

Zuckerman, S. 1932. *The Social Life of Monkeys and Apes.* London: Kegan Paul, Trench, Trubner and Co.

Index

Beyond Boundaries: Humans and Animals
Barbara Noske

Beyond Boundaries steps out into hitherto unknown territory in taking an interdisciplinary approach to the subject of animals. Vast in scope and vision, this book synthesizes an array of disparate research and scholarship, and in so doing is certain to spark a furore of philosophical debate.

> A fascinating section is the review of human-animal continuity in the fossil record, in the psychological studies of chimpanzees' ability to learn, and in anthropological-style studies of animal communities. Even more stunning is the recorded cases of animal species raising human children. —*Australian Tribune*

BARBARA NOSKE has an MA in cultural anthropology and a Ph.D. in philosophy, both from the University of Amsterdam. In addition to this book, she is at work on an *Encyclopedia of Animal Rights and Animal Welfare*.

253 pages, bibliography, index
Paperback ISBN: 1-55164-078-3 $23.99
Hardcover ISBN: 1-55164-079-1 $52.99

Evolution And Environment
Peter Kropotkin, with an Introduction by George Woodcock

The Origin of the Species was published when Peter Kropokin (1842-1921) was seventeen and from boyhood onward into old age he maintained a lifelong interest in science. But the geographer had a social and political concern that transformed his interest in science into a larger ecological concern. Unwilling to accept the arguments of the time that based all change on the drive for survival (what he regarded as the "vulgar Darwinism of Huxley and his followers"), Kropotkin argued that there must be something more than chance variation to explain the complexity of evoluton, and that one needs to accept the direct action of the environment as a potential factor. His insight, now acknowledged by ecologists, insisted on the selective pressure of the environment.

This volume, comprising seven essays on evolution, written between 1910 and 1915, and never before published, provides excellent background to the continuing evolutionary controversy.

262 pages
Paperback ISBN: 1-895431-44-1 $24.99
Hardcover ISBN: 1-895431-45-X $53.99

ALSO AVAILABLE from BLACK ROSE BOOKS

Artful Practices, *Henri Lustiger-Thaler, Daniel Salée, editors*
Certainties and Doubts, *Anatol Rapoport*
Civilization and Its Discontents, *John Laffey*
Commonwealth of Life, *Peter Brown*
Defending the Earth, *Murray Bookchin, Dave Foreman*
Designing Utopia, *Michael Lang*
Every Life is a Story, *Fred Knelman*
Geography of Freedom, *Marie Fleming*
Green Cities, *David Gordon, editor*
Humanity, Society, and Commitment, *Kenneth McRobbie, editor*
Mutual Aid, *Peter Kropotkin*
Nature and the Crisis of Modernity, *Raymond Rogers*
One God, *Ernesto Lorca*
Participatory Democracy, *Dimitrios Roussopoulos*
Perspectives on Power, *Noam Chomsky*
Prehistory and History, *David Tandy, editor*
Writers and Politics, *George Woodcock*

Send for a free catalogue of all our titles

C.P. 1258, Succ. Place du Parc
Montréal, Québec
H2X 4A7 Canada

Or visit our website at http://www.web.net/blackrosebooks

To order books
In Canada: (phone) 1-800-565-9523 (fax) 1-800-221-9985
email: utpbooks@utpress.utoronto.ca

In United States: (phone) 1-800-283-3572 (fax) 1-651-917-6406

In UK & Europe: (phone) London 44 (0)20 8986-4854 (fax) 44 (0)20 8533-5821
email: order@centralbooks.com

Printed by the workers of
MARC VEILLEUX IMPRIMEUR INC.
Boucherville, Québec
for Black Rose Books Ltd.